Captain William H. Whitfield. Circa 1880. (Courtesy Millicent Library,
Fairhaven, Massachusetts)

The Life
and Times
of John Manjiro

Donald R. Bernard

McGraw-Hill, Inc.
New York   St. Louis   San Francisco   Auckland   Bogotá   Caracas
Lisbon   London   Madrid   Mexico   Milan   Montreal   New Delhi
Paris   San Juan   Singapore   Sydney   Tokyo   Toronto

All activities, persons, and backgrounds in this astonishing story have been checked and verified by the author in careful basic research. The facts presented here coalesce in a remarkable tale of adventure and achievement.

The wording, spelling, and punctuation of all materials taken from original sources have been reproduced exactly as they appeared, in order to retain their historical interest.

The Life and Times of John Manjiro

Copyright © 1992 by McGraw-Hill, Inc. All rights reserved. Printed in the United States of America. Except as permitted under the United States Copyright Act of 1976, no part of this publication may be reproduced or distributed in any form or by any means, or stored in a data base or retrieval system, without the prior written permission of the publisher.

Page 243: "Fair Haven to Weigh Plan for Japanese 'Sister City,'" THE STANDARD-TIMES, December 19, 1961. Reprinted by permission of THE STANDARD-TIMES, New Bedford, Massachusetts.

1 2 3 4 5 6 7 8 9 0   DOC DOC   9 0 9 8 7 6 5 4 3 2

ISBN 0-07-004947-5

This book was set in Caledonia by ComCom, Inc.
The editors were Seibert Adams and Larry Goldberg;
the designer was Carol Couch;
the production supervisor was Kathryn Porzio.
The idea for the jacket came from the author.
The copy editor was Georgia Kornbluth.
R. R. Donnelley & Sons Company was printer and binder.

Library of Congress Cataloging-in-Publication Data

Bernard, Donald R.
    The life and times of John Manjiro / Donald R. Bernard.
        p.   cm.
    Includes bibliographical references (p.   ).
    ISBN 0-07-004947-5
    1. Nakahama, Manjiro, 1827–1898. 2. Japan—Officials and employees—Biography. 3. Japan—History—19th century.
    4. Japan—Relations—United States. 5. United States—Relations—Japan. I. Title.
    DS881.5.N3B47   1992
    952'.025—dc20   92-2782

About the Author

Donald R. Bernard has been recognized in Massachusetts as a local historian since 1967. He has lectured on a variety of historical subjects before local organizations, state social study organizations, Asian study groups, and schools in the Greater New Bedford area. He is the author of *The Tower of Strength* (Reynolds Dewalt, New Bedford, Mass., 1975), a book of local military history. He has organized many reenactments and commemorations of events in U.S. history, such as battles of the American Revolution and the Civil War.

It was Bernard's involvement in preparations for the U.S. Bicentennial that led to his initial awareness of the story of Manjiro, on which he has become an acknowledged authority. His expertise on the subject is well known not only in Greater New Bedford but also in areas of Japan. Through his work on Manjiro, he has become acquainted with Japanese historians and descendants of Manjiro as well as Japanese royalty.

Donald R. Bernard was instrumental in the formation of a Sister City relationship between Fairhaven-New Bedford and Tosashimizu City, Japan. He has received awards from historical organizations such as the Daughters of the American Revolution, as well as the prestigious Foreign Ministers Award in Tokyo.

To my mother, Alice Bernard,
and to the memory of
my father, Paul H. Bernard,
this book is lovingly dedicated.

Contents

To the Reader

The contents of this book are accurately reflected in the title *The Life and Times of John Manjiro*, though the actual tale continues long after Manjiro's death, encompassing present-day community commemoration of his life and achievements, in both Japan and Massachusetts.

Starting out as a poor, uneducated Japanese fisherboy in the mid-nineteenth century, with no apparent prospects for a better life, Manjiro (whose given name is simply "Manjiro" but who is called, in the West, "John Manjiro," "John Mung," or "John Mungero," and who, in Japan, after he is given the privilege of adopting a last name, chooses to be known as "Manjiro Nakahama") eventually achieves fame and respect in his own country, after a decade of perilous adventures and valuable education abroad. Shipwrecked by a storm that arose during a fishing trip, he and four companions are rescued by the *John Howland*, a whaleship from New Bedford, Massachusetts, and taken to Hawaii.

The captain of the whaleship, William H. Whitfield, becomes attached to Manjiro, impressed by the boy's intelligence and curiosity. He takes Manjiro to Fairhaven, Massachusetts, to live with the Whitfield family and get an American education. Manjiro loves his American family, but his steadfast goal is to return to his homeland—a difficult matter because the Tokugawa regime's policy of isolation means that foreign ships cannot enter Japanese ports. (Relevant aspects of Japanese history are discussed in the book.)

Besides studying English and the standard curriculum of American schools of the day, Manjiro also learns navigation and the whaling trade. When he is unable to earn enough at whaling to pay for his return trip to Japan, he joins the forty-niners in California. Mining for gold does enable him to accumulate enough money to begin his long journey back to Japan. He starts by returning to Hawaii, from whence he and two other crew members from the shipwrecked fishing boat finally do get back to Japan, with the help of Hawaiian friends and supporters.

The shogunate greets Manjiro and his companions with much suspicion because they have spent time in foreign lands. After being questioned relentlessly for many months, they are finally set free and allowed to return to their homes. Manjiro has only a brief visit with his widowed mother before he is pressed into the service of his country in various capacities, including teacher, shipbuilder, whaler, interpreter, and translator. Though he achieves much respect and many honors in his native land, and though he is consistently loyal to Japan, he remains under suspicion for the rest of his life.

The impact of Manjiro's foreign travels and achievements upon his own life and upon others was considerable. The education, status, and possibilities of his descendants were startlingly improved, as compared to what their lives would have been like had they been descended from a poor fisherman. His work as an educator and translator had a profound effect upon the educational system and the political climate of his times. Donald R. Bernard makes a convincing case for the idea that Manjiro may have been instrumental in the opening of Japan to foreign trade by Commodore Perry in 1854. The full extent of Manjiro's influence upon the subsequent history of Japan, and indeed of the world, may never be fully known.

Manjiro and Captain Whitfield kept in touch throughout their lives, and their descendants have kept up the tradition of maintaining a connection between Tosashimizu (the present-day name of Manjiro's home town, which was then called "Nakanohama") and the Massachusetts community of Fairhaven. A Sister City relationship was formalized in 1987.

In telling the story of Manjiro, this book reveals much about his nature, as well as that of Captain Whitfield. Both were men of courage, sincerity, and wisdom. Manjiro appears to have possessed unusual intelligence and charisma, and his story is engrossing. It should give much pleasure to the general reader as well as to the book's intended audience, the biological and spiritual heirs to the Manjiro legacy.

Georgia Kornbluth

Preface

This book is based on more than fifteen years of involvement and research. I became interested in Manjiro in 1975, when I was working with the Historical Commission of Fairhaven, Massachusetts, on preparations for the U.S. Bicentennial. It was the late Rita E. Steele, director of the Millicent Library in Fairhaven, who first revealed to me the story of Manjiro's extraordinary odyssey.

Manjiro—or "John Mung," as he was known in the United States—began life as a Japanese fisherboy, developed great dreams for his people and his country, and rose to a position of influence and acclaim in Japan. In the course of a dangerous and uncertain life, he constructed an enormous symbolic bridge linking a small whaling village in the United States with his own fishing village in Japan and touching upon many Pacific islands along the way. This mutual relationship of respect and understanding continues to flourish even today, a hundred and fifty years later—a warm bond between cultures on opposite sides of the world.

Until the publication of this book, many details of Manjiro's life had been known only in Japan. His tribulations and his successes were hardly known in the United States, even though it was his studies in Fairhaven, Massachusetts, that enabled him in later life to make valuable contributions to his own country. Although many books about him had been written by Japanese historians, most of them had been published only in Japan and were thus inaccessible to the English-speaking world. One of my goals in compiling and writing an accurate version of Manjiro's story was to create an English-language account of the far-reaching effects of one simple act of kindness—that of William H. Whitfield, the American whaling captain who gave Manjiro the opportunity to acquire an education.

Researching the many details that enhance this narrative, though extraordinarily time-consuming, has nevertheless been an engrossing and worthwhile endeavor. The result is a chronicle of a man whose life was significant not only in American and Japanese history but also in the history of the world. It is my sincere hope that this book will serve as a suitable tribute to Manjiro's achievements.

Donald R. Bernard

Acknowledgments

The research and writing of this book have been both time-consuming and rewarding. Without the assistance of many individuals, the final product could not have been realized. To name everyone who contributed would be impossible, but not to mention certain people who provided special assistance would be inexcusable. It is with a deep sense of obligation, gratitude, and appreciation that I acknowledge the assistance of those listed below.

The late Rita E. Steele, former director of the Millicent Library in Fairhaven, Massachusetts, inspired my interest in the Manjiro adventure. Her enthusiastic encouragement provided the guiding light by which I set for myself the goal of writing this book.

I am greatly indebted to Dr. Hiroshi Nakahama, the great-grandson of Manjiro, and to his gracious wife Tomoko (Grace) Nakahama. Together they constituted an invaluable resource in my research. Dr. Nakahama's willingness to share with me many intimate details of his great-grandfather's life enabled me to develop an appropriate perspective on Manjiro.

I am also indebted to Carolyn Longworth, director of the Millicent Library. She gave freely of her time and expertise during the development of this book.

Special thanks to Anne W. Jepson for her tireless efforts in transcribing the manuscript on a computer keyboard, as well as for her research assistance, which enhanced the final product. Georgia Kornbluth did extensive copy editing and polishing. Also deserving of mention is Alice Berard for the many hours she spent typing the first draft.

I hereby recognize my good friend, Kazuo (Jim) Narita of Nagoya, Japan, who is a prolific journalist as well as a recognized historian and the author of many articles on the Manjiro legacy. Mr. Narita eagerly shared with me his extensive knowledge of Manjiro Nakahama. Professor Takashi Miyanaga of Hosei University, Tokyo, helped in research on related information.

The following individuals contributed to my documentation of the many facets of this astonishing story: Gail Enos, formerly of the Fairhaven School Department; Mabel Hoyle Knipe of the Millicent Library; Paul Cyr and Ernestine Furtado of the New Bedford Free Public Library; and Elaine Rocha, Fairhaven Town Clerk. In addition, I am eternally grateful to Don Canto and Mark M. L. Baron, and to everyone else who contributed.

Donald R. Bernard

1

The Rescue of Manjiro by Captain William H. Whitfield and the John Howland

Far away and long ago, a chance meeting between two fishermen, a thirty-six-year-old American and a fourteen-year-old Japanese, became an incident of profound importance. This encounter would influence the course of world history for the next hundred and fifty years.

This is the story of Manjiro, a Japanese fisherboy from the village of Nakanohama. The substance of the story, as strange as it may appear, is factual. No novelist could have invented a more dramatic and meaningful tale.

In the year 1805, in the town of Fairhaven, Massachusetts, a baby boy was born to a young woman named "Sybil Whitfield." Sybil was the third daughter of Joseph and Parnel Whitfield of Dartmouth, Massachusetts. She named her newborn boy "William Henry Whitfield." William was to become a sailing shipmaster, carrying on a Whitfield tradition in a sense, for his uncle, (his mother's brother) George Whitfield, was also a whaler, serving aboard the whaleship *Martha*. The *Martha* was built at Scituate, Massachusetts, in 1805. Weighing in at 271 tons, she measured 92 feet 8 inches (about 28 meters) in length, 25 feet (about 8 meters) in breadth, and 12 feet 11 inches (about 4 meters) in depth. The *Martha* had two decks, three masts, and a square stern showing no galleries or figureheads. Her surveyor was Rounsevel Spooner.

In June 1818, at age twenty-nine, George Whitfield served as crewman aboard the *Martha,* sailing out of Nantucket, Massachusetts. George lived in New Bedford, Massachusetts, and was of average size, at 5 feet 8 inches tall. He had brown hair and a fair complexion. Later that same year, having been appointed master of the *Martha,* he sailed to South America to take on a cargo of sperm oil. Nearly a year later, in June 1819, he again sailed to South America, this time to transport still another consignment of whale oil.

Two months later, in August, he once more sailed from New Bedford. Records show that his fifteen-year-old nephew, William H. Whitfield, of Fairhaven, Massachusetts, had signed on as a crewman. William resembled his uncle George, and was only half an inch taller. On July 26, 1820, both Whitfields, George as master and William as crewman, again sailed out of New Bedford aboard the *Martha*. They went south to pick up a cargo of oil. On May 14, 1821, and again in May 1822, both George and William served on the whaleship *Pacific*, sailing out of New Bedford.

In 1823, George was again master of the *Martha*, but his nephew signed on as second mate aboard the merchant ship *Missouri*. In 1824, William signed a merchant contract as first officer aboard the sailing ship *William Thompson*. Up to that time, the ships that both George and William served on had been outfitted by Seth Russell and Sons of New Bedford.

In 1835, George Whitfield assumed command of the *Newark*, sailing out of Poughkeepsie, New York. The records of the town clerk of Fairhaven reveal that George married Pamela Wood, daughter of Richard and Mary Hitch of Fairhaven, on August 14, 1820. William married Ruth C. Irish of Fairhaven in 1835, and he and his new bride lived in his Aunt Amelia's house at 11 Cherry Street in Fairhaven. Aunt Amelia was sister to William's mother Sybil. Ruth died in 1837. Devastated and despondent over his wife's death, William spent a year in seclusion, avoiding all social and business encounters.

After his year of mourning, William's attention was drawn to a young lady from Bridgewater, Massachusetts, a small town thirty miles north of Fairhaven. Albertina Peters Keith frequently visited with her uncle, Alexis Keith, a landlord and next-door neighbor to the Whitfields. On one of her visits, William and Albertina met, and a courtship began.

In the summer of 1839, William asked for Albertina's hand in marriage. She promised to marry him, and he decided to return to the sea to earn enough money to provide a proper home for his new bride. This pivotal decision would eventually involve him in the tale of adventure and intrigue that is the focal point of this book.

After pondering several offers from both merchant and whaling interests, William Whitfield decided to once again embark on a whaling expedition. He was retained by the J. & J. Howland Company of New Bedford to take command of the whaling ship *John Howland,* which was named after the principal owner of the company. The *Howland* had been built at New Bedford in 1830. She weighed about 377 tons. Her length was 111 feet 10 inches (about 34 meters) and her breadth 27 feet 5 inches (about 8 meters), and she drew 13 feet 8½ inches (about 4 meters). The *Howland* had two decks, three masts, a square stern showing no galleries, and a scroll head. She had been constructed by J. & Z. Hillman, master carpenters. Once assured of Whitfield's commitment, the *Howland's* owners publicly posted the upcoming expedition. Many applicants were eager to serve aboard the rugged whaling ship, and twenty-eight men were hired, satisfying the ship's complement. During the next several weeks, the crewmen, under Whitfield's watchful eye, prepared the ship for an anticipated three-year adventure. They would be searching for valuable prey—the "black whale."

Once the ship was ready, Whitfield submitted to the officials at the Customs House of New Bedford the required list of the crew members, written in his own hand:

Crew of *John Howland*

Captain William H. Whitfield

Master of the ship, *John Howland* bound for the Pacific Ocean sailing from New Bedford, on October 30, 1839.

Name	*Residence*
Parden G. Winslow	New Bedford
Edward Southworth	Dartmouth
Warren Woodward	Buffalo
Isaacar U. Akin	Fairhaven
Jacob B. McBride (boat steerer)	Goshen
Hiram Talbot	New Bedford
William Sanford (steward)	"
John Baldwin (carpenter)	"
William N. Stannard	"
Frederick R. Deming	"
Lyman Holmes	"
Hazen Warren Furber	"

James Price	New Bedford
Hiram Rockwood	"
John Conory	Boston
LaFayette Willcox	Fairhaven
Thomas F. Adams	New Bedford
Edward F. Thompson	New York
Richard Vernon (blacksmith)	Eastport
Lewis D. Hicks	New York
William Rhodes (seaman)	New York
Antonio Lopes	New Bedford
Francis Josephs (cooper)	"
Manuel Frisk	"
John Francis	New Bedford
Alexander Harris (cook)	"
John Gridley	"

Before noon on October 30, 1839, at high tide, the *John Howland*, assisted by several barges, was skillfully maneuvered out of her berth. An array of well-wishers, including the ship's owners, were on hand to bid the *Howland* and her crew Godspeed, and to wish them a safe journey home.

Getting the cumbersome vessel out of her berth and into the main channel was a tedious task, but the bargemen's skill soon carried her into the mainstream between Palmer's Island, off the New Bedford shore, and Fort Phoenix, the old Revolutionary battery on the Fairhaven side. From his station on the quarterdeck, Captain Whitfield bellowed familiar commands that caused the crewmen to scurry about, both on the main deck and aloft. Light morning winds from the south-southeast gently lifted the sails from their spars. In about the time it would have taken an hourglass to empty, the *John Howland* was in full sail, pressing southward toward the Elizabeth Islands and Buzzards Bay. From the vantage point of well-wishers, the vessel gradually diminished in size as it left the harbor and set sail toward the whaling grounds of the Pacific Ocean. Once clear of New Bedford harbor, the ship headed southwest toward Cape Horn, the dreaded southernmost peninsula of South America.

A legend among mariners, Cape Horn was a subject of great concern to shipmasters and crewmen alike. Without question, the route via Cape Horn was by far the shortest way to the Pacific Ocean, but it entailed serious risks. It was surrounded by endlessly aroused seas and strong riptides. Ice floes were often present. A heavy fog frequently compounded the other dangers. Lookouts, always fearful of collision with a passing floe, dared not let their attention wander even for a moment. The annals of sea life abound with tales of countless ships that were either lost or heavily damaged while passing Cape Horn. Even when the elements showed signs of fair sailing in general, the weather in the vicinity of the cape was unpredictable. A calm rhythmic sea could suddenly and without notice change into a snarling instrument of destruction. Nevertheless, most shipmasters chose this route over any other, mindful of the responsibility entrusted to them by the ships' owners—to acquire the greatest possible amount of whale oil and bone in the shortest possible time.

Captain Whitfield, then, was only following tradition when he chose the Cape Horn route. The *Howland* was able to successfully clear the dreaded Cape Horn area and sail steadily on into the calmer waters of the South Pacific. Captain and crew turned to the true purpose of the expedition—the hunting and taking of whale. Captain Whitfield ordered the crow's nest to be manned from sunrise to sunset. The lookouts strained to catch any glimpse of whales thrashing about, or basking in the sun on the surface of the ocean, or blowing their characteristic spouts of water and air, which from a distance look like smoke or fog. The effort was successful, as the days became weeks and the weeks months. The ship's log recorded frequent captures of whales, and hand-drawn pictures often accompanied the detailed written accounts, which as a matter of course included the longitude and latitude.

The logbook also revealed that Captain Whitfield and his crew made stops on several of the many islands that dot the Pacific. They were always careful to select friendly ports, mindful that hostilities would have jeopardized not only the crew but the ship as well.

Late in the spring of 1841, when nearly sixteen months had passed since they left the harbor of New Bedford, the *Howland*'s hold was nearly half-filled with barrels of precious whale oil. Captain Whitfield turned the search in an easterly direction, away from the isolationist country of Japan. It was well known that Japan had maintained a self-imposed policy of isolation for nearly 200 years. Captain Whitfield was following an unwritten rule when he kept the *Howland* a respectable distance from the territorial waters of Japan.

Several months earlier, in January 1841 according to the Western calendar, a young Japanese peasant boy named Manjiro was helping to eke out a bare living for his family in a small fishing village called Nakanohama on Shikoku Island. The community was typical of the many villages that graced the eastern coastline of Japan. Fishing was the main industry and had been since ancient times.

The fishing is good in these parts because of the Kuroshio Current (the name means "black stream"). From a great distance, the current looks dark blue; from directly above the sea surface, it looks ultramarine or cobalt. Like the other major oceanic current, the Gulf Stream in the Atlantic, the Kuroshio Current consists of a continuous flow of warm water and provides an ideal habitat for many species of fish. A very strong current that extends deep into the ocean, it flows north from Okinawa along the eastern coast of Japan, then veers to the northeast and out into the Pacific. Men from villages like Nakanohama have relied upon this natural phenomenon for hundreds of years for assistance in their quest for fish.

Fourteen-year-old Manjiro was one of five children of a fisherman named Etsuske and a peasant woman named Shio. Japanese peasants in those days did not have surnames; they were known only by the names given them at birth. Manjiro was born in 1827, and his father died nine years later. Shio was left alone to support and provide for her children. She worked long hours for little return, earning barely enough to feed her family. Schooling, no matter how rudimentary, could not even be considered. Each child, as soon as he or she was old enough, began to work.

Such was the case with Manjiro. Unable to find steady work in his village of Nakanohama, he decided to venture to the coastal village of Usa, nearly 90 miles (145 kilometers) to the north, where the prospects of obtaining permanent employment might prove better. Manjiro was able to convince one of the boat owners of his village who was planning to fish in the vicinity of Usa to give him passage.

While he was sleeping near the shore, a man later identified as Fudenojo came upon the lad. Since the boy was unfamiliar to him, Fudenojo decided to stop and question him. After listening to Manjiro's story, the elder Fudenojo offered to take the boy home where he was given food and shelter.

On the morning of January 5, 1841, Manjiro was assigned to a small fishing boat, serving under a boatman named Fudenojo, who was called "Denzo." Denzo's duties included serving as helmsman for the craft. At age thirty-eight, he was the oldest member of the crew. Under him, besides Manjiro, were Denzo's fifteen-year-old brother Goemon, a man named Jusuke, and a twenty-seven-year-old fisherman named Toraemon.

The small boat, with its five-man crew, left the shore of Usa at approximately ten o'clock in the morning. During a day that began to seem endlessly long, the men on the tiny boat sailed far from the sight of land but met with no success. Again and again they hauled in empty nets. When the sun began to set, the crew hauled in their nets for the last time. Slowly the boat made its way toward the silhouetted Cape of Yaso in Okitsu. In the calm of leeward, they dropped anchor for the remainder of the night. The lack of fish must have dominated the evening's conversation.

At first light, the determined crew once again set out in search of fish. This morning, they used fishing rods instead of nets. Again they drifted along the prevailing currents, and again their luck was not good. Light to moderate winds prevailed for the better part of the day and carried the craft nearly 30 miles (48 kilometers) out to sea. As before, they hoisted sail and made their way toward landfall, this time the leeward side of the cape near Shirahama. On the following morning, January 7, with Denzo at the helm as usual, the crew again ventured many miles off the coast of Okitsu. At midmorning, thick clouds began to gather, and a fresh northwest wind began to blow. Soon the crew forgot about fishing, thinking only of the adverse weather. By noon the wind and waves had calmed enough to allow them to resume fishing, but soon the northwest winds picked up again. Denzo decided to seek refuge but had great difficulty in controlling the boat.

Just northeast of Cape Ashizuri of Shikoku, the boat began to drift uncontrollably. Before dawn the next morning, the small fishing vessel was held captive by the agitated sea. The southeasterly wind was howling with mounting fury. Denzo was having difficulty in steering. Soon the craft was blown well off course.

The frightened crew unexpectedly found themselves in the middle of a large school of mackerel. They threw all available nets out over the disturbed waters but soon regretted their impetuosity. The swelling seas were threatening to engulf the nets. Denzo ordered the nets to be hauled back. By this time, the men were weary, but they quickly responded to Denzo's order, struggling to recover their valuable gear. The intensifying storm proved too strong. The men were able to retrieve only about half of their nets.

What was worse, the mainsail was snatched away by a wave and pulled down into the foaming sea. The men hurried to lash down every piece of equipment on board. The vessel was assaulted by wave after wave. Finally the rudder splintered and was carried away, leaving the boat and the men totally at the mercy of the elements. Hanging onto the framework of the craft, the men were swiftly swept toward the southeast, totally at the mercy of the Kuroshio Current.

At first Denzo assured his comrades that the whale lookout at Mountain View Lodge atop the steep hillside of Cape Muroto would be sure to see them and would arrange a rescue, but the sweeping tide soon carried the small fishing boat well out of view of the watchman's house. The last bit of land they saw was Mount Kiki. The threatening skies turned dark as night set in. The crew were weary, cold, and hungry. In an attempt to warm themselves, they tore planks off the boat, gathered small bits of straw from between the planking, and made a fire. They ate some of the fish they had caught during the height of the gale. By this time, they had no idea where they were, as they had lost sight of all known landmarks. Icy winds prevailed, and their boat continued to drift for four days.

On January 11 the vessel finally broke free of the Kuroshio Current, but it continued to drift helplessly toward the southeast for the next two days, traveling approximately 225 miles (362 kilometers).

On January 12, the morning darkness was accompanied by a cold, piercing drizzle. Goemon became ill. His body was burning with fever, and the others tried to encourage and warm him. The crew's small supply of drinking water and mackerel was gone, but they were able to gather a few icicles from the boat's rigging. They divided them equally, and thus were able to satisfy their intolerable thirst to some degree.

Finally, on January 13 in the late morning, the gale began to subside. Goemon's fever persisted, and the boat continued to drift. Suddenly, one of the men noticed a small flight of birds in the distance, an indication that land was nearby. The men watched the direction of the birds' flight and began rowing, using broken boards as oars. For several hours they rowed toward what they hoped was land. Manjiro helped to row and also to bail out the seawater, so as to lighten the vessel.

At about four o'clock in the afternoon, Denzo rose excitedly to his feet, hoping he saw land but not sure. As twilight fell, he realized that a profile of land was indeed visible. With new hope, strength, and joy, the crew rowed toward the welcome sight. As they drew closer to the island, however, they heard the dreadful sound of rolling surf, a distinct signal of danger, especially so close to land.

What they heard was waves crashing onto coral reefs which dominated the coast. This strange island had no beach and was fortified by high stone walls. Towering cliffs overlooked the treacherous reefs. Denzo and his crew made every effort to stay well away from the reefs that ringed the island. Using all their seafaring skills, they circled the island in search of a safe approach. As night came on, they agreed not to risk losing their boat and belongings. They anchored and waited for daylight.

As the moon brightened, the men saw fish splashing about near the anchored boat. They quickly cast out their nets, close to the protruding rocks, and retrieved them filled with fish. After a banquet of raw fish, they huddled close together in an attempt to keep warm.

At dawn on January 14, the crew woke feeling rested and enthusiastic, for the first time in days. Denzo ordered the anchor to be raised so they could again survey the island for a safe approach. The anchor, however, was firmly wedged into the sharp coral. Time and again the men tried to free it, to no avail. Several possible methods of dislodging the anchor were discussed. Finally, they agreed to cut the anchor rope and to try to steer the craft through the dangerous shoaled waters toward the island. Toraemon suggested that they enter the turbulent waters and guide the craft through the reefs to the base of the high cliffs. The dangerous plan was agreed to; each man was fully aware that it was a one-chance opportunity.

Denzo, as helmsman, stayed on the boat while the other four slipped over the side of the boat into the water and positioned themselves on either side of the bow in the hope of guiding the boat safely to the island. The anchor line was cut free, and the boat was quickly drawn into the racing current and toward the shoals. Denzo, relying upon his experience as a helmsman and using his makeshift rudder, attempted to guide the vessel through the swirling waters toward the base of the palisade. The boat was rocked again and again as it glanced off the coral reefs. The men in the water tried in vain to guide the craft through the treacherous passage. Denzo fought desperately to hold the craft on course. Finally, captured by the quick, turbulent current, the helpless boat crashed into a crevice in a gigantic towering wall of protruding rock. Denzo leapt clear of the boat, and the men swam courageously in an attempt to escape from the uncontrolled craft, which was bearing down upon them. They all managed to swim clear, just as a huge following wave crashed down upon the battered vessel, splintered it into several sections, and finally buried it beneath the surf. Moments later, the foaming, disturbed water dissipated. Only fragmentary, splintered remains of the boat could be sighted.

Manjiro was momentarily pulled below the turbulent waters but quickly surfaced and swam to a nearby rock. Denzo too was trapped when the vessel floundered, but somehow he, Goemon, Toraemon, and Jusuke managed to fight their way to the rocky base of the cliff, assisted by the rise of a following swell. Jusuke sustained a severe injury to his leg. Nevertheless, the men were able to scale the projecting cliff and make their way to the summit of the isolated island. All the men finally reached the top and fell to the ground, exhausted from the struggle.

After resting for a while, the crew confronted the task of evaluating their situation. Each man was assigned to search a different area of the island for inhabitants and edible vegetation. The search went quickly, and its results were dismaying. They were alone. Worse, the island was free of vegetation except for some small bushes and the seaweed that ringed its base. The island was estimated to be approximately 2 miles (3 kilometers) in circumference.

The men held a conference to decide on their next course of action, and agreed to make another search of the island for signs of life and for food. Again they found no other people and no food, but they did discover a small cave. Approximately 12 feet (3.5 meters) square, the cave contained evidence of shellfish. The men became convinced that other persons had at one time occupied the cave—probably other fishermen like themselves. During their search, they also found several crevices in the rock formation where rainwater had collected. This discovery was very welcome to the shipwrecked crew, since their water supply had been almost completely depleted. The supply of rainwater was meager but would, they figured, be adequate if they were careful.

Now that their water problem had been solved, they focused their attention on obtaining food. The only possibility seemed to be an abundant population of albatross, seagoing birds which clustered heavily on this lonely coral island in the Pacific. These birds were numerous and were initially unafraid; the men were able to walk among them and capture them easily. Soon, however, the birds became aware of the danger and began to take flight when the men came near them. Manjiro, the youngest, learned how to cast sharp stones at the birds with a great degree of accuracy. The men's diet was confined mainly to the birds, but Manjiro also found some albatross eggs. For a change of diet, they would eat the seaweed that was plentiful all around the atoll, first carefully wiping off all possible salt in order to curb their desire to drink fresh water. After several months, the men noticed that the bushes scattered over the atoll were bearing small nuts. They harvested the nuts and included them in their meager diet.

The months passed slowly. With each day, the crew's hopes of being found and returned home to Japan faded. As summer approached, the birds, which had been plentiful, began migrating to other locations. The water supply also was being rapidly depleted as the seasonal rainstorms became less frequent. Denzo, still the recognized leader of the stranded

crew, realized that they would soon be facing a serious shortage of both food and water. He therefore introduced a plan of
rationing, and each man was required to pledge that he would
not violate the rules. Nuts became their main course, and
each man was allowed only one shellful of water after each
meal. This method of rationing enabled the crew of the
wrecked fishing boat to subsist for a while longer.

Manjiro, like the others, was often preoccupied with
thoughts of home. Still a young boy, he thought especially of
his mother. His heart was heavy whenever he remembered
that he had not had the opportunity to embrace her prior to
the ill-fated departure of the fishing boat from Usa. This
young fisherman had, in only a few months, developed into a
manly state—not only mentally but physically as well. He was
sharing the burden of work equally with the grown men.

At this time the Tokugawa regime was the prevailing authority in power in Japan. For over 200 years, a policy of strict
isolation had not only prohibited any foreign entry into Japan
but also provided cruel punishments for those who left and
subsequently attempted to return to the country. Well aware
of this dangerous situation, the crew of the wrecked fishing
boat often discussed it during their confinement on the island.
Though they felt certain that they could explain their unfortunate dilemma, the question remained: Would they be put to
death if they were able to return to Japan? This dire prospect,
however, was not their main concern at the moment. Instead,
their thoughts were centered on their hopes of being rescued
from this barren, miserable isle.

Jusuke was still suffering from the injury he had received
while attempting to leap to safety during their landing. The
other men also had contracted various physical disorders.
Only Manjiro remained in good health, having somehow
warded off the diseases which the others had contracted.
Being youthful and strong, the lad was able to perform many
of the chores, which included obtaining and preparing the
daily meals as well as taking his turn as lookout on the cliffs.
The men clung to a hope that they would someday see and
capture the attention of a passing ship.

One day in early June, when the men from Usa had been
prisoners on the lonely island for six months and thirteen

days, Manjiro ascended to his perch high atop the cliff. As he gazed out over the ocean, he thought he noticed a small speck on the southern horizon. Could it be, he wondered, a ship moving in their direction? His adrenaline started to flow at the mere thought that a ship might be sailing toward their barren prison. Though his heart was pounding like a drum, he sat motionless for a long time, watching the speck. When he became sure it was not a mirage but truly a ship, Manjiro could no longer contain his emotions. He shouted with glee, hoping to get the attention of the others. Quickly he descended the steep bluff and hurried to the cave to tell his friends about his sighting. Goemon and Toraemon hurried to the top of the cliff, but Denzo and Jusuke were too weak to climb. Once Goemon and Toraemon reached the summit, they stared as in disbelief in the southwest direction that Manjiro indicated. A new sense of hope inspired them, and they began jumping up and down with joy. One of the men quickly removed a shredded piece of clothing, attached it to a staff and began waving it frantically in the hope of gaining the attention of the oncoming ship.

As they watched, the unidentified ship suddenly changed course and headed due east. The stranded fishermen were in a near panic, but shortly, the ship came about, taking a north by northwest heading and once again steering toward the island. Closer and closer she sailed. Soon her billowing sails were completely visible, as she labored heavily, plowing through the running sea. The crewmen aboard the large vessel became visible and could be seen moving about on the pitching deck as the ship lurched forward through each swell.

Manjiro's thoughts returned to their attempt to land on this barren island, and the destructive barrier of coral rock which encircled it. He wondered whether the ship's lookouts could sight the hidden reefs, and he feared that the ship's crew would also become prisoners on this small lonely island. His fears diminished somewhat as the gigantic ship began to lower her sails.

The Japanese fishermen began shouting and dancing at the thought of being rescued. They watched as the sprit of the vessel swung about and her bow caught the wind. After what seemed like an eternity, they could see a whirlwind of activity on the main deck. Several small longboats were lowered into the water, and their bows were directed toward the island. As the men in boats rowed closer, it became apparent that they were experiencing the same landing problems that the Japanese fishermen had had nearly six months before.

Fearful of disaster among the treacherous reefs, the strangers began motioning to the men on the island, trying to tell them to swim out to the waiting rescue boats. The stranded fishermen were not sure at first what the men in the boats were trying to tell them, but then Manjiro caught on. He slipped out of his weather-beaten clothing and rolled it up into a ball, which he held over his head with one hand as he entered the turbulent water and swam slowly out toward his rescuers. When he was finally able to reach the first longboat, several crewmen extended their hands and hoisted him aboard. He sprawled near the garboards at the rescuers' feet, in a seemingly religious gesture which was not understood by his liberators. The crewmen shouted and gestured to Manjiro, who was equally unable to comprehend them.

The other Japanese had watched Manjiro's swim with great interest, and they soon realized that they must follow his example. After both Goemon and Toraemon were safely aboard the boats, one of the rescuers shouted something in a strange tongue and the crew immediately resumed their posts and began pulling rhythmically on their oars, rowing the small boats back toward the waiting ship, which was anchored at a considerable distance from the island.

The rescued party reacted with much excitement, for they now realized for the first time that the men in the boats could not be aware that Denzo and Jusuke were still in the cave on the island. The Japanese men kept screaming and pointing back to the island. Finally the man who was steering the first boat realized that they wanted to return to the atoll. Bewildered, the boatman nevertheless brought the boat about and started back toward the island.

As the boat again neared the churning waters, Toraemon jumped in and made his way toward the base of the rocky wall. Two of the boat's crewmen stripped off some of their clothing and followed Toraemon. When the Japanese fisherman reached the ledge at the base of the rock, he struggled to pull himself up out of the water and then began scaling the wall, working his way up toward the hidden cave that held

Denzo and Jusuke. The men from the rescue boat followed close behind. When they reached the cave, Toraemon tried to explain to his friends, who were delirious in their illness, what had happened. The two strangers attempted to assist the sick men to rise to their feet, but Denzo, misunderstanding their intentions, tried vainly to assume a position of combat. Denzo was easily overpowered, and Toraemon continued explaining that there was a very large ship waiting for them beyond the reef barrier. Denzo finally came to realize that the strangers meant no harm.

With Toraemon leading, the five men slowly descended the cliff toward the waterline and the waiting boats. The strangers helped the sick men to make their way through the turbulent waters and to board the longboats. Then they again began to row back toward the ship. The Japanese fishermen, especially Manjiro, were awed by the great size and magnificence of the strange vessel. Her three large masts seemed to tower into the heavens. Never had the men from Usa seen such an enormous ship. However, as the small boats drew closer to the ship, a strong and familiar odor told the rescued party that this ship of mystery was undoubtedly one which plied the fishing trade.

When the last longboat, carrying Manjiro, reached the broadside of the larger vessel, the ship's crewmen lowered a long rope ladder which dangled below the water line. The Japanese were instructed by motions that they should climb the rope ladder.

They now encountered yet another strange sight—a huge black man who smiled broadly as he helped them to climb the ladder and board the large ship. Having reached the sweeping main deck, they were brought before a stern-looking man who at first said not a word. Instead, he simply gazed at the ragged men, looking somewhat surprised. Manjiro, sensing authority, quietly assumed a humble, prone position on the hard deck. The others followed his example. Manjiro mumbled several words in his native tongue, but the men of the large ship understood nothing that he said. The stern-looking man, who was obviously in charge of the ship, said something to another man, who immediately left the deck. He returned a few minutes later, carrying a large platter that held an assortment of food. The stern man benevolently extended his hand to the prostrate Japanese crew and encouraged them to rise. He removed some of the food from the platter and offered it to the Japanese men. Slowly, hesitatingly, the hungry men tasted the food, which was like nothing they had ever tasted before but did satisfy their hunger pangs. After they ate, they were led to a nearby companionway and motioned to make themselves comfortable.

Their kind host then bellowed several sharp commands which sent men scurrying in all directions. The longboats that had been used in the rescue were hoisted slowly out of the water and raised just above the main deck. The Japanese men watched and listened in awe as the head man again bellowed instructions. Men climbed high into the rigging in response to their leader's commands. Soon the creaking of the capstan could be heard, along with the fluttering of the overhead canvas as it caught the moderate wind.

Realizing that they were being taken on a mysterious voyage with an unknown destination, the Japanese fishermen wondered what fate was in store for them. Soon the canvas swelled and billowed, and the huge vessel set off in the direction she had come from. The distraught fishermen watched as the desolate island which they had called home for six months—and which they later found out was called "Torishima" (meaning "Bird Island")—began to fade beyond the horizon and finally disappeared.

2

The Wake of the John Howland

Once Denzo and his crew were safely aboard the mysterious sailing ship, they became concerned about what their future had in store. Their inability to communicate intelligently with the crew of the *John Howland* was a mutual hardship. With communication impossible, the Japanese were at the mercy of their emancipators.

It was some time before the distraught fishermen learned the identity of the great ship. At first, they were confined to their own area, so that they would not interfere with regular shipboard duties. In confinement, they continually speculated about the enormous ship. Where did she come from? Where was she bound?

As the days passed, they gradually began to find some answers. They learned that the man in charge of the ship was Captain William H. Whitfield. They also discovered that the ship was called *John Howland*, that she had been at sea for nineteen months and seventeen days up until the time of the rescue, and that she was a whaling ship out of a port in the United States known as "New Bedford." However, neither "New Bedford" nor "United States" meant anything to them, because the Tokugawa regime's policy of isolation had suppressed all information about the outside world. The fishermen from Shikoku knew nothing of other countries and probably didn't much care.

Among themselves the Japanese were forever discussing the nagging questions of where they were being taken and how long it would take to get there. What would become of them once they were landed? Did the captain understand what they were trying to tell him—that they were Japanese? Were they being taken back to Japan? Only time would reveal the answers.

After many days, the fishermen regained much of the strength that they had lost during their months on Torishima Island. Jusuke, whose leg injury had continued to be very troublesome, was attended to by the ship's physician and soon recovered nearly full use of the damaged limb. The doctor's kindness and close attention to Jusuke during treatment favorably impressed the Japanese.

Soon the Japanese were allowed to walk about on the main deck of the ship. They observed mutual respect and a close working relationship between Captain Whitfield and his crew. Manjiro especially noted that when members of the crew were occasionally disobedient, the captain would sternly lip-lash the offenders with words that were unfamiliar to the Japanese but in tones left no doubt in their minds about his message. During such reprimands, however, neither Manjiro nor his shipmates observed even one act of physical punishment. The ship's master was always quietly authoritative with his men, and he quickly settled all problems. Again, the Japanese were favorably impressed.

Their newfound friends explained that the ship had been searching for turtles near Torishima when they discovered the stranded fishermen. Eventually the Americans tried to tell the Japanese that soon they would be landing in a place called Honolulu, on the island of Oahu, which was one of the islands then known as the "Sandwich archipelagos" (now called the "Hawaiian Islands").

They explained that most ships, whalers and merchant ships alike, would visit Honolulu to refuel and to take on provisions, including fresh fruit and water. They said that fresh fruit was a major deterrent to scurvy, a dreaded disease of seamen. Ship repairs also could be made in Honolulu, and the ship's crewmen looked upon it as a place where they could relax, enjoy themselves, and get away for a while from the gruesome task of taking whale.

In addition, Honolulu served as a meeting place for sailing ships from all over the world. Mail could be transferred from one ship to another and carried on to other places. Honolulu was indeed a welcome port of call, especially to the whalers, who often sailed for upward of three years. Some of the letters that were exchanged would be between one and two years old. Honolulu was also a port where many sailors changed ships for one reason or other. Some who left their ships were never heard from again.

Even while en route to Honolulu, the *Howland* continued searching for the prized whale. Though they had been rescued from their island, Denzo and his companions still felt somewhat confined—this time on a floating island made of timber and sailcloth.

Several weeks after the rescue, a lookout perched high above in the ship's mast shouted excitedly, "She blows!" The ship's mate was quick to answer with, "Where away?" The lookout, pointing with an outstretched arm, answered the call of the mate with phrases that the Japanese could not understand. The commotion brought crew members, along with Denzo and his friends, rushing to the rail to scan the horizon. What they saw was an object that emitted short puffs, like water spouting from a fountain in a mist. The ship's master also rushed to the rail, near the mate. He was promptly handed a telescope, and the sighted object was pointed out to him. He was very pleased and immediately blasted orders to the crewmen. He gave further instructions to the helmsman. Repeating the orders, the helmsman responded by spinning the large wheel that steered the ship. He spun the wheel with such force and confidence that the vessel pitched and yawed as it dipped into a passing swell. The ship's bow, forced against the running tide, came about smartly in the direction of the sighting. Still more commands from the ship's master followed. Soon the creaking of the blocks could be heard, and more canvas was fed to the wind. The ship's speed increased noticeably as the canvas swelled overhead.

Manjiro and his comrades were caught up in the excitement that rippled through the entire ship. They watched intently as the crewmen hastily prepared the longboats which had been securely locked into the davits. The Japanese party were not at all accustomed to this type of fishing; they knew only of fishing with the use of hand lines, rods, and nets. The largest fish they had ever encountered was the sea bass, which could not begin to compare in size with a fully developed whale. They had often heard about the large mammals but had never seen one. Denzo commanded his comrades to stay well out of the way of the busy crewmen. The fishermen from Usa were completely stunned. Their eyes were fixed on

the enormous floating whale, but suddenly and without warning, it disappeared beneath the surface. The ship continued
on course. Soon the mammal was again spotted near the
surface, only a short distance away. Excitement mounted as
the large ship closed in on the surfaced whale. Captain Whitfield ordered the sails trimmed to slow down his vessel, so that
the confused target would not be spooked. At this point, several longboats were lowered into the running tide and the
boat crews rapidly jumped aboard. Each boat had a six-man
crew. Moments after the boats hit the water, they were in hot
pursuit of the frightened whale.

Each whaleboat measured about 28 feet (8.5 meters) in
length and was very shallow. Each carried an assortment of
related gear, including two tubs (or barrels) of line, one containing approximately 225 fathoms (1350 feet) of line, while
the other carried an additional 75 fathoms (450 feet), to be
tied to the first if the whale sounded to a greater depth. The
Howland stood off at a considerable distance and watched the
proceedings.

The longboats raced one another toward the surfaced
whale, competing to throw the first iron into the flesh of the
leviathan. Soon the lead boat was within throwing range. The
whale took fright and began to dive. The harpooner was
experienced and skillful. He stood firmly in the bow, reared
back, and threw his harpoon at the whale, using all his body
strength. The steel-tipped weapon found its mark and buried
itself deep in the flesh of the frightened whale. The large
mammal flinched, rolled sharply to one side, and quickly disappeared beneath an oncoming swell.

The striker's iron was connected to a long rope, which was
coiled in a wooden barrel. Next to the barrel was a short
wooden post around which the crewmen could wrap the rope,
to relieve the strain created upon the boat when the harpooned whale sounded. Often, when a whale was diving rapidly, it would be necessary to pour water over the post, to cool
the post and line. This was done to prevent the post from
being weakened by friction burn and to protect the line from
breakage due to heating of the hemp strands of the rope.

The whale's reaction to the initial harpooning was probably
the most dangerous time of the entire hunt for the men in the
longboats. Wounded by the harpooner's iron, the whale

would attempt to escape in unpredictable ways. A whale might try to elude the persistent whalemen by frequently and abruptly changing direction. It might use its tremendous strength to roll and flip in an effort to shake loose the painful iron. As long as the harpoon was buried in the mammal's flesh, struggle would only prove fatal. When the whale dove deep toward the ocean floor, the men in the boats above would pay out whatever line was still available in the cask. When the whale suddenly charged upward (an act which was called "breeching"), the trailing line would become limp; the men would cease rowing and await the next move of the wounded and dangerous whale. Every man would search the waters around their small craft for any indication of the movements of the huge mammal. At the first sign, the cry "She breeches!" would alert the other crew members. The men would quickly resume rowing in hot pursuit of their prey. Once they were again within range, the striker would let fly with another harpoon to ensure a strong hold so that they could move in for the final kill.

As the Japanese fishermen watched from the *Howland,* several longboats followed the lead boat, on the trail of the harpooned leviathan. The enraged mammal again disappeared below the surface, carrying with it the rope connected to the lead boat. The men immediately withdrew their oars and secured their boat as the whale made its final attempt to escape the menacing hunters. Though wounded, it swam with increasing speed, pulling the whaleboat in what has often been called a "Nantucket sleigh ride." Unable to escape, the whale soon became exhausted and returned to the surface. The other boats soon closed in, and the harpooners thrust even more of their deadly irons into the flesh of the doomed giant. When the men were sure that the whale was too tired to endanger them, some of them climbed out of the boat and placed a line on its tail. They then signaled the larger ship that the whale had been captured.

Captain Whitfield, aboard the *Howland,* had taken great care to keep his ship on a circular course so as not to interfere with the chase. When he received the signal, he ordered the *Howland* to proceed with all dispatch toward the captured whale. Once the ship came alongside, the huge mammal was securely tied to the larger vessel. Several men thrust long, spear-like lances deep into the carcass of the dying leviathan, probing for the vital spot in which they could finally kill the valuable prey. In its last moments, the wounded whale began gasping and blowing through its spout, showering a mixture of blood and water over everyone and everything nearby. It emitted several screeching cries and rolled over, still desperately trying to ward off its enemies' lethal blows by flipping its destructive tail. Despite the whale's colossal size and tremendous strength, it eventually became motionless on the surface of the water. It was now merely another statistic in the long list of victims of deadly whale hunters.

Manjiro and Denzo were awed by what they had witnessed. They continued to watch as the dead whale was secured to the side of the ship. Manjiro wondered how the crewmen of the *Howland* intended to lift such a heavy prize, and where on board they could place it. His questions were soon answered as the crew began to prepare for "trying out" the whale, or processing its carcass. They prepared a wooden cutting platform by rigging it to fit into brackets on the rail of the vessel. (Such brackets were usually located on the starboard side, at approximately midship). The platform, when in place, extended approximately 10 feet (3 meters) out from the ship and was approximately 6 feet (2 meters) above the waterline.

The carcass was hauled alongside the ship and maneuvered underneath the platform. Several men began working from above the whale, using cutting implements to accomplish the gruesome task of cutting the flesh into manageable pieces. They rolled the whale over as they worked, and removed the blubber in uniform sections. Blocks and tackles were used to raise the freshly cut slabs of blubber onto the main deck of the New Bedford whaleship. These slabs were then placed near a strange-looking object called a "tryworks" located on the main deck near the center of the vessel, under which a fire had already been lit. Working on deck, crewmen would subdivide the slabs into still smaller, more manageable pieces. The two huge kettles called "trypots" were installed within the tryworks. The tryworks was permanently constructed before each cruise and, when the ship returned to port, completely dismantled and rebuilt again prior to the next cruise. When "trying" the whale, each pot was filled with pieces of whale

The building of a tryworks on an American whaleship. (Courtesy Fairhaven Selectmen)

fat, which soon melted into oil. The small portions of carcass
which remained unmelted were fed into the fire to serve as
fuel, and heavy wooden barrels were filled with the oil. One
man's job was to continually spread sawdust on the deck to
soak up the excreted body fluids of the whale.

The Japanese fishermen could not understand why the
American crew were boiling down whale's flesh. According to
Japanese custom, the purpose of killing such a huge whale
would be to eat its flesh; they were not aware of the financial
value of whale oil in the West. In the United States, whale oil
was used as the primary means of illuminating homes. In
addition, since the early 1800s, when America had embarked
on the process of industrialization, whale oil had been found
to be an excellent and economical means of lubricating industrial machinery.

The process of boiling down the whale blubber continued
through the remainder of the day and well into the night.
Finally, all the flesh had been boiled down into oil. By the

time the final ladle of oil had been poured into its huge cask, the crewmen were quite weary—but the job was not yet finished. The entire working area had to be scrubbed clean of all traces of the whale's fluids and carcass.

Although Manjiro had not participated in the work, he had never left the deck, he was so interested in what the ship's crew were doing. The Japanese now had much more to talk about. What they had witnessed would certainly command the ears and attention of all the fishermen back in Usa.

After the capture of the whale, the days aboard ship again became comparatively uneventful. The search for whales continued, and the rescued party were becoming more and more at ease with the crewmen of the American ship, although the communication barrier still existed. Though most Japanese-American communication was accomplished through sign language, the Japanese knew they were among friends. Whitfield, in particular, took a keen interest in Manjiro and would often try speaking with him. He tried to teach the lad by using sign language and by speaking slowly and clearly. Manjiro was eager to learn and soon became able to identify objects on the ship in English. He tried hard to build his vocabulary and to retain the things the captain taught him. Whitfield had quickly learned to pronounce the names of the Japanese, but most of the crewmen found their names very difficult. They decided to give the boy an American-sounding name, and the name they chose for him was "John Mung." His new first name was derived from the name of their vessel, the *John Howland,* while the last name was shortened from "Mungero," an Americanized pronunciation of "Manjiro."

Trying to repay the captain and his crew for their kindness, the Japanese would often try to assist with the ship's chores. At first, the captain discouraged their attempts, but eventually, because of their persistence, he let them help. Even young Mung was allowed to lend a hand. One of the duties which the young boy eagerly performed was that of lookout. He would take his turn at climbing high into the ship's rigging and carefully scanning for any sign of whales.

One day, Mung's sharp eyes noticed something splashing, far out toward the horizon. Through his long glass, he identified a fair-sized whale and a young calf. He immediately began shouting the alarm, and excitedly waved his arms and pointed at the surfaced mammals. The mother whale made frantic attempts to escape and to protect her offspring, but the experienced whalemen made short work of capturing and killing her. However, the men of the *Howland,* after a close inspection of the calf, agreed that it was much too small to be taken. They allowed it to swim free, hoping that it would survive and that they could someday recapture it, after it had grown to a more valuable size.

Whitfield had high praise for Mung's sharp attention to duty, and Mung relished his attention. The captain presented John with a sailor's cap as a reward for his part in the sighting and resulting capture of the good-sized whale. The other Japanese fishermen also received rewards for their efforts during the trying-out periods.

As the ship continued to sail toward the Sandwich Islands and the port of Honolulu, John Mung, always noticeably inquisitive, would often watch the actions of the helmsmen very closely, hoping to learn the secret of steering. After many hours of observation, he was allowed to take control of the massive wheel. In addition, whenever the captain was working with his charts, Mung would be close at hand. He watched with great interest every move the captain made as he manipulated his instruments over the strange-looking documents. His exceptional interest in sailing matters did not go unnoticed by Captain Whitfield.

This time aboard the *Howland* was Mung's first educational opportunity. His English vocabulary grew larger every day, which meant that communication between the Japanese and the Americans became easier—a welcome relief to all concerned. Mung's aspiration was to discover how the captain could understand what the ship's position was by using the charts.

During the first five months after Whitfield rescued the Japanese from their imprisonment, the *Howland* took fifteen whales. The Japanese passengers acquired a great deal of knowledge about the capturing and killing of whales. Mung had learned even more than the others because of his deep interest and his fearless approach. Whitfield and the members of his crew were quick to befriend the boy because of his cooperative attitude and his willingness to perform nearly any task. They also appreciated the aggressive manner in which he attempted to learn their language. Mung was enthusiastic about his newly acquired knowledge and eager to explain everything he had learned to the other Japanese fishermen, but his attempts to share his knowledge were frustrating.

In November 1841, late in the whaling season, the *Howland* sailed within sight of her destination—Honolulu, the port where all the sea-lanes of the Pacific Ocean met. Captain Whitfield had promised that his young friend would see many ships like the *Howland* and would hear many new languages, some of which his American friends on the whaleship could not understand. Honolulu was also the place where Mung and his friends might hope to secure passage back to their homeland on a vessel sailing in that direction.

As the *Howland* approached the harbor, her progress was hampered. Captain Whitfield noted in the ship's log on November 20, 1841, "Wind out, could not get her in."

Instead, scores of islanders came out to the whaleship in boats that looked strange to the Japanese. After securing lines to various parts of the great ship, they began to paddle, skillfully applying their own strength to help guide and tow the broad-beamed *Howland*. After a considerable delay, the island's pilot, with the assistance of the islanders, was able to guide the ship through the intricate approach and into the safety of the inner harbor.

The Japanese fishermen, along with the ship's company, lined the rail as the huge vessel was slowly towed toward a protected anchorage. The busy harbor was alive with ships of every description; their masts looked like a wall against the light blue sky. Never before had the rescued men witnessed such an impressive sight. Upon reaching its anchorage, the ship came to an easing stop. Moments later, the large anchor, dropped from its holding position, disappeared into the water below. The New Bedford vessel was quickly besieged by many Hawaiians in little boats, all shouting excitedly and waving their arms in a friendly and welcoming manner. It was easy for the Japanese to understand that they were receiving a friendly reception, and they enjoyed the exciting and pleasurable experience.

The arrival of the *Howland* was noted in the island newspaper, *The Polynesian*, under the heading "Marine News," as follows: "ARRIVED: Nov. 20, 1841, *John Howland*, New

Bedford, 24 mons 1400 sperm" (meaning "twenty-four months at sea, carrying 1400 barrels of sperm whale oil").

The crew of the *Howland* were noticeably excited and enthusiastic, but they made the ship secure before going ashore for some well-earned rest and relaxation. The Japanese fishermen also were excited; it had been nearly a year since they had set foot on any land other than the hard rock of their island prison.

Once the ship was properly secured, however, the captain had the Japanese brought before him. He explained that he would go ashore to seek permission from the governor of the island for the Japanese men to come ashore. He hoped to gain the governor's sympathy for their plight and his help in seeking some means of returning them to their homeland—if and when it could be determined exactly where that homeland was. The captain had trepidations, however; he feared that if the men he had rescued were allowed to come ashore, they might have great difficulty in finding a way to support themselves, and he was also concerned that not all the people in this port would be as kind to and understanding of these Japanese as the crew of the *Howland* had been.

Whitfield also explained to Denzo and his men that he would try to have passage booked for them on some vessel that would be cruising in the vicinity of the Sea of Japan, but that he could not promise that this would be possible. He told them to remain on board the ship until he returned. Denzo, speaking as the leader of the stranded men, agreed to do what the captain said.

Long, lonesome days slipped by with no word or sign from Captain Whitfield. The Japanese fishermen were not at all comfortable during their restless wait. They silently watched as the ship's crewmen, in alternate shifts, went ashore to seek various pleasures, and they saw many of the crewmen staggering when they returned to the ship, under the influence of grog, a favorite drink of the visiting sailors. No matter what they saw, though, they all knew that Denzo had given his word. The disciplined group of Japanese therefore waited for the promised return of the captain.

As they waited, they discussed among themselves what types of work they would like to try if they were allowed to go ashore. They all agreed that they must continue to learn

the strange language of the Americans. Mung's English had
already improved markedly. He was by far the quickest to
grasp the new language. The slowest was Denzo, the oldest of
the five. They all practiced their English by asking for the help
of the sailors who were standing watch. It was easy for Manjiro to get help, as he was well liked by most of the ship's crew.

After several days of waiting, finally the Japanese got their
reward: the captain returned. He told them that they were to
accompany him to the governor's office, located within a fort
near the harbor on the main island. When they finally went
ashore, they experienced great difficulty in keeping their balance because they had spent such a long time on the rolling
and pitching deck of the *Howland*. On the dirt roadway leading to the governor's office, they had further opportunity to
observe the scantily clad people of the island, most of whom
had skins several shades darker than the Japanese. The
thatched-roof houses lining the road were another new sight
for Denzo and his men.

The captain directed their attention to a large stone building that was under construction. The ship's master hailed a
man working on the roof, who acknowledged the American
seaman with a smile. The man dropped his tools, quickly
descended the ladder, and offered a firm handshake and a
quick embrace to his old friend. He then probably pointed out
that the new church he was building was nearly finished.
Whitfield complimented him on his fine artisanship and then
introduced his Japanese companions to his friend, Dr. Gerrit
P. Judd. Dr. Judd was a medical missionary who had first
come to Hawaii in 1828 and was later to hold important
positions in the government of the Hawaiian Kingdom. He
asked the fishermen where they had come from, but before
they could answer, Whitfield explained that they had been
picked up by his ship early in the summer, and that they could
neither speak nor understand English. He added that he was
deeply committed to making arrangements to have them
safely returned to their homeland, wherever that might be.

The task of discovering where the shipwrecked fishermen's
home was had been made doubly difficult by the isolationist
policy of the Tokugawa government. Because the Japanese
people had long been shielded from outside influences, they
knew nothing of other places, peoples, countries, or politics.

Dr. Judd decided to make an attempt to determine where the captain's friends came from. He asked them a number of questions but received only puzzled silence in reply. Dr. Judd pondered for a moment and then remembered that, several years earlier, another group of shipwrecked men had been rescued and had left Honolulu on the whaleship *James Loper* under Captain Cathcart. They had left behind with Dr. Judd a package which he still had in his possession. The package contained some metal coins, pipes and tobacco, and several other strange-looking articles. He sent a Hawaiian boy to his house for the package. Upon the boy's return, Dr. Judd showed some of the articles to the Japanese, hoping for a reaction. Mung let out a cry of joyous glee. Other members of the Japanese party were also excited. Dr. Judd was encouraged. He next laid before them an old chart, hoping that they might recognize the area from which they came. Even the doctor was not fully aware of just how illiterate these men really were. Denzo and his friends showed no emotional response whatsoever when they looked at the chart. The doctor decided to try a different approach. He held his arms by his sides and bowed forward into a very low position. Once again, the Japanese did not react.

The missionary then went back to get the package. Again he removed some copper and silver coins, as well as several long-stemmed pipes with small bowls. Using Mung as translator, he asked the men whether they could recognize any of the items. Denzo smiled faintly and half nodded. Soon the others were also nodding in the affirmative. This settled the question of their origin to the doctor's satisfaction.

He explained to Whitfield that he was quite sure that these men were either from Japan itself or from the Ryukyu Islands which lay south of Japan. In any case, he was sure that they were Japanese. The Japanese were quite pleased. They fell to the ground and assumed a prostrate position before the doctor and the captain, in acknowledgment. "Dai Nippon," they cried. Captain Whitfield also was pleased, as his months of wondering about their origin were finally over. This confirmation that his charges were from Japan would be of great value in his attempts to make arrangements for their passage home. However, he mentioned to Dr. Judd, their need to become self-supporting was the first order of business.

Dr. Judd said that he was sure the government would take care of their expenses until other arrangements could be made. He gave each of the fishermen a silver dollar and told them that no chores or duties would be required of them, as they were the guests of the Hawaiian government. The Japanese, unaccustomed to this kind of treatment, were overjoyed.

Dr. Judd invited Captain Whitfield and his Japanese friends to visit him in his home and to meet his wife. He continued to ask questions as they walked toward his residence. First, he asked Mung if he knew of a place called "Osaka."

The boy quickly replied, "Oh yes, I know that place. But me not see Osaka. Denzo, he know that place. It big, big place."

"Yes, indeed, it is a big place," said the doctor. "It is the best harbor in Japan."

The doctor told them that they must register at the government office in the fort near the harbor entrance. "It is the custom for all foreigners to register," he explained. The Japanese men accompanied Dr. Judd and Captain Whitfield to the government office, and the Westerners explained to the authorities the dilemma of the rescued party. The government officials were completely sympathetic. The Japanese men were then confined to the fort near the government office and were to remain there as guests until other arrangements could be made, confirming Dr. Judd's earlier statements.

Captain Whitfield had grown exceptionally fond of Mung. Despite his very young age, John had displayed an ability to learn quickly. He had a good grasp of the things his new friends aboard the *Howland* had taught him. His abilities, coupled with his ever-present inquisitiveness about almost everything, and especially about navigation, had drawn Captain Whitfield's attention. During the months at sea, the *Howland*'s master had had many opportunities to observe Mung's behavior closely. Often the captain had thought about taking Mung home with him to Fairhaven. He felt that he would like to give the youngster an opportunity to receive a formal education, which would free him from a life of poverty. The weight of this decision lay heavily on Whitfield's mind, especially now that it had been established that the boy came from Japan. The captain, as mentioned before, was well aware of the Tokugawa doctrine, as were most seamen in that latitude. Even so, he was bothered by a nagging question: "Should I leave the boy to the mercy of his destiny?" He felt certain that if he made no attempt to help Mung he would live to regret that decision.

The captain called the Japanese fishermen together, in hopes that they would help him to make his decision. He told the Japanese what he had been thinking about, and offered to take John with him when he left. He assured Denzo that, as soon as the *Howland* returned to Massachusetts, Mung would be enrolled in a school and educated properly. Whitfield's offer completely stunned the already indebted men. They were initially left speechless. John himself said nothing and showed no outward sign of any kind. Denzo took great care to show no sign of disrespect or embarrassment to the captain.

The Japanese moved away from the captain and discussed the captain's suggestion in a huddle. Soon they returned and told Whitfield that his offer had put them in an awkward position. They indicated that they would like to say yes but were concerned about what the authorities and people of the village would say if they were to return home without Manjiro. Further, what could they tell his poor mother and other members of his family? Denzo said that the decision was too difficult for them to make and respectfully asked the captain to forgive them for not offering a solution to the problem. Then one of the Japanese suggested that the question be put to Manjiro himself, thereby relieving his shipmates of the responsibility. Whitfield welcomed this suggestion and asked Mung whether he wanted to go to Fairhaven to get an education. Mung thought for a moment and then answered that he would like very much to accept the captain's offer. This pleased the captain immensely. Mung asked Denzo to explain to his mother the circumstances of his decision, if Denzo returned to Japan before Manjiro did. Denzo agreed to do what Manjiro asked, and the other fishermen all nodded their approval. Manjiro then suggested to the others that they should try, if at all possible, to wait for him to return to Hawaii, rather than attempting to go home without him.

The captain then vowed that he would assume total responsibility for Mung's well-being and promised to do everything in his power to assure that no harm would come to his ward.

Thus it was settled that Mung would sail with Captain Whitfield aboard the *Howland* when she left the port of Honolulu.
The captain's plan was to keep the boy with him during the
rest of the whaling expedition, and then to take him home to
Fairhaven.

Soon the island newspaper, *The Polynesian*, under the
heading of "Marine News," announced: "SAILED: Dec. 1,
Am. Whale Ship *John Howland*, Whitfield, to cruise."

The four other Japanese men were soon assigned living
quarters, with the help of the authorities. They remained in
Honolulu for nearly a year, initially living at the expense of
the government, which showed a great sense of humanity in
their behalf. During this period, all four were able to learn to
speak their new language, which of course made living in
Honolulu a lot easier. Eventually, Denzo and his young
brother Goemon found employment as servants at the Royal
School in Honolulu. Toraemon became an apprentice to a
carpenter on the island. As for Jusuke, the injury he had
received at the time of the shipwreck had taken a turn for the
worse, and he was not able to handle steady employment.

Long after the departure of the *Howland*, Mung's former
boatmates were still discussing and wondering about their
young friend. They were concerned about whether or not
they would ever see either Manjiro or Captain Whitfield
again.

3

Mung's American
Experience

Leaving the port of Honolulu late in December 1841, the New
Bedford whaler *John Howland* sailed once again into the open
sea, setting a course for the whaling areas of the Pacific.
Captain William Whitfield, in company with his young ward
John Mung, watched solemnly as the outline of Honolulu
faded from sight. Manjiro was thinking sadly about the
trusted friends he was leaving behind and also about his
mother, Shio, back in Nakanohama. Even so, he was certain
that sailing as a member of the crew of the *Howland* was the
right choice. Whitfield's promise to help him get an education
in Fairhaven was an opportunity that John Mung could not
pass up. The young boy's destiny was in the hands of the
American sea captain who was his sole guardian now that he
had parted company with Denzo and his companions.

The spring of 1842 was at hand by the time the ship returned to the routine of hunting whale. After leaving the port
of Honolulu, the *Howland* had sailed almost steadily toward
the south-southeast, taking whale from time to time. Captain
Whitfield proudly and eagerly accepted the challenges of his
new role as guardian to young "John Mung," as Manjiro was
now called. Although the captain was engaged to be married
to Albertina Peters Keith, who was waiting for him back in
Bridgewater, Massachusetts, he was still mourning his first
wife's untimely death, and his relationship with John Mung
filled a void. The response of the boy, whose father had died,
leaving him with a similar void, was by now quite evident.
The two spent much of their free time together. It was a
happy period for both. Mung also struck up warm friendships
with several members of the crew who, like him, were still in
their early teens.

When the ship's supplies of fuel and water reached a dan-

gerously low point after a few months, Captain Whitfield
decided to replenish them at the Gilbert Islands. Many scantily clad islanders met the *Howland* almost before she
dropped anchor. Standing by the rail, Mung watched with
interest and amusement as people with rich brown skins offered for trade items such as freshly picked fruit, bows and
arrows, spears, and other primitive weapons. Members of the
Howland's crew had been saving broken chains and other
scraps of metal, which were no longer useful as shipboard
equipment, for use on just such an occasion. The bartering
was lively and apparently mutually satisfactory.

Restocked with the necessary supplies, the *Howland* departed once again in search of whale. Her next stop was the
Pacific island of Guam. Mung's shipboard education continued under the ever-watchful eye of Captain Whitfield.
Leaving Guam, the ship changed course, sailing northeast to
the seas east of the island of Formosa. Captain Whitfield
called to Mung's attention the fact that they were quite near
his homeland of Japan, and said that he was truly sorry that
he could not sail in and return the boy to his mourning
mother, who had not seen nor heard from her son in well over
a year. Whitfield added that he was fearful for his young
friend's life should he chance the return alone. Being so near
to home was an emotional strain for Mung. The thought of
being so close to his homeland and especially his widowed
mother, and yet unable to see them, caused him immense
anxiety. His heart was heavy because he feared he might
never see his mother again. The captain quickly sensed
Mung's distress and tried to ease it by assuring him that
someday he would be better prepared to undertake the haz-
ards involved in returning home. The New Bedford ship continued with her whaling, sailing far and wide across the vast
blue waters. The end of the whaling season was approaching
when the *Howland* again returned to Guam, sometime in
February 1843. She stayed just long enough to secure the
necessary provisions. Her hold was nearly filled with sperm
oil. The captain decided that, after three years of whaling, it
was time to sail for home.

The *Howland*'s log recorded sighting Cape Horn in April
1843. Even though they were homeward bound, the ship's
master and crew stayed alert for signs of whale. Whitfield

spent many hours telling Mung about Fairhaven, in anticipation of the time when young John would see the place that the
captain had so often referred to as home.

Although the *John Howland*'s complement had never been
physically abused, they were all eagerly awaiting their landing in familiar, friendly surroundings—the peaceful harbor of
New Bedford. Many of the crew had families that they had
not seen since they left the port over three years earlier. Some
of their wives had even borne children since the men left.

The large vessel forged northward along the path of the
prevailing Gulf Stream, which runs parallel to the Atlantic
coastline. The crew worked busily, preparing the ship to enter
port.

At long last they heard a welcome cry from the lookout—
not the familiar cry that told of a whale sighting, but rather a
cry that the familiar silhouetted coastline of Block Island, off
Rhode Island, had been sighted. Tranquil green hills against
a pale blue sky were enhanced by the intermittent shrills of
the gulls that followed the ship. The whalers knew that,
within the hour, Cuttyhunk, the southernmost key of the Elizabeth Islands chain, would be visible. The men of the *Howland* looked upon this dramatic moment as the beginning of
the end of their long, prosperous journey.

The captain called Mung, who was now sixteen years old,
to his side as the vessel slowly moved north into the Acushnet
River, the lifeline of the port of New Bedford. With great
pride, Captain Whitfield pointed out to his young friend the
various landmarks. Sconticut Neck protruded out into Buzzards Bay on the eastern shore. Across the way, in New
Bedford, was Clark's Point. On the opposite shore, the Fairhaven bank, stood the old Revolutionary battery, Fort Phoenix—the perennial sentinel of the harbor. The boy himself,
excited at the sight of the place he had so often heard about,
attempted to identify some of the structures.

As the morning sun rose over the eastern peninsula of
Sconticut Neck on the Fairhaven shore, it seemed to absorb
the morning mist that shrouded the quiet harbor. Many of the
trees surrounding the harbor displayed new spring blossoms,
as if welcoming the weary crew back to New Bedford. The
harbor teemed with various types of vessels, none of which
escaped the attention of the Japanese boy.

The logbook of the *John Howland* disclosed that she had been away for three years, seven months, and seven days. Her hold was bustling with 2761 barrels of sperm oil, a fine haul.

The great ship moved into a quarantine area, apart from the other ships, which was designated for vessels arriving from foreign lands. Such ships had to stay in the quarantine area until the harbor authorities were satisfied that the ships and their crews were not transporting diseases or parasites. The stillness of the New England harbor was suddenly shattered by the rattling chain of the ship's anchor as it plunged into the muddy bottom of the riverbed.

Mung keenly scanned the nearby shorelines on both sides of the narrow harbor. He noted needlelike spires that protruded high above some of the structures, although at this point he did not know that the spires topped churches. Looking north, he saw a peculiar sight. A bridge spanning the river opened up, and a ship passed through. Mung was so fascinated by this unfamiliar sight that he later sketched it, to preserve it in his memory.

Though the houses that surrounded the waterfront were foreign-looking to the young man from Nakanohama, the view was as beautiful as the captain had promised. As Mung stared, fascinated by the quaintness of this typical New England port, his thoughts were interrupted by Captain Whitfield's voice. The captain walked over, placed his hand on his young friend's shoulder, and proudly announced, "Well John, this is my home—Fairhaven!" Pointing to the other side, he said, "Over there on that side of the harbor is the place called New Bedford. I know that you've heard of that place many times." The boy nodded in agreement, and the two gazed together at the beauty of the harbor, warmed by the sight.

Already they could see a small crowd gathering near the ship's landing—undoubtedly the friends and relatives of the ship's company. Soon, a small open boat from the nearby wharf headed toward the *Howland*. As it approached, the ship's master was able to recognize several of the passengers.

The small boat came alongside and was made fast. The first man to reach the main deck was the quarantine officer, who greeted the captain with an outstretched hand. One of the owners of the *Howland* soon followed, beaming with pleasure at the sight of Whitfield.

Mung moved aside so as not to intrude upon the joyful reunion, but Captain Whitfield soon summoned him and introduced him to the men from the small boat. John bowed politely in the Japanese manner. Unfamiliar with this kind of salutation, the men from shore appeared to be somewhat puzzled. Soon afterward, their initial conference concluded, the men returned to their small boat and departed for shore.

The captain returned to his cabin and after a short while emerged carrying a leather portfolio and a large carpetbag. He ordered a boat to be brought alongside and issued a number of instructions to the first mate. Then he beckoned to Mung, and together they climbed down into the waiting longboats.

By the time the boat approached the landing in New Bedford, a sizable crowd had gathered. Captain Whitfield and young John started out for the shipowner's place of business, so that the captain could report on the results of the expedition and explain the facts of the rescue of the five Japanese.

As they walked the roadway, they were frequently delayed by acquaintances of the captain who expressed their pleasure in his safe return. At J. & J. Howland's offices, Captain Whitfield introduced young Mung to those present and then asked him to sit by the large window near the front door while he discussed business with the owners. The young man could see the busy street in front of the building. He was captivated by the sight of so many people scurrying about, and was especially interested to see the Western women, who wore long dresses that contrasted sharply with the scanty attire of women on the Pacific islands that the ship had recently visited.

After what seemed to the Japanese lad like an eternity, the captain came out of the owner's offices. As they left the *Howland*'s place of business, he told Mung that he was now required to file a report with the port's Customs House. Prior to his departure, he had listed the names of all the crewmen who were sailing with him on the *Howland*. Now that he had returned, he must submit a list of the crewmen who returned with the ship.

They climbed the hill that sloped up from the waterfront and entered the Customs House. Captain Whitfield submitted the following report:

Whale Ship *John Howland*

New Bedford, Massachusetts

William H. Whitfield—Master

Return from Pacific Ocean whaling expedition arrived New Bedford, Massachusetts, May 7, 1843. This list was returned to the Customs House upon arrival of the ship in New Bedford, Massachusetts:

Name	Residence
Parden G. Winslow	New Bedford
Edward Southworth	Dartmouth
Warren Woodward	Buffalo
Isaacar U. Akin	Fairhaven
Jacob B. McBride (boat steerer)	Goshen
Hiram Talbot	New Bedford
William Sanford (steward)	"
John Baldwin (carpenter)	"
William M. Stannard	"
Frederick R. Deming	"
Lyman Holmes	"
Hazen Warren Furber	"
James Price	"
Hiram Rockwood	"
John Conory	Boston
LaFayette Willcox	Fairhaven
Thomas F. Adams	New Bedford
Edward F. Thompson	New York
Richard Vernon (blacksmith)	Eastport
Lewis D. Hicks	New York
William Rhodes (seaman)	"
Antonio Lopes	New Bedford
Francis Josephs (cooper)	"
Manuel Frisk	"
John Francis	"
Alexander Harris (cook)	"
John Gridley	"

The following did not return with the ship:

° William Sanford	— Richard Vernon
— John Baldwin	# Lewis D. Hicks
' Frederick R. Deming	— William Rhodes
— Hazen W. Furber	° Francis Josephs
— James Price	— Alexander Harris
— Hiram Rockwood	— John Gridley

° Discharged at their request
Discharged by direction of consul
' Deserted before sailing
— Deserted from ship and didn't return to U.S.

When they left the U.S. Customs House, the captain and his ward went to the business office of Chapman & Bonney, an accounting firm on Second Street. One of the partners, Josiah S. Bonney, not only served as Whitfield's financial and business adviser, but was married to the captain's cousin, Parnel M. (Post) Bonney. The Bonneys had a daughter named Anne.

Bonney was openly pleased at hearing of the success of the expedition. As it was near lunchtime when the two men concluded their business, Bonney invited Whitfield and his Japanese friend to have lunch at his home, just a few blocks from his business office. At first Whitfield reluctantly declined, saying that he had much to do to prepare for Mung's stay, but Bonney insisted, especially because he wanted to hear more about the dramatic rescue of the Japanese fishermen. Eventually the captain agreed, and the three went to Bonney's house at 18 Fifth Street (which is the present site of the Franciscan Fathers Chapel, at 600 Pleasant Street), where they were greeted by Mrs. Bonney and their daughter Anne. Manjiro thus ate his first meal in America at the Bonney's home. A spirited conversation about the rescue continued well past the allotted lunch hour.

After lunch, the captain and John walked along a long, narrow roadway leading to the bridge that crossed the river to Fairhaven. Mung told the captain about having seen the bridge separate, and asked for an explanation. Grinning, Whitfield replied that the wooden structure was called a "drawbridge" and was known as the New Bedford–Fair-

(Top left) *Josiah Bonney.* (Right) *Parnell M.* (*Post*) *Bonney.* (Bottom) *Anne M. Bonney. Circa 1865.* (All courtesy Dr. Hiroshi Nakahama)

haven Bridge. Mung accepted the captain's explanation with
a nod, but again tried to tell his friend, this time using his
hands, that he had seen the structure separate in order to
allow a ship to pass through. Whitfield explained that the
structure was constructed in such a way as to serve the needs
of both ship passage and wagon traffic. John appeared to be
somewhat amused by the captain's explanation but nodded
his acceptance. Their progress over the narrow span was
interrupted several times by goods-laden wagons going in
opposite directions, which forced them to step aside.

Once they reached the Fairhaven side of the river, they
walked north along the main road. The dirt road was considerably muddy because of a recent rainfall, a common occurrence in spring. About a quarter of a mile along the road, in
a neighborhood called "Poverty Point," they reached Oxford
Lane and headed west to where the lane crossed Cherry
Street. Just around the corner on the east side of Cherry Street
was a low-roofed dwelling house which appeared to need
repairs.

Captain Whitfield said, "Well, my young friend, this is my
home." Following in his mentor's footsteps, Mung entered a
rather dark parlor which was neat and well-furnished. He
was intrigued by the strange furnishings and the fireplace,
typical of New England homes. A woman opened the door
from the kitchen. At first she seemed apprehensive when she
saw the two seamen, but suddenly she called out, "Is that you,
William?" The captain quickly responded, "Yes, it is, Aunt
Milly." The two rushed to each other and embraced. The
woman was clearly delighted to see her nephew. Mung
watched the reunion quietly.

Whitfield soon beckoned to his ward and said "John, this is
my Aunt Amelia. We call her 'Aunt Milly,' and she looked
after me in my growing years. But since my grandmother's
death, she lives alone."

Mung bowed respectfully before the captain's aunt. He
glanced about the room as the two elders continued their
conversation. He was particularly impressed by the fine furnishings he saw, as the home where he had grown up in the
village of Nakanohama had contained only shabby, rudimentary furniture.

Aunt Milly offered to prepare an evening meal for the two

whalers, and the captain gratefully accepted. Soon the three sat at the kitchen table and enjoyed Aunt Milly's home cooking. While they ate, the captain described the details of the cruise and especially the rescue to his aunt. He also told her about his plan to enlist the help of his old friend Eben Aiken. He hoped to have the boy stay with Aiken while he and his fiancée, Albertina Keith, traveled to Scipio, New York, to visit with his Uncle George. He planned that they would marry in Scipio and then return home to Fairhaven.

Soon after eating, the two seafarers went to 14 Oxford Lane, just a short distance west of the Whitfield house. On the way, Whitfield told Mung that Eben Aiken was an old friend with whom he had served on a previous voyage. He knocked on the front door, and Aiken warmly invited them in. The reunion was lively, as the two men competed in exchanging stories. Mung said nothing and was unable to comprehend much of the conversation. The men paid little attention to him, but he sat patiently.

When Captain Whitfield told the story of the rescue of his Japanese ward and his former shipmates, their host was intrigued and took a particular interest in the details. The conversation continued for several hours.

After the excitement of the reunion had subsided and three years of news had been exchanged, the conversation took a more serious turn. Whitfield explained Mung's situation and said that he hoped to have the boy stay at the Aiken house for several weeks, if that was acceptable to both Aiken and his wife, while he himself went to New York to visit his Uncle George and to be married. He explained that he felt that it would be unfair to his Aunt Milly to ask her to take in a strange young man on such short notice, because she lived alone.

(Top) *Manjiro's drawing of the drawbridge opening of the New Bedford-Fairhaven Bridge. Circa 1845.* (Courtesy Dr. Hiroshi Nakahama) (Middle) *Photograph of the actual drawbridge opening. Circa 1870.* (Courtesy New Bedford Free Public Library, New Bedford, Massachusetts) (Bottom) *An easterly view overlooking the New Bedford–Fairhaven Bridge. Circa 1870.* (Courtesy New Bedford Free Public Library, New Bedford, Massachusetts)

It was common knowledge in Fairhaven that the Aikens had from time to time taken in young wards to board with them in their home. This was why Whitfield was making his proposal, and he assured his friend Aiken that he would underwrite the costs. The two men discussed the matter and agreed that the Aikens would shelter and care for Mung until Whitfield returned.

Once the details were settled, Whitfield thanked his old friend for his help and understanding, and Captain Whitfield and John returned to the Whitfield home at 11 Cherry Street.

By this time, it was getting late. Whitfield led Mung up a dark narrow stairway to the attic. There they discussed the arrangements the captain had made with Aiken, as well as his travel and marriage plans. Mung was somewhat puzzled, but his trust in and respect for his friend helped him to realize quickly that the captain was acting in his best interest. After listening to the entire proposal, he nodded in agreement, which evidently pleased Whitfield.

The captain showed John a corner and told him that he should sleep there. The two said goodnight, and John, following his own tradition, bowed before the captain.

When he was alone, Mung unrolled a small bundle. Through all his adventures, he had managed to keep a tattered kimono which his mother had given him. His thoughts returned to her and to his home in Japan. Lonesome in the solitude of the attic of the Whitfield home on his first night in America, Manjiro clutched his only tie to his mother and quietly wept in despair. Then through the low window of the attic, he gazed out over the dark harbor and wondered whether he would ever see Japan again.

The following morning, Captain Whitfield and Mung returned to Aiken's house. John carried the small, rolled-up bundle which contained all his clothing and personal belongings. Aiken assured the captain and Mung that John's stay in the Aiken home would be a pleasant experience and that the lad had nothing to fear. Whitfield, in Aiken's presence, instructed Mung to listen to Mr. Aiken and to respect his wishes. He again thanked his friend for his cooperation, and left his ward in his new temporary home.

Later that same day, the captain paid a visit to Jane Allen, who resided at 10 Oxford Lane, just west of the Aiken house, with her sister Charity Allen. Jane Allen was a teacher in the public school in Fairhaven. In addition to her regular classroom duties, she tutored children who needed special attention, conducting her classes in the basement room of her home, which was set up for use as a classroom. Whitfield asked her to help John by giving him basic elementary instructions, so that he could become qualified to take his place in a public school classroom.

After a lengthy discussion, Whitfield convinced Jane Allen to accept the Japanese lad in her after-school class. Therefore, each afternoon for the next week, when Miss Allen returned home from her regular teaching duties, Mung was waiting by the fence gate to join the other children in her basement classroom.

While John was beginning to learn the rudiments of a public school education, the captain was busy attending to many personal and business matters. He managed to visit with his young friend each day even if only for a short while. He took a special interest in John's well-being and in his progress in Miss Allen's class. However, after clearing up his most pressing business matters, Whitfield departed for Bridgewater, Massachusetts, from which he would begin his trip to New York.

Mung became the center of attention, both in Fairhaven and in New Bedford. People had heard about the *Howland*'s humanitarian rescue of the distressed Japanese fishermen, and they were curious.

John soon showed an exceptional ability in academic studies. After a week of tutoring him, Miss Allen declared that he was ready to be enrolled in a public school classroom. Acting on his behalf, she applied for his admission to the Point School (also called the "Stone School House") on Bread and Cheese Lane (now North Street) in Oxford Village, which was part of District 11 of the public school system. The report of the Fairhaven School Committee for the year 1843–1844, printed below, reviews the condition and facts of the Point School, District 11.

In Oxford Village

We are glad to find a School-house which approaches respectability; we don't mean by this, that the house in this District is

(Top) *The Point School, District 11—also called "the Old Stone School-house."* (Bottom) *Interior view of the Old Stone Schoolhouse. Circa 1890.* (Both courtesy Millicent Library, Fairhaven, Massachusetts)

just what it ought to be, for in many respects it could be made much better than it is. In the first place, it is located in a very pleasant place, and with a very little expense might be made eminently so; but it wants a spacious play ground connected with it, but it may be thought that the street answers every purpose; any one may judge how good a substitute it is, when they see the children almost invariably trespassing upon the adjoining fields, and making them their play ground, of which the fields and walls themselves bear testimony.

The house is built of rough stone, durable and proof against jackknife impressions; but whether this counterbalances its prison-like appearance, is a question in which men may differ; everything in and about a school-house should be made as pleasant as possible, no expense should be spared to make it attractive to children. The school-room is not large enough by 10 feet, to say the least, for the number of scholars. The floor is almost wholly covered with seats, so that scarce any space is left for recitations; the room is 21 feet by 32, the height is 10 feet; 2 feet higher would be better. The windows are all 4 feet and 3 inches from the floor, altogether too high, it gives the room a gloomy appearance. The seats are very uncomfortable, not so much on account of their height, (though they are somewhat too high, being from 15½ inches to 17½, when they should only be from 10 to 16½) as from the awkward position they place the scholar in, the perpendicular back prevents his leaning back, while he sits fair in the seat; this leaves the whole line of the back from the shoulder downwards with nothing to rest against; this produces curved and diseased spines, to say nothing of the present wearisome pains. The seats are all placed some 7 or 8 inches from a perpendicular with the front of the form, consequently whenever the scholar uses his form, he must sit on the very edge of his seat in order to reach it; which makes his seat about as comfortable as if he were sitting on a board set up edgewise. Now this evil was created in order to shun another, if seats, containing two or more scholars, run under the form, or even perpendicular with it, every time the scholar stands up to read, or recite in his seat, or for any other purpose, it puts him in the uncomfortable shape of a grindstone crank, and he can't stand still in such a position more than two minutes at a time; and every time the scholar goes in and out of his seat, he is obliged to drag his feet after him, making more noise, than a dozen would if the seats were such as they ought to be. The fact is, no seat ought to contain more than one scholar, the forms may be long or short, but let the seat be separate, made something in the form of a chair, easy and comfortable, then place it, in relation to the form just where you would place a chair to a table or desk, upon which you were going to write, let there be an aisle back of every seat; then the scholar can go to, and from his seat without noise, or in any manner disturbing another scholar;

the teacher has free access to every scholar, either side of him. But the cost. We know, therefore we state it more than the present seats cost, we can seat every scholar in that school in the manner above described. The only question then is, will the advantages pay for the trifling cost? If so, then it is economy to do it.

The room is heated with a close, wood stove, and there is no ventilator, nothing but the door and windows by which the teacher can change the air of the room. We do know that if the parents of this district well understood the injurious effect of a vitiated atmosphere upon their children, they would spare no pains, stint no cost, to give them the pure air, designed by Heaven for man's richest blessing.

There is a blackboard, and during the winter term it was well used. There is no other school apparatus, but in place, hats, coats, bonnets, and shawls, are hung up all around the school-room, as if exhibited for sale, and as we entered the room we involuntarily looked around to see which was the best article.

Parents do not visit the school. Is the school-room door a bar to a parent's love, a parent's care, a parent's anxiety? If not, why should they not look upon them, even in the school-room?

There is a library connected with the school. The amount apportioned to this district was $272.48.

The whole number of children between the ages of 4 and 16, is 104.

The winter term was taught by Mr. _____ Bartlett five and a half months, at $36 per month, whole number of scholars attending school 46, average attendance 38.

The summer term was kept by Miss Sarah W. Allen twenty-two weeks, at $4 per week, whole number of scholars 42, average 36, two out of every three, in the district, absent from school. Is this as it should be? But this, in part, is accounted for, by the fact that the district voted that no scholar over ten years of age should attend the summer school, and none under ten, should attend the winter school.

Mung's application was accepted by the school authorities. Once enrolled, he quickly adapted to the daily routine of reading, writing, and arithmetic. However, his mind was constantly clouded with thoughts of his mother and the pain and anguish she must have endured since his unexplained disappearance nearly three years previous. In addition, his interest in navigation was always uppermost in his mind. His hope was that someday he would fully understand the secrets of navigation. He wanted to know how it was possible to sail well out of sight of land and then to return to the precise place of origin without the aid of landmarks.

(Left) *Captain William H. Whitfield.* (Courtesy Dr. Hiroshi Nakahama)
(Right) *Albertina (Keith) Whitfield.* (Courtesy Dr. Hiroshi Nakahama)
(Bottom) *The Whitfield farmhouse at Sconticut Neck. Circa 1890.*
(Courtesy Millicent Library, Fairhaven, Massachusetts)

It was at the Stone School House that John Mung first learned the English alphabet. He was so impressed that it remained with him for the rest of his life, and he eventually taught it to Japanese students, once he was back in his homeland. Even today, Japanese students of English echo a musical version of the alphabet that Manjiro took back to Japan. In addition, Manjiro's artistic drawings can still be seen at the Kochi Castle in Kochi City, Kochi Prefecture, on the island of Shikoku, Japan.

Manjiro had a burning desire to break through the language barrier, and this desire, coupled with his voracious appetite for knowledge of all kinds, soon propelled him academically to the head of his class.

The days slipped by rapidly, though Mung was constantly aware of the absence of his friend and benefactor, Captain Whitfield. Finally, word was received at the Aiken home that Whitfield had returned, but that he was not alone. Much to the surprise of many townspeople, but not of Mung, the captain had taken a wife. His bride, Albertina Keith, was from Bridgewater. She was the daughter of Howe Keith, Jr., also of Bridgewater, who was the brother of Alexis Keith of 13 Cherry Street in Fairhaven. They had been married in Scipio, New York, on May 31, 1843, just four days after Whitfield had completed the acquisition of a parcel of farm property located on Sconticut Neck in Fairhaven. He had purchased the property from Alice P. Fuller for the sum of $1000, and it included 14 acres of land, a dwelling house, and a barn. The deed to the property is recorded in the Bristol County Registry of Deeds (Book 8, pages 188–189). It reads as follows:

Deed of Captain William H. Whitfields Sconticut Neck Farm

Know all men by these presents, that I Alice P. Fuller of Fairhaven, in the County of Bristol, and Commonwealth of Massachusetts, widow, in consideration of one thousand dollars to me paid by William H. Whitfield of Fairhaven aforesaid master mariner, the receipt whereof I do hereby acknowledge, do hereby give, grant, sell and convey unto the said William H. Whitfield, his heirs and assigns, a lot of land, situated in Fairhaven aforesaid, and bounded as follows viz: Beginning at the Northwest corner of said lot, and at the Southwest corner of John Tabers lot by the road leading into Sconticut Neck; thence east ten degrees north thirty one rods and seven tenths of a rod;

thence south twenty-eight degrees east five rods; thence east ten degrees north seventy-eight rods and the same course into the river. Then began again at the first mentioned bound, running south fifteen degrees east, eighteen rods to the school house lot; thence east thirteen degrees north four rods; thence south fifteen degrees east, three rods; thence west fifteen degrees south four rods to the road; thence south fifteen degrees east two rods and six tenths of a rod to the corner of Elisha Tobey's land; thence east fifteen degrees north twenty one rods; thence east nine degrees north twenty-two rods; thence east seven degrees north, nineteen and seven tens rods; thence east twenty-eight degrees north five and seven tenths rods; thence north thirty degrees west five and two tenths rods; thence east thirteen degrees north seventy rods to the shore or sea; thence northerly by the shore to the north line, containing about fourteen acres, together with the buildings thereon standing. To have and to hold the afore granted premises to the said William H. Whitfield, his heirs and assigns, to his and their use and behoof forever. And I the said Alice P. Fuller, for myself, my heirs, executors and administrators, do covenant with the said William H. Whitfield, his heirs and assigns, that I am lawfully seized in fee of the afore-granted premises; that they are free of all encumbrances; that I have good right to sell and convey the same unto the said William H. Whitfield, and that I will warrant and defend the same premises to the said William H. Whitfield, his heirs and assigns forever against the lawful claims and demands of all persons . . . in witness whereof, I the said Alice Fuller have here unto set my hand and seal, this twenty-seventh day of May in the year of our Lord one thousand eight hundred and forty three.

Signed and sealed and delivered   Alice P. Fuller
[Seal]

in presence of John Taber.

Bristol County; May 27, 1843. Then the above named Alice P. Fuller acknowledged the foregoing instrument to be her free act and deed before me.

Edmund Gifford, Justice of the Peace

May 27, 1843 then received and recorded Berg T. Congdon

Registrar

The new Mrs. Whitfield showed warmth and tender understanding to John Mung, even at their first meeting. After introducing the two, the captain explained to his young friend that he planned to start a new life on his recently acquired farm on Sconticut Neck. He made it clear that his plans included John, and he was hopeful that his young friend would accept his and his wife's invitation to live on the farm as a member of their family. John answered almost immediately that he would like that very much. Both the captain and his bride had hoped for this answer, and therefore, the matter was settled satisfactorily.

Whitfield settled his account with Aiken and took Mung to Aunt Milly's house. He assured his aunt that John would not cause her any problems if she would let him live with her until the school term ended. This arrangement, he told her, was necessary because the farmhouse was some five miles from the Stone School House. Aunt Milly agreed to look after the boy until the school term ended in late June.

With a new sense of enthusiasm, Mung continued his studies until the class was dismissed for the summer months. While school was still in session, he often spent his weekends assisting the captain on the farm, and when school ended, he quickly gathered his scant belongings. He thanked Aunt Milly for all her kindness and generosity, and Aunt Milly grasped John's hand and wished him well. Mung reciprocated with his traditional bow. Then he and Whitfield climbed into a waiting horse-drawn wagon and departed for their new home on Sconticut Neck.

Mung worked very hard throughout the summer, tending to many of the farm's chores. Despite his longings to see his mother, he enjoyed the hard work and responsibilities given him by Whitfield. He had some of the happiest times of his young life while living on the Whitfield farm. There he first learned to ride a horse, an accomplishment of which he was especially proud because in Japan, the riding of a horse was reserved for samurai and other high-ranking officials.

When Mung had free time after tending to his duties on the farm, he could often be found fishing in the sparkling waters known as "Little Bay" at the eastern boundary of the Whitfield farm. Fishing was easy and enjoyable for Mung, because it was the trade he had learned as a young boy in Japan. "How beautiful is this place called 'Sconticut Neck,'" thought Mung. He had learned that the name "Sconticut" was derived from an Indian word meaning "the place of the first light."

Not long after Mung moved to the Whitfield farm, it seemed, the cornstalks began transforming the fields with various hues and the surrounding trees came alive with vivid colors. Summer was almost over. Soon the autumn winds would snatch the dying leaves off the trees and scatter them across the landscape to enrich the soil. John knew that it was almost time for him to return to his studies.

Because the Stone School House was so far from the Whitfield farm, the captain made arrangements with school officials to have Mung attend the public school on Sconticut Neck Road, which was listed as Public School District 14. The school's land abutted the west boundary of the Whitfield farm.

The report of the Fairhaven School Committee for the year 1843–1844 reviews the facts of District 14:

Sconticut Neck District

The house in this district is old, and out of repair. It is located in a pleasant place—that is, so far as Nature is concerned—but Art has not lent her a helping hand at all. There is hardly any yard room at all; nothing but the street, or the neighbor's grounds, for a play-ground; nothing attractive about it. The house is 18 feet by 25, unpainted, hip-roofed. You know which side is the front, because one side has a door and no window. The entry is 16½ feet by 3½. The school-room is 17 feet by 20,

The Sconticut Neck Schoolhouse, District 14. (Courtesy Helen Radcliffe)

and 9 feet high. It is badly seated. The seats are built up on three sides, the old-fashioned, uncomfortable box seats, all upright backs, and much too high. There is no ventilator, unless a large space where the plastering overhead has tumbled down, serves as one. The room is heated by a close, wood stove. The whole appearance of the room is wanting in neatness and comfort.

There is a black-board, but it has been used the last winter but very little, if any, although the Committee urged the necessity of it upon the teacher again and again. The first time the Committee visited the school, in the winter, he drew an outline map of New England on the black-board, in order to interest the children in that exercise; and at the next visit, more than a month afterward, the same map was there, and not another mark appeared to have been made. Nothing but laziness deprived these children of much knowledge, which they might have acquired by the use of the black-board.

This district has no school library. This fountain of instruction, to them, is dry. They have no school apparatus; and unless they have somebody beside whalemen for teachers, it would be of but little use to have any. But with a teacher who understood his business, and was willing to devote his time to it, school apparatus would do inestimable service.

This district is so situated that a union of it with any other would not be of much, if any advantage; it is alone by itself. There is but a small number of children in the district, and not half of them attend the school. What can be done to better it? Give the children half an acre of land for a play-ground— enclose it with a neat fence—ornament it with trees—make it the pleasantest spot in the whole district; put a handsome front on the school-house; lengthen it 8 or 10 feet, and paint it, and put blinds upon it; affix to it a good ventilator; throw away the old, awkward seats, and put in convenient and comfortable ones; build a wood-house, that the fuel may be kept dry, and not, with wet wood, compel the teacher to keep a salamander heat, or none at all; procure a good library, to interest and instruct yourselves and your children; get a good set of school apparatus, that every lesson may be illustrated and explained, that they may not be kept in the fog, or stuck fast upon the shoals of ignorance,—do this, and then select a teacher who is worthy of such a house and fixtures, and your children will reap a harvest, the very first year, that will more than pay the whole cost.

The whole number of children in this district, between the ages of 4 and 16, is 33.

The amount apportioned was $104.80.

The summer term was kept by Miss Gould, 8 weeks, at $2, and by Miss Terry, 10 weeks, at $2, and boarded. Whole number of scholars, 20; average attendance, 16.

The winter term was kept by Mr. Quintus M. Bellows, 3½

months, at $28 per month, and "boarded round." Whole number of scholars, 23, average attendance, 14; more than 38 per cent absent.

Despite Mung's enjoyment of his summer vacation, he had never completely abandoned his books. He considered books to be full of magic, and he believed that someday they would help him to become more like William Whitfield, whom he had first known as a sea captain, not as a farmer.

Mung had worked very hard on the farm, but he knew that farming would never satisfy him. It was the sea that had captured his heart. He saw the sea as an international "roadway," and its mystery, its fury, and its pulsing beauty occupied his mind and permeated his imagination. The life of a seafaring man was the only life that young Manjiro would accept.

When the new school year started, Mung began attending the Sconticut Neck School. It was indeed much smaller than the Stone School House, and the classroom was arranged differently, with the teacher sitting in the rear of the classroom facing the backs of the students.

During the time that he was attending this school, John momentarily set aside his usual seriousness, and centered his attention on a classmate of the opposite sex, Catherine E. Terry. More than fifty years later, on July 5, 1916, *The Fairhaven Star* made a passing reference to this brief romance under the title "Story of Nakahama," as follows:

> Probably the only person living who went to the Sconticut Neck School with Mung, is Mrs. Elbridge G. Morton of Fairhaven. She recalls the pleasing little incident of being the recipient of a May Basket with a note within from the Japanese boy which reads as follows:
>
> > Tis in the chilly night
> > a basket you've got hung.
> > Get up, strike a light!
> > And see me run
> > But no take chase me.

By the time Mung attended the Sconticut Neck School, his story was well known in the town. John Mung was accepted by most people who knew him. His polite manner, likable personality, delicate sense of humor, and serious attitude about his studies were generally appreciated.

However, he did encounter prejudice on one Sunday morning. The Whitfields, accompanied by John, went to the Congregational Church, which was near Four Corners in the center of Fairhaven, for the weekly services. Like many other citizens, the Whitfields had paid a nominal annual fee to have a section of pew set aside solely for their use. Sitting in the family pew, the Whitfields and Mung participated in the ecumenical service. Afterward, a spokesman for the elders of the church discreetly drew the captain to one side. He said that they were all pleased by seeing the young boy attending services, but he suggested that, in the future, it might be well to have the Japanese boy take a place in the section set aside for Negroes. It was the feeling of the elders that Mung's presence was a distraction to worshipers sitting near the Whitfield pew.

Captain Whitfield showed no emotion but merely acknowledged that he had heard the spokesman's discriminatory remark. Leaving the house of prayer, the Whitfields returned home. The captain, a man of sterling character who was held in high esteem within the community, mentioned the incident to no one outside his immediate family. Instead, he promptly made financial arrangements to acquire a new family pew in the Unitarian Church on Washington Street, just two blocks north and east of the other church.

Because of the incident, the Whitfields never again resumed their membership in the Congregational Church, though church officials attempted many times to reconcile the unfortunate matter. Captain Whitfield remained steadfast in his refusal.

As the months passed, the bond between the captain and the teenage boy grew stronger. Whitfield observed with pleasure the lad's continuing, relentless quest for knowledge. Mung's progress was remarkable. He excelled especially in mathematics, which prompted Whitfield to consider enrolling his young friend in a navigation course.

In pursuit of this possibility, Whitfield visited still another old friend, Louis L. Bartlett. Bartlett had been principal of the Fairhaven Academy on the west side of Main Street, north of Bridge Street, but on October 3, 1842, he had opened the

Louis L. Bartlett School of Mathematics, Navigation, and Surveying. The school was housed in a building at 42 Spring Street, on the north side of the street. The building had been built in 1835, and the school was unique in that it offered extended courses in mathematics. The school was rather exclusive, and its clientele consisted mainly of the sons of prominent shipowners and shipmasters.

Louis Bartlett at first rejected Whitfield's proposal that John Mung attend his school, but the captain persisted. He insisted that the Japanese boy was a member of his family, an adopted son. The schoolmaster thus had little choice, and he accepted Mung in February of 1844. Mung promised Whitfield that he would work very hard so as not to disappoint his trusted friend.

Despite his initial reluctance, the schoolmaster soon became aware of the Japanese lad's extraordinary ability. John's eagerness to excel in the manly art of navigation quickly elevated him to the position of one of the leaders in his class. He hoped that his labor of love would enable him someday to return to his homeland and his mother. He often thought too that it would be wonderful if he could share his knowledge of navigation with the fishermen of Nakanohama.

The Louis L. Bartlett School of Mathematics, Surveying, and Navigation. (Courtesy Millicent Library, Fairhaven, Massachusetts)

While attending the Bartlett School, Mung formed a strong
bond of friendship with a schoolmate named Job C. Tripp.
Tripp and Mung enjoyed playing mischievous pranks and
making jokes. The friendship between the two boys flourished
long after their days at the Bartlett School.

John Mung was a year older than his American friend, who
was born in Fairhaven on August 9, 1828, and was attending
the Bartlett School after having finished his public school
education. He went on to the Bridgewater Normal School and
was graduated in 1847. He then became a bookkeeper in the
office of Morgan & Pope, whaling agents, in Fairhaven. Later
he was confidential clerk for Charles W. Morgan. In 1854, Job
became a whaling agent on his own account, and was successful until the discovery of petroleum in 1859 in Pennsylvania,
which wiped out the whaling business in the United States. In
the early days of the schools, when the town was divided into
districts, he was on the Prudential Committee for Districts 12
and 13. He was elected to the School Committee in 1856. He
served as postmaster for four years starting in 1890, and for
eighteen years, he ran an insurance and real estate business,
before retiring.

Job Tripp was one of Fairhaven's best-known citizens. He
died on Friday, July 13, 1917, following a shock; he was
eighty-nine years old. He is buried in the Riverside Cemetery
in Fairhaven.

In spring 1844, when the Bartlett School closed for the
summer, Mung began another enjoyable summer of farming
and fishing on the Sconticut Neck farm. The Whitfields' first
son was born on July 20, and they named him William Henry
Whitfield, Jr. John was delighted with the new addition to the
family.

Meanwhile, Captain Whitfield was planning another whaling expedition. He was negotiating with the Henry Taber
Company of New Bedford, owners of a 321-ton whaleship,
the *William and Eliza*. The planned destination was the
Pacific Ocean, and preparing the ship took several months.
For Captain Whitfield, this voyage would be somewhat different from previous ones, for he would be leaving behind a
wife and an infant child, as well as his young ward, John
Mung.

It was during this summer that Captain Whitfield explained

to his young friend that schooling in itself would not be enough to help Manjiro fulfill his hope of returning to Japan by way of a whaler. Manjiro would have to acquire some additional skills that would be useful on a whaling expedition. Therefore, Whitfield offered to speak to William M. Hussey, a local cooper, who operated a cooperage shop by the Acushnet River in Fairhaven, where he made whale-oil casks for the New Bedford whaling fleet. Whitfield's idea was for Mung to become an apprentice in Hussey's shop. The shop was a considerable distance from the Whitfield farm, which meant that it was necessary for John to live at Mr. Hussey's shop, rather than returning to the farm each evening. Mr. Hussey lived at 194 Middle Street in the city of New Bedford.

Also living at the shop were two other apprentices who were learning the art of barrel making. Mung worked long hours at Hussey's Cooperage. The food that was provided was often old and stale. John was not at all happy with the condi-

Interior view of an American cooper shop. Circa 1885. (Courtesy Fairhaven Selectmen)

tions at Mr. Hussey's place of business. John's other two
companions were also discontented, so much so that they
slipped away one evening and were never heard from again.

Mung, unlike his friends, realized that learning the trade
was far more important than the discomforts he was experiencing. Besides, he had given his word to Whitfield that he
would become an accomplished cooper. His mother's early
teachings had given him the virtues of patience and self-
sacrifice, and those qualities helped him to persevere despite
the deep and lasting depression that he suffered while serving
under Hussey. After a while, however, his body could no
longer endure; he became quite ill and was forced to return
to the farm for proper care and attention.

As he recuperated, the ice floes that huddled against the
Fairhaven shoreline began to melt. Spring was coming, which
meant that the workload at the Whitfield farm would increase
and Mung's help would again be needed. By the time the
ground became pliable enough to accept a plow, Mung had
become healthy again and was able to do many of the farm
chores. It felt good to once again be in the service of the
Whitfields. He willingly worked long hours to show his appreciation for Mrs. Whitfield's kindness. He also gave much attention to young William Henry and somehow always found
time to entertain the child.

In addition to taking care of all his responsibilities, John
retained his intense interest in reading and in practicing the
skills he had learned at Mr. Bartlett's school. No longer was
Manjiro the poor rescued Japanese fisherboy. He had become
an accepted and respected lad who eagerly learned the ways
and lifestyle of the Americans.

Wherever he went in the Fairhaven area, he was observing
and learning. Even so, his thoughts always wandered back to
Nakanohama, his native village. He yearned to hear the voice
of his mother once more. "Is she still alive and well?" he
asked himself. "How proud she will be," thought Mung, "if
and when I return and tell her about this great adventure in
America and the knowledge I have attained."

The summer passed, and fall was at hand. John reluctantly
returned to the dreaded dampness of the dark cooperage. His
reluctance, however, was tempered by the thought that soon
he would be going back to the Bartlett School for further

training in the field that interested him the most. Though he was willing to endure whatever hardships he encountered at the cooperage, again he became violently ill, and again he had to return to the Whitfield home to recuperate. After several months of care, he was able to resume his studies at the Bartlett School. He later returned to Hussey's Cooperage a third time and finally completed his apprenticeship.

At the Bartlett School, the studies that most interested Mung were contained within the covers of Nathaniel Bowditch's *The New American Practical Navigator.* Of all his books, he cherished this one most dearly, for it contained the information that he was seeking.

Whenever possible, John would wander along the Fairhaven shore studying and sketching. He always took great care to observe the behavior of whalers. He took a special interest in whaleships when they returned from their long voyages. He was ever on the alert for news from Honolulu which might include a mention of his Japanese comrades, and for any information about the area near the Sea of Japan. One of John Mung's favorite observation posts was the old ruins of Fort Phoenix, overlooking the Acushnet River on the Fairhaven bank. He spent many hours in meditation at this high spot.

4

Denzo and Goemon Attempt a Return to Japan

While Manjiro was obtaining an education in Massachusetts, his shipwrecked companions—Denzo, Goemon, Jusuke, and Toraemon—were being cared for under the watchful eye of Dr. Gerrit P. Judd in Honolulu. After Manjiro's departure on the New Bedford whaleship, three of them had been able to find work, with Dr. Judd's help. Denzo and Goemon were now working as house servants at the Royal School for a Mr. Cooke, who was a schoolteacher from America and lived in a house owned by the government. Goemon's responsibilities included tending to the Cooke children. Toraemon was apprentice to one of the island's carpenters.

Jusuke, however, had not been able to obtain long-term employment, because of the leg injury which he had received while landing at Torishima Island in January 1841. Dr. Judd supervised Jusuke's care and well-being. When the shipwrecked Japanese had first arrived at Honolulu, Dr. Judd had been a practicing physician as well as a missionary, but after the *Howland*'s departure, he had become a government official and curtailed his medical practice. He did not, therefore, act as physician to Jusuke, but he did help pay for Jusuke's medical care.

One day, while Denzo was tending to his chores, some children told him that a large American ship had landed near the south harbor and that the ship was carrying two Japanese. Denzo hurried to the harbor, where he saw a man with Japanese features. He immediately asked the man whether he was Japanese. The stranger appeared startled but responded that he was. Overjoyed, Denzo asked him what section of Japan he was from. The man replied he was from Edo and his name was Yasutaro. He and seven other men had been returning to Edo from Mutsu, carrying a large cargo of salt, but had become lost. Their ship had floundered aimlessly for many months, during which their food and water had dwindled to nothing. The frightened men were on the brink of despair until they encountered a large school of tuna and were able to catch a sizable number. After satisfying their pangs of hunger, they had dried the remaining fish. Their boat had continued to drift, and soon all the dried tuna had been consumed. The men started dying one at a time, of famine and thirst. Only Yasutaro and one other had survived until an American whaleship rescued them. Ever since they were rescued, they had been working for the American captain on the whaling ship.

Denzo offered his condolences over the loss of the five fishermen and said he would like to continue their conversation. He invited Yasutaro and his friend for a visit and gave him directions on how to find his house. Yasutaro was obviously pleased with the invitation and promised that he and his friend would come to visit.

On the following day, Yasutaro and his friend appeared at Denzo's house as requested. Goemon was also present. Yasutaro introduced his friend Tobie. Denzo and his brother were pleased to see their countrymen, and the conversation lasted most of the day. Many stories were exchanged. Yasutaro described again how he and Tobie had been rescued and nurtured back to health. Then they were assigned to look after the captain's children, who were accompanying him on the whaling expedition. Yasutaro also explained to Denzo that he and Tobie would soon be transferred to a French trade ship which was sailing to China. If Denzo and Goemon wanted to join him and Tobie in attempting a return to Japan, he said, they should visit the American ship's captain and plead with him to take them along with Yasutaro and Tobie. The two brothers decided to follow Yasutaro's suggestion.

Together the four Japanese went to the American whaleship and asked to speak with the ship's master. Yasutaro introduced Denzo and Goemon to the captain. Then Denzo explained that he and Goemon had become hopelessly lost at sea while fishing and had been rescued by an American whaleship, the *John Howland*, sailing out of New Bedford. Therefore, he and his friend would like to be taken on board the French ship which was bound for China.

Taken by surprise and shaking his head in disbelief, the American captain refused Denzo's request. He explained that he had already made the arrangements with the French captain for passage of two men and to request two additional passages would not be proper. Denzo pleaded with the captain, promising that he would work very hard while on board the French ship, if only he could be allowed to sail with Yasutaro and Tobie. Again the captain refused. In a last desperate attempt, Denzo pleaded once more. He said that perhaps if he and Goemon were to offer to pay for their passage, the French captain might be more receptive. The captain did not answer. Then Goemon took Denzo aside and reminded him that they had no money. The American shipmaster soon returned to his duties, leaving the four Japanese alone to discuss the matter further.

At first they said nothing, but searched their minds for a possible solution. Suddenly, Tobie jumped to his feet excitedly and reminded Yasutaro that they still had possession of the clothing of the other men of their ill-fated voyage, who had all died of starvation. Surely, he said, the clothing had some value. They could offer it for sale and use the money to pay passage for Denzo and Goemon. In addition, they would all work while en route. The four agreed to try Tobie's plan, but the plan proved to be a failure. They were not able to sell even one piece of the clothing.

Still determined, Denzo and Goemon again pressed the American captain to attempt to persuade the master of the French ship to take them on board. However, the captain could not be swayed.

Each time Denzo and Goemon visited their Japanese friends on board the American ship, they were given food by Yasutaro, which was taken from the regular crew's mess. After they had a few such meals, the ship's cook began to express his anger about the two outsiders coming on board and taking food. At first the Japanese acted as though they did not hear the disgruntled cook's protests, but finally, Yasutaro received a direct order: He must tell his friends that they were no longer welcome to share the ship's rations.

Denzo and Goemon now realized that their attempts to persuade the American captain to speak in their behalf were hopeless. They thanked Yasutaro and Tobie for their assistance, and departed. Several days later, they watched enviously as the French vessel cleared the harbor carrying their newfound friends. Whether Yasutaro and Tobie would thus be able to return home, only time would tell.

In 1844 Jusuke's leg took a turn for the worse. The leg, in fact, was deteriorating so badly that it was diagnosed as incurable. Denzo told his younger brother Goemon that he wanted to help Jusuke, for Denzo had been in charge of the boat at the time of the shipwreck and he felt responsible. If Jusuke did not receive better medical attention soon, he might die. Denzo said he had heard of a good doctor in the village of Kaneohe, about eleven miles from Honolulu, and he wanted to take Jusuke there for treatment.

Together Denzo and Goemon went to see their friend, Dr. Judd, to discuss Denzo's idea with him. Dr. Judd had been assisting Jusuke by paying for much of his medical care, and he agreed to help in any way he could. Pleased with the doctor's answer, Denzo and Goemon purchased a palanquin (carrying chair) in which to transport Jusuke to the new doctor's village. En route, carrying Jusuke in the palanquin, they met a man who was leading a horse in the opposite direction. The man greeted them and explained that he had been instructed by Dr. Judd to come to their assistance. Denzo asked the stranger to take over as bearer so that he could ride ahead and make the necessary arrangements prior to their arrival at the village.

By the time Goemon and the stranger arrived with Jusuke, Denzo had already met with the doctor to explain the situation, and the doctor was waiting to examine Jusuke. While the doctor conducted the examination, the others walked about the village. They came upon an American house of worship and met the American in charge, the Reverend Benjamin Parker, who was an acquaintance of their friend and benefactor, Captain William Whitfield. The Reverend Parker had already received word of the coming of the Japanese fishermen and was aware that they were friends of Whitfield. Because of that relationship, he made every effort to assist the Japanese and to facilitate Jusuke's treatment.

Over the weeks, however, Jusuke's condition continued to deteriorate. The village doctor's treatments were not beneficial. Slowly the sick fisherman became weaker and weaker, and eventually he lost his long-term battle and died. His remains were placed in a wooden coffin and buried close to the temple in the village of Kaneohe.

After the burial, Denzo and Goemon stayed at Reverend Parker's house for a while, and then Denzo went to see a man named Puupun in the nearby village of Koorau. King Kamehameha III, the great ruler of the islands, soon arrived in Koorau for his annual visit; he visited all the villages every year. Accompanying him was the leading official of the island, a man named Tsuwanahawa, who knew Denzo and Goemon from Honolulu. Tsuwanahawa stopped at Puupun's house and was surprised to find Denzo there. Greeting Denzo warmly, he inquired about his well-being. Denzo thanked him for his kind and sympathetic attention and said that since Jusuke's death, he had not been able to motivate himself to return to Mr. Cooke's household. Tsuwanahawa listened attentively and offered his assistance. Denzo asked permission to make a claim on an unused portion of land near the place where his friend was buried. He wanted to be close to Jusuke's grave so that he could visit it often. Tsuwanahawa awarded him the use of the land, and Denzo thanked the island leader for his generosity.

Denzo hurried to tell Goemon of the good news and to ask him also to live and work on the land, so that they could build their own hut and no longer be dependent on others. Together they started clearing the land, with the help of some islanders who lived nearby, and soon they had constructed their hut. Next they cleared some more land and planted a variety of vegetables, including sweet potatoes, corn, gourds, and millet. Their new self-reliance gave the two Japanese a sense of hope. They did become alarmed one day, when they saw a man collecting taxes from their neighbors, but were relieved when the tax collector told them they were not required to pay taxes because they were considered guests of the government and not permanent residents.

On November 29, 1846, Captain Whitfield arrived on the island of Oahu for the purposes of replenishing provisions and making some necessary repairs to his ship. He was not in the familiar *John Howland* but in the *William and Eliza*. This stop at Oahu allowed Captain Whitfield the opportunity to meet with his Japanese friends, Denzo, Goemon, and Toraemon.

Once anchored in the protected harbor, Whitfield came ashore. His first order of business was to inquire about the Japanese whom he had rescued. The local officials told him where Denzo and Goemon were living. As soon as the captain had completed some business concerning his ship, he set out to find his former wards.

He arrived at the village on a Sunday and so went directly to the church of his old friend, the Reverend Parker. Goemon was at the church, and Whitfield approached him quietly and placed a hand on his shoulder. Surprised and overjoyed, Goemon could hardly believe his eyes. Upon seeing the captain, he automatically began to look for his old shipmate Manjiro as well. Whitfield sensed whom Goemon was looking for and said that Manjiro was in Fairhaven and was doing quite well, studying hard and getting an education. Goemon was pleased. The captain then asked about the well-being of the other Japanese fishermen. Goemon explained that Toraemon was learning the trade of carpenter. Speaking in a subdued tone, he also told the captain of Jusuke's death and added that Jusuke was buried near the church. Whitfield expressed his sorrow and then asked Goemon to take him to their hut to see Denzo. Denzo was excited when he saw their old benefactor, and he immediately asked about Manjiro. Whitfield told him that Manjiro was studying hard in the hope that the education he was acquiring would be beneficial if and when he returned home to Japan.

The three men talked for a long time. Captain Whitfield made jokes about their hut and especially its furnishings, which consisted of old boxes and pickle barrels. Denzo and Goemon were much amused and cheered by his jokes.

Following his visit, Whitfield returned to his ship. After the necessary repairs had been made, the *William and Eliza* sailed from the harbor of Honolulu on February 12, 1847, and resumed cruising for whale. Nine months later, the *William and Eliza* reappeared in the harbor of Honolulu. Whitfield once again visited with his Japanese wards, for a jovial reunion.

Prior to leaving Denzo and Goemon's hut, he gave them two silver dollars and invited them to visit him on the *William and Eliza* within the next few days, saying that he had something to tell them. They hurried to the whaleship the very next day and thanked Whitfield for his benevolence. The captain revealed a new plan. He had not forgotten that they were stranded many thousands of leagues from home, and he offered them an opportunity to try to return home. He had heard that the *Florida*, a large ship from New Bedford had arrived in Honolulu on October 23, 1847, and was planning to sail in the vicinity of the Sea of Japan. This was the opportunity the Japanese fishermen had long been waiting for. Whitfield said that if they were willing, he would make the necessary arrangements with Arthur Cox, the ship's captain, who was a friend of his. Knowing that he didn't even need to discuss the offer with Goemon, Denzo excitedly accepted Whitfield's plan. The captain told them to gather their personal belongings and report back to his ship, where they would be lodged until the *Florida* was ready to sail.

Before the Japanese left the *William and Eliza*, the Fairhaven master gave them five overcoats, five pair of trousers, two pieces of white linen, some tobacco, and some sandals. Goemon wept with joy and again thanked Whitfield.

The very next day the two men from Usa, inspired by a new sense of hope, divided their assigned land among some of their neighbors. They gave the former proprietor all the crops they had cultivated and left their hut standing empty. When they were ready to leave, many of their neighbors, including the Reverend Parker, gathered to bid them a safe journey home to Japan. The American clergyman gave them two overcoats and a pair of gloves. They thanked him for his support and generosity throughout their stay in the village and especially for his assistance at the time of Jusuke's death.

Denzo and Goemon then gathered their livestock, which included four ducks, six chickens, two fighting cocks, two pigs, and two dogs. Herding the livestock and carrying their personal possessions, they left the village and headed for Honolulu, where they paid a final visit to their good friend Dr. Judd. Then they reported to the New Bedford whaleship and offered the captain their livestock, in appreciation for his assistance. Whitfield selected several animals and returned the rest.

Once Denzo and Goemon were settled on board the American vessel, Denzo again sought out Captain Whitfield and reminded him that his offer had included no mention of

Toraemon. Whitfield nodded in agreement but said, "Toraemon did not show any interest in me, and therefore, I shall not
trouble myself about his affairs."

Denzo was surprised and alarmed. He pleaded with his
friend to overlook Toraemon's behavior. He said further, "He
was my neighbor in Japan and I feel responsible for his pre-
dicament, for it was I who employed him on the fishing boat.
If I have to leave him, I shall have nothing to say to his
relatives. We understand your attitude toward him, but
please secure passage for him for our sakes."

Whitfield sat motionless for a while, saying nothing. Finally
he said, "It would be quite difficult to add another person to
that ship, whereas the accommodations were limited to only
you two." He paused for a moment as if searching his mind
for a satisfactory solution. Then he continued, "I heard of
another ship, a big one, that will soon be sailing toward Japan.
I will try to ship Toraemon on it."

Denzo was much relieved and thanked Captain Whitfield
on Toraemon's behalf. The two Japanese left the ship to
search for Toraemon. When they told him the good news, he
was excited and began at once to gather his personal effects.
In a very short time he was ready to go to the *William and
Eliza* to thank Whitfield and await further instructions regarding his passage back to Japan. Back at the ship, the homeless
Japanese learned that both of the ships on which they were
scheduled to sail were whaling vessels.

The captain had made the arrangements for Denzo and
Goemon to sail on the 330-ton American whaleship *Florida,*
which was bound for the Indian Ocean via the seas near
Japan. They had much difficulty in finding the right words to
thank their dear friend Whitfield. They knew that they would
never see the likes of him again. With heavy hearts they
embraced him for the last time. The captain too was moved,
and they wished one another the blessings of good fortune.

Captain Whitfield escorted the two Japanese to their ship.
Before they sailed, Denzo looked over to the ship that was
carrying Toraemon, hoping to catch a glimpse of him. He was
standing in the prow of the vessel, waving frantically and
beckoning. Denzo and Goemon immediately rushed over toward Toraemon's ship to find out the reason for his excited
behavior. He shouted that he had decided not to sail aboard

the vessel but wanted to wish them a safe journey home. Surprised, Denzo asked Toraemon to explain this sudden change. He replied that the officers on board the ship were not kind to him and did not want him on their vessel. Thus he had decided not to sail with them but rather to return to his home on the island.

Denzo and Goemon were heartbroken, but their own ship was making ready to raise her anchor. Denzo had no time to argue with Toraemon about his decision, for he could not take the risk that both he and Goemon might miss their long-awaited opportunity to try to return home. The three tearfully exchanged confused goodbyes, and Denzo and his brother rushed back to the *Florida*. On the morning of December 13, 1847, both the *William and Eliza*, under the command of Whitfield, and the *Florida*, under the command of Arthur Cox, sailed out into the open sea once again.

The *Florida*'s sails soon swelled, and she slowly made her way out of the protected harbor. Distressed about leaving Toraemon, the two fishermen silently watched as the harbor faded from their view.

Oahu was astern, and the ship's compass revealed that she was sailing southwest. After several days, they passed the large island of New Guinea, in the vicinity of Australia. The next port of call was an island known to whalers as the "Nude People's Island." Geographically, the island was flat, with few elevations. The people of the island wore no clothes, though the women did hide parts of their bodies from view with leaves taken from the coconut trees that grew abundantly on the island. The men cut their hair short, leaving their necks bare, and they also plucked out their beards and mustaches. Their living quarters were holes dug in the ground and covered over with leaves. Instead of using pots and kettles for cooking, they roasted seaweed on long poles over a fire. They drank the juice of coconuts. Several times each day, the women covered their faces and bodies with coconut oil, which made their naturally brown bodies shiny.

Denzo and Goemon were captivated by the behavior of the islanders and wished to look at the village more closely. They left the ship and strolled about among the people, taking a great interest in many of the strange sights they saw. They noticed an odd-looking man who wore ragged clothes and had dirt encrusted all over his body. When they looked closer, they discovered that they had known him in Oahu. Denzo asked what he was doing on this strange island, and he replied that he had been exiled some time ago. He also said that the people of this island lived like beasts. They had no knowledge of how to cultivate the soil, nor did they care to learn. He himself, however, had planted some potatoes and wheat by a small nearby hill. He collected urine and excrement from the natives and used them as fertilizer for his crops. Denzo felt sorry for the tattered-looking man and offered him several pieces of his own clothing. The derelict's eyes filled with tears and he accepted Denzo's offer.

After a short stay on the island, the American whaling ship weighed her large anchor and again sailed into the open sea, heading north by northeast until she reached the Pacific island of Guam. The crewmen were allowed to go ashore in turns, and there was always a watch aboard ship. Most of the crew, including the captain, checked into the local hotel, to experience the pleasure and comfort of clean bedding and other amenities.

Guam was a beautiful island. It had numerous hills, and a large mountain in the center protruded up high into the clouds. This mountain supplied the island with ample fresh water and fuel. The land was so rich that rice crops could be grown year round. The climate was moderately warm all year, but never exceedingly hot. The language of the islanders was familiar to Denzo and Goemon, being similar to that spoken on Oahu.

While in the port of Guam, the ship underwent some minor repairs. After nearly a month, she again set sail, taking a course directly north by northwest, into the Sea of Japan.

It was now the spring of 1848. Denzo and Goemon were excited by the thought that they were so close to their homeland, which they had not seen for nearly seven years. They could hardly contain their joy, feeling that they would soon be on Japanese soil once again.

Captain Cox skillfully maneuvered the whaleship close to shore. Members of the crew, assisted by the Japanese, prepared to lower a small, flat-bottomed landing boat. When the whaleship was as close to land as safety would allow, the Japanese men thanked the captain for his assistance and climbed down into the small boat.

As the boat approached the shore, its occupants could see

some men driving oxen and horses through orderly well-manicured fields. As they got closer to the beaching area, however, the winds and waves began to rise. Suddenly and without warning, the wind began to excite the surrounding water, so much so that it became impossible to find a safe place to land. Denzo and Goemon were reminded of the dreadful day when they had attempted to land on the island of Torishima. The small craft continued circling about for most of the day. Finally, unable to find a suitable landing site, the crew abandoned the plan and returned to the ship, which was watching from a safe distance. The larger vessel quickly recovered the smaller landing craft and secured it on deck. The captain decided to make another attempt, at Ezo, in the southern part of Hokkaido. Upon reaching Ezo, they rounded a peninsula and sailed in toward the shore. As they approached, they could see many small fires being lighted, as well as rockets being fired into the air as if to warn others of their approach. Denzo was familiar with this type of behavior by the Japanese. He had heard many such stories while fishing in the waters off Usa.

Despite the pyrotechnics, Captain Cox again ordered the small boat to be lowered. This time, the captain accompanied the two Japanese, and they made a landing. Once they were on shore, the people quickly fled in all directions. Denzo called out to them in his native tongue, attempting to calm their fears by saying that he too was Japanese. The people did not respond. Denzo, Goemon, Captain Cox, and the crew members entered a small hut, only to find that the inhabitants had fled. Denzo pointed out a Japanese stove to the captain, along with other Japanese implements. These Japanese utensils were a familiar and welcome sight, proving to Denzo and Goemon that they were indeed back in their own homeland.

The captain, however, was not satisfied with their reception. He told Denzo that they should return to the whaleship. Denzo pleaded with the captain to leave him and Goemon on Ezo. His feeling was that the people were panic-stricken at the sight of the foreign ship, but would be more receptive to their countrymen once the ship departed.

The captain said that he had been instructed by Whitfield to offer a letter of explanation to whoever received his passengers, and to ask for a receipt stating that Denzo and Goemon had landed in Japan and would be safe. He refused to leave the Japanese on Ezo without such a receipt, saying that he must fulfill the terms set forth by his friend Whitfield. The Japanese were insistent that they should be allowed to chance their own fate at the hands of the Japanese, and were very frustrated by the position taken by the captain. They had no recourse, however, and so returned to the waiting vessel with the captain. Shortly thereafter, the ship sailed away from Ezo. Even though it was spring, the weather in that latitude was still extremely cold. The whale hunters continued to sail in a northerly direction. They passed many seals along the way, and took a great number of whale. After sailing in the northern latitudes for approximately two months, they came within sight of land. The captain told Denzo and Goemon that the land belonged to a country called "Russia." The Japanese were interested to see that along this promontory of land there ran a mountain range, identified as the "Sikhote Alin Range," which protruded high into the sky and extended for many, many miles. On the upper peaks the snow was piled high and deep, the result of many seasons of snowfall.

Continuing to sail north along the coastline, the *Florida* became enshrouded in a seemingly endless bank of heavy fog. So dense was the fog that it often blotted out the daylight, creating an eerie simulation of night. Lookouts were placed all about the ship in strategic locations, with instructions to be alert for the sight and sound of a passing ship. Whenever a passing vessel was discovered, the ship's lookouts would bang together pieces of wood or beat the gunwales, to alert the passing ship to their presence and avoid collision.

The temperature continued to fall, and wind and snow made movement about on the deck dangerous. Nevertheless, the *Florida* continued to hunt for whales. Finally, after a prolonged period during which they found no whales, the captain decided to leave the treacherous fog bank and set a new course that would take them back to the Sandwich Islands. The ship continued to take whale along the way.

In the early fall of 1848, the *Florida* sailed into a driving westerly wind that caused her to labor heavily. Her prow was battered continually by the running sea. The vessel's pitching and rolling forced the ship's cook to curtail heavy cooking. For three days they ate nothing but steamed dumplings called "bechiteeburu." This diet was not well received by the members of the crew, but it was all the ship's cook could offer under the circumstances.

Suddenly the winds shifted to a more easterly direction, which allowed the captain to come about into the wind and take a more direct course toward the Sandwich Islands. The men of the *Florida* were much relieved.

5

John Mung and the Whaling Bark Franklin

Back in Fairhaven, Massachusetts, John Mung was still living on the Whitfield farm and had become adjusted to the American way of life. He had become an accomplished navigator and cooper as well. Despite these achievements, he still yearned for his mother and his homeland.

In the early spring of 1846, Mung decided to pay a visit to the J. & J. Howland Company in New Bedford, the owner of the whaleship *John Howland*. There he met with one of the principal owners of the firm, John Howland. Mung reminded Mr. Howland that he and his friends had been rescued by Captain William Whitfield, and inquired whether the firm had any plans to sponsor a whaling expedition that would sail anywhere near Japan. Howland said that his firm had no immediate plans for such a venture but that he would make every effort to find out whether other ship owners might be planning such an expedition. John was disappointed and somewhat discouraged, but he was able to base a shred of hope on Mr. Howland's promise. He returned to the Whitfield farm on Sconticut Neck in Fairhaven and resumed his chores.

One day in March, when the vernal equinox had arrived and buds had begun to swell on the abundant trees and shrubs of Sconticut Neck, an unexpected opportunity came calling. A man arrived at the house in a wagon drawn by a single horse. When Albertina Whitfield answered the door, the stranger introduced himself as Ira Davis and explained that he was a former shipmate of her husband, having served as a harpooner on a previous voyage. Mrs. Whitfield invited him into the house, and he told her that he wanted to speak with Mung. By chance, John was working nearby. Mrs. Whitfield called him in and introduced him, telling him that Mr. Davis had some business to discuss with him. She then left the two alone and went back to her own work.

Davis explained that he had heard about Manjiro from his employer, George W. Paine of the West & Paine Merchant Company of New Bedford. He knew that the Japanese boy had been rescued by Captain Whitfield several years before and that he was seeking passage back to his homeland. Mung listened intently as the older man spoke, and nodded as if approving each point in Mr. Davis's explanation. Davis revealed that he was hiring a crew for a proposed expedition on the whaling bark *Franklin*, which would be sailing in the waters near Japan. Davis had recently been appointed as master to the 273-ton vessel. He offered to sign Mung as a bona fide member of the crew. John's heart pounded with excitement about Captain Davis's offer, but he soon remembered that he had promised Captain Whitfield to help Mrs. Whitfield with the farm and with other related duties.

Trembling with anxiety, Mung hesitated. Again Captain Davis made his offer. The boy from Nakanohama stuttered and searched his mind for an acceptable solution. Finally, he requested permission to discuss the matter with Mrs. Whitfield before answering. Davis thought for a moment, then agreed.

Mung realized that he might not have another opportunity in the foreseeable future to return home. With Davis's help, he expounded the offer to Mrs. Whitfield, trying carefully to assess her reactions. She was obviously interested in the offer and listened intently to each detail.

Mrs. Whitfield resembled her husband in being able to control her reactions to complicated questions that required thought. She proposed to Captain Davis that John be given a little time to consider such an important choice. Captain Davis said that John could have a day or so in which to make his decision. Mung promised to have an answer within the required time. Captain Davis thanked Mrs. Whitfield for her hospitality and assistance, and climbed back into his wagon to return to New Bedford. Mrs. Whitfield told her ward that they would discuss the matter further after the evening supper, and they both returned to their chores.

That night, Mrs. Whitfield explained to John that, although he had promised the captain to look after things in his absence, she believed that, if her husband were there, he would undoubtedly consent to Davis's proposal. She further assured Mung that if he chose to go ahead with the plan, both she and

her child, William Henry, Jr., would be just fine and that he
should not concern himself about their well-being. She reminded John that he had been waiting for this opportunity
ever since his arrival in Fairhaven. John thought it over and
then nodded in agreement. He thanked his benefactor for her
strong words, and for her support and encouragement in this
difficult decision.

The following morning, Mung mounted a gelded horse and
rode to New Bedford. At the New Bedford waterfront, he
located the whaleship *Franklin* lying to at the Packet Pier.
Shouting from the dock to a worker who was carrying a sizable beam, Mung inquired whether Captain Davis was
aboard. In a few moments, the captain appeared on the quarter deck and beckoned Mung aboard. Mung said that he had
decided to sail on the *Franklin,* with the understanding that
he would leave the ship if he had an opportunity to reach his
homeland. Captain Davis assured Mung that he fully understood the circumstances and promised to cooperate in any
way possible. Mung smiled in agreement, and the two men
shook hands. Captain Davis advised Mung to return to Fairhaven and take care of his personal business, so that he could
report back to the ship no later than May 6.

During the next several weeks, Mung visited with a number of his newfound friends and acquaintances, to say goodbye and thank them for their friendship and encouragement.
He also visited his tutor Mr. Bartlett, of the Louis L. Bartlett
School of Mathematics, Navigation, and Surveying.

One of his last visits was to his close and dear friend Job
Tripp, with whom Mung had studied at the Bartlett School.
The two reminisced about some of the practical jokes they had
played while they were in school. John promised that someday
he would return to Fairhaven for a visit. He had become fond of
this place, where he had received much kindness.

On May 6, with much emotion, Mung embraced the American woman who had become a sort of stepmother to him.
Words were difficult for both John and Mrs. Whitfield. The
necessity for parting touched them both. He promised that,
no matter what fate had in store for him, he would never
forget Captain and Mrs. Whitfield, who had taken the outcast
fisherboy from Nakanohama into their home. He turned to
William Henry, Jr., whom he looked upon as a stepbrother,
and embraced him with tear-filled eyes. He had no way of

knowing that this was the last time he would ever see the child.

Tearfully, Mung gathered up his belongings and walked along the rutted lane that led to the main road. He turned several times and waved farewell.

Later that afternoon, John reported to the business office of West & Paine. Mr. Paine explained to Mung that he was required to sign a document known as the "Whalemen's Shipping Paper"—a formal written agreement containing rules as well as governing factors designed to protect both the crewmen and the owners. John signed the document. It listed him as a steward and stated that he was to receive $1/140$ of any profits which might result from the expedition. Below is a copy of that agreement.

Whalemen's Shipping Paper

1st: It is agreed between the owner, Master Seaman and Mariners of the Bark *Franklin* now bound from the port of New Bedford for the Indian Ocean and Pacific Ocean on a whaling voyage.

That in consideration of the share against each respective seaman or mariner's name here under set, they severally shall and will perform the above mentioned voyage; do hereby agree with, and hire the said Seamen or Mariners for the said voyage, at such shares of the net proceeds, or of the actual products of the voyage, to be paid pursuant to this agreement, and the custom and usage in the port of New Bedford.

2nd: And they, the said Seamen and Mariners do severally hereby promise and oblige themselves to do their duty and obey the lawful commands of the officers on board said bark or the boats thereunto belonging, as become good and faithful Seamen or Mariners while cruising for whales, and at all places where the said Bark shall put in, or anchor at, during the said voyage; to use their best endeavors to obtain a cargo of oil; and for the preservation of the said vessel and cargo, and not to neglect or refuse doing their duty by day or by night, and they shall not go out of said vessel on board any other vessel, or be on shore, under any pretence whatsoever, until the afore said voyage be ended, and the vessel discharged of her loading, without leave first obtained of the Captain or Commanding Officer on board; that in default thereof, he or they shall be liable to all penalties and forfeitures mentioned in the Marine Law, enacted for the Government and Regulations of Seamen in the Merchant's service: it being understood that said forfeiture shall be estimated according to his or their respective shares of the net proceeds of the voyage, and the length of the same conjointly.

3rd: And it is further agreed by all the parties to this contract, that such regulations as a just regard to the good order, effectual government, health and moral habits of the Officers and the Men shall be established and observed on board the said vessel. And to ensure proper attention to this important object, it shall be the duty of the Officer having care of the Log Book, to note therein daily all flagrant breaches of the same. It shall especially be his duty to record all instances of drunkenness, all cases of absence from the said bark by any Officer or Seaman with or without permission after sunset, or beyond the time prescribed for their absence, every instance of absence by any Officer or Seaman through the night, whether on shore or on board of any other vessel, every instance of the introduction of any woman or women into the ship for licentious purposes, every instance of disability for the performance of the Ship's duty, which may occur, with the cause of it, if occasioned by sickness or infirmity, the nature and origin of the same, if known, to be particularly stated, especially if it be the consequence of their own misconduct. And in case of the Officer who may usually have charge of the Log Book being implicated in any of the misdemeanors or disabilities herein mentioned, it shall be the duty of the Master to make or cause to be made by another hand an entry of the same on the Log Book. And it shall be the duty of the Master to see that a proper record is kept therein of all the matters mentioned in this article according to its true intent and meaning.

4th: The Officer having charge of the Watch on Deck for the time being, shall be responsible for the maintenance of the Regulations in regard to the admission of women—and in case of any getting on board unperceived, they shall be forthwith expelled by him, or if not able to do so in the case shall be immediately reported to the Captain or Commanding Officer on board, whose duty it shall be to enforce their immediate expulsion. On the failure of any Officer in this part of his duty, either willfully or through negligence, each and every Officer so failing, shall forfeit twenty days pay for every such offence, and any Officer or Seaman who shall abet any breach of the said regulation—or refuse when lawfully called upon to aid in sustaining it, or shall be proved to have had a criminal intercourse with any such woman or women on board, shall forfeit for each such offence, five day's pay—for every instance of drunkenness two days pay shall be forfeited, and a similar forfeiture shall take place for each day that any Seaman or Officer shall be off duty from sickness or disability caused by intemperance or licentiousness—the forfeitures in all these cases to be estimated as in the second article, and to go to the use of the owners of said.

5th: All expenses which may be necessarily incurred during the voyage with direct reference to any of the misdemeanors or disabilities enumerated in the third article—or to any attempt at desertion or other disobedient or mutinous conduct, shall be charged to the individual or individuals by reason of whom they may have been incurred.

6th: It is further agreed that if any Officer or Seaman, after a fair trial, if his abilities and disposition shall be judged by the Master incompetent or indisposed to the proper discharge of the duties of his station, the Master shall have the right to displace him and substitute another in his stead—a corresponding reduction of the lay of such Officer or Seaman with reference to the duty which he may afterwards perform, thenceforth to take effect; and a reasonable increase of the lay of the individual who may thereupon be promoted to a higher station, shall be made on the final adjustment of the voyage.

7th: It is understood and agreed that if any Officer or Seaman shall be prevented by sickness or death from performing the voyage, his legal representatives shall be entitled to such part of the whole amount of his stipulated share, as the time of his services on board shall be of the whole term of the voyage.

8th: It is further agreed that whatever apparel, or stores belonging to the said vessel, may be given in charge by the Master to any Officer or Seaman, shall be accounted for by him, and in case anything shall be lost or damaged through his carelessness or neglect, it shall be made good to the Owners by such Officer or Seaman. And whatever Officer or Seaman the Master shall appoint for the duty, shall take charge of any portion of the cargo or ship's stores required to be landed or brought on board in any boats or lighter, and faithfully perform the service assigned, and see that the said cargo or stores are safely landed and delivered, or brought on board the said vessel as the case may be.

9th: Each and every Officer and Seaman, who shall well and truly have performed the above mentioned voyage, complied with the regulations and duties herein specified, and committed no dishonest or unlawful acts, shall be entitled to the payment of his share of the net proceeds of the voyage pursuant to this agreement, as soon after the return of said Bark to New Bedford as the oil and other products of the voyage can be sold and the settlement adjusted by the Owner or agent of said Bark.

10th: In testimony of our assent, consent and agreement, faithfully to perform the various duties and obligations implied in the preceding articles, and in the acknowledgement of their being voluntary, and without any compulsory or clandestine means being used, we have, each and every of us, severally, hereunto affixed our names, on the day and the year against them respectively written. And it is hereby understood, and mutually agreed, by and between the parties aforesaid that they, the said Seamen and Mariners will render themselves on board the said vessel, on or before _____ the _____ day of _____ at _____ o'clock in the _____ noon.

NO DISTILLED SPIRITUOUS LIQUOR will be put on board
this vessel by the Owner, except for the strictly medical use:—
and by their signatures, the other parties to this contract, pledge
themselves not to take of these articles with them as their private Stores, or for traffic, either from this port or any other port
or place where they may be, during the voyage. And in case of
violation of this pledge by the Master or any Officer or Seaman,
his entire share of the voyage shall be thereupon forfeited to the
use of the owners of the Bark.

Time of entry	*Name*	*Quality*	*Witness*	*Shares*
1846				
May 13	Ira Davis	Master	Ralph B. Alden	1/7
" "	Issachar H. Aiken	Mate	George W. Paine	1/27
" "	Joseph H. Alden	2nd Mate	Gordon E. Page	1/40
" "	Henry T. Chase	3rd Mate	Leonard A. Chase	1/55
" "	William Webster	°Bt. Ste.	George W. Paine	1/80
" "	Geo. L. Sylvester	°Bt. Ste.	Joseph H. Alden	1/80
" "	Fred. S. Gammon	°Bt. Ste.	George W. Paine	1/80
" "	Edward D. Read	Cooper	Frederick H. Read	1/55
May 6	Corydon E. Page	†Gr Hand	James B. Smith	1/170
" "	Francis x Silva his mark	Seaman	Ephraham H. Aiken	1/145
" "	Learner R. Chorse	Seaman	Ephraham H. Aiken	1/145
" "	John E. Smith	Boy	Corydon E. Paine	1/170
" "	John P. West Jr.	†Gr Hand	Corydon E. Paine	1/170
" "	Phillip Wilcox	†Gr Hand	James N. Mann	1/170
" "	**John Mung**	**Steward**	**George W. Paine**	**1/140**
" "	John Winston	Cook	Parker Watkins	1/135
" "	D. C. Smith	†Gr Hand	George W. Paine	1/170
" "	Addison Hazer	†Gr Hand	George W. Paine	1/170
" "	John Dolan	Seaman	Joseph H. Alden	1/140
" "	Jacob Mieos	Seaman	Joseph H. Alden	1/145
" "	John Snow	Boy	John H. Snow	1/180
" "	William H. Smith	Seaman	Shubet Smith	1/160
" "	Isaue D. Holt	†Gr Hand	Edward L. Reed	1/170
" "	George B. Childs	†Gr Hand	Edward L. Reed	1/170

°*Boat Steerer*
†*Green Hand*

Once John Mung had signed the whalemen's contract, his commitment was legal and binding. George Paine and Captain Ira Davis congratulated him. Captain Davis told him to report on board the *Franklin* to Henry Chase, the third mate, who would provide him with further instructions. Carrying a faded carpetbag containing all his worldly possessions and feeling somewhat exhilarated by his new venture, Mung reported on board the ship as directed. Mr. Chase welcomed Mung and led him to an area below the main deck of the ship. His berthing space was nearly adjacent to the ship's galley. The third mate explained to the new steward that his duties for the most part would be under the direction and control of the ship's cook, John Winston. Before returning to the quarterdeck, the third mate advised Mung that the ship was scheduled to leave for the whaling grounds on the sixteenth instant—that is, on May 16. He further suggested that Mung spend as much time as possible familiarizing himself with the ship and his duties.

Mung's exhilaration faded as he looked about the ship which was to be his new home. He soon developed the same feeling he had had when he left his Japanese friends in Honolulu and sailed to America with Captain Whitfield—a feeling of emptiness. He began to question the wisdom of his decision to leave the Whitfield farm without Captain Whitfield's advice and consent.

On the early morning tide of May 16, 1846, the whaling bark *Franklin* was slowly eased away from her berth alongside the Packet Pier. Several barges strained as they swept her to midstream, and then she began to sail under her own accord. Feeling forlorn and homeless, Mung watched silently as the familiar harbor faded from sight. The *Franklin*, measuring nearly 170 feet (52 meters) in length, was soon well under way. More canvas was lowered into the wind, and the vessel was soon caught up in the running tide. Mung gazed aloft at the ship's tall masts. His thoughts turned to Japan and his mother—how proud she would be if she only knew of her adventurous son's accomplishments. His thoughts were shattered suddenly by the shouts of the second mate. Men began to bustle about on the weather deck. The ship heaved momentarily as she laid her broadside against the starboard swells. Coming to a new heading, she aimed her bowsprit north, catching the wind at her stern.

Mung was not without friends aboard the *Franklin,* for two members of the crew had served with Captain Whitfield on previous voyages, and were also his neighbors in Fairhaven. Also included in the *Franklin's* crew were two young boys— both much younger than Mung—who were taking their first voyage aboard a whaler.

It had been five years since John had been rescued by the men of the *Howland.* He felt certain that he was at long last beginning his journey home.

The *Franklin* sailed first to the large port of Boston. The ship cautiously plied her course through the many small islands that cluttered the port's access. The young man from Nakanohama was awed by the sight of several forts which protected the harbor's approach and by the size and physical appearance of the protecting palisades. These consisted for the most part of multiple tiers of breastwork, and numerous guns could be seen protruding out of the many openings. The young sailor was so impressed that he decided to sketch the scene. This sketch and others have been preserved, along with other documents, in collections related to the Manjiro story. They may be viewed at the Kochi City Public Library in Kochi City, Kochi Prefecture, Shikoku, Japan.

Following a short stay in the Boston port, the *Franklin* headed east, helped along by the prevailing southwest winds. The whaler's first destination was the Azores, a small group of Portuguese islands located some 2500 miles (4022 kilometers) due east from the U.S. mainland.

After leaving the Azores, the ship headed south, toward the Cape of Good Hope, the last point of land on the southerly tip of Africa. Having rounded this famed promontory, the vessel again sailed in an easterly direction, passing a number of islands. During the course of the voyage, a lookout spotted an object floating near the water's surface. The sighted object turned out to be a huge sea turtle—a favorite delicacy of many mariners. Mung recalled that it was a search for turtles that had brought Whitfield and the crew of the *John Howland* close enough to Torishima Island to rescue him and his Japanese boatmates, some five years earlier.

The large ship was brought about into the freshening winds, and soon a longboat was lowered into a passing swell. The men in the longboat rowed closer to the swimming reptile, which then disappeared below the water. Several mo-

ments later, however, it reappeared; it was headed toward
the *Franklin*. Mung climbed aloft to watch the action. The
men in the longboat were soon within harpoon range, and the
striker, standing in the bow, let fly with his harpoon. The iron
missed its mark, but the striker quickly retrieved it. In a
second attempt, the harpoon struck the turtle a glancing blow
and was sent astray. Before the striker could position himself
for a third attempt, the large sea turtle commenced to de-
scend. Watching from aloft, Mung realized that the giant
turtle was about to escape. He rose quickly to his feet, pulled
a knife from its sheath and placed it between his teeth, and
dove into the sea. He was able to catch hold of the rim of the
turtle's shell just behind its protruding neck. Still underwater,
Mung hauled back his prey and, at the same time, reached for
his knife. Quickly he slashed the turtle's throat. Grasping its
rear leg, he pulled himself and his quarry to the surface just
as his lungs were about to burst. Upon seeing the Japanese lad
surface with the turtle, the men of the *Franklin* shouted a
wild burst of approval. The longboat rushed to Mung's assistance and hauled both him and his prize safely on board. The
fatal blow had been struck with such skill and determination
that the crewmen were overwhelmingly impressed. Because
of Mung's intrepid act, the men of the *Franklin* gained much
respect for him—and their respect would one day have a
positive effect upon his career.

The large turtle was hoisted from the chase boat to the
ship's deck by a block and tackle. The ship's cook came forward to take charge, and over the next several days, the men
on board the New Bedford whaleship enjoyed savory turtle
soup, thanks to Mung.

The *Franklin* continued to sail the lonely Pacific and to take
whale, weaving in and out among both known and unknown
islands. One island on which they landed was under the protection of the Dutch flag. Many of its houses and other structures resembled those seen in the vicinity of Japan, but John
soon learned that they had been designed and constructed by
men of Chinese ancestry. Mung was not personally familiar
with the Chinese, although during his studies in Fairhaven,
he had been told of such a people. Because Japan had been
in isolation for such a long time and because he had never
encountered any Chinese people, either in Fairhaven or on

board the *Howland*, the word "Chinese" was just that to him—a word. When he had an opportunity to go ashore, Mung encountered a number of Chinese people. He found them to be similar to his fellow countrymen of Japan, although he could not understand their dialect.

As the New Bedford whaleship continued to move from island to island, John was exposed to many strange-looking people. Some dressed in unusual clothing, whereas others wore no clothes at all. This exposure to different people and their customs was an educational and interesting experience for John Mung. He became frightened, however, at any mention of cannibals, but Captain Davis, like most experienced whalemen, was careful to avoid islands that were inhabited by cannibals.

Aside from occasional stops at islands, the days and weeks aboard the *Franklin* were monotonous and uneventful. The crew continued to take whale. When rumors began to spread that the ship would soon be putting into the port of Guam, a small island in the Philippine Sea, Mung welcomed the news. He had been to Guam with Captain Whitfield and cherished his memories of the island. Captain Davis promised his men that they could have a much-needed rest on the serene island of Guam.

Once the ship was securely anchored in the quiet, sun-drenched harbor, the crewmen were allowed to alternate shore leave. Captain Davis invited Mung to accompany him on visits to several other whaleships that were anchored in the harbor. It was customary for newly arrived ship captains to visit the captains of ships already in port, to exchange news of current events and to forward mail on homeward-bound vessels. In addition, Captain Davis was hoping to hear some news that might be helpful to Mung.

John found the opportunity to visit other ships very interesting. He listened attentively as the shipmasters exchanged stories and news of the day, and was quite amused by many of the tales he heard.

During the course of conversation, the subject of experiences in the Ryukyu Islands often arose. These islands were located off the southern point of Kyushu Island, Japan, and bordered on the west by the East China Sea. Historically, at least, there had been some question whether the Ryukyu

Islands belonged to the Japanese or to Russia. Several captains spoke bitterly about the treatment they had received when they attempted to establish friendly relations with the islanders. Each had his own tale of resentment toward the Japanese government. Mung did not fully understand the politics involved, and he only listened silently.

While in Guam, John mailed a letter to his old friend and benefactor, Captain Whitfield. The letter was carried by another American ship that was returning home after a successful expedition. The letter, which was written in Mung's own hand, reads as follows:

Guam, March 12, 1847

Capt. Wm. H. Whitfield
Ship *William & Eliza*
New Bedford, U.S.A.

Respected Friend:

I will take the pen to write you a few lines and let you know that I am well and hope you were the same. First thing I will tell you about the home, the time I left. Well sir your boy, William, is well all the summer but the cold weather sets in he will smart a little cunning creature I ever saw before. He will cry after me just as quick as he would to his mother. Your wife and Amelia and Mr. Bonny's family and your neighborhoods they all well when I last saw them. I did went to Mr. Huzzeys and stayed there about six months and then I left them. Reason is this— they were a good family but very poor living. They only gave us dry hard bread for supper and breakfast and dinner. That's doing well for apprentices, only gave us old Nantucket Dumpling. He have got three apprentices. That is two more besides me. They were left all to once. I was last one in the whole. I thought after them two apprentices left I will stand a better chance, but in vain, so I left too and I was sick in that month three or four times. Then I went to see your wife. Mrs. Whitfield very glad to receive me, so I went to your home and go to the school. After the school out I did try find the place to finish my studies. One gentlemen wished to receive me but the same time United States talks about the war and then I thought make up my mind to go the sea. I went to see Mr. John Howland. He says to me if that I like any kind of a trade he will get it for me. I told him the Bark *Franklin* the last voyage saw a great many of Japanese fishing boats and the (punck) Capt. Ira Davis thought that I might get a change to reach these; so I shipped for the steward 140th lat. we have caught 30 barrels of sperm oil and

have sent it home fifty barrels same last summer we have got in
about 50 barrels, 50 bushel apples, 115 bushels potatoes and
eight or nine tons of hay, and have sold between three to four
tons of hay and we have plenty of milk to drink. I wish you had
some of that milk. Your wife is careful and industrious respectful
and good woman. I am glad for that you have such good wife.
I hope you will forgive me. I hope you never will forget me for
I have thought about you day after day. You are my best friend
on earth beside the great God. I do hope the Lord helps us
whole my friend. Oh my friend, I wanted to see that boy more
than little. His cunning little thing I ever saw before. When you
get home give my best respects to whole. We were ten months
out, sixteenth of this mo. After this we shall go North and
Westward toward the Loochue Islands, Japan, and I hope get a
chance to go ashore safely. I will try to open a port for purpose
for the whaler come there to recruit. We came here to anchor
3rd of this month and saw number of whalers. One of them
touched the Loochue Islands and send the boats ashore in order
to see if they can get some of refreshment. Natives gave them
two boats and tell go away. One of chief officers says to them in
two days if you no sail he cut you float name of this Abram
Howland of New Bedford, Capt. Harper. He is going to Japan
Sea. He want me to go with him but Capt. Davis he would not
let me go. When you see Mr. Warren Woodward give him my
best friendly respects. Here I have got letter for you written by
your wife. She will tell you more about the home.

John Mung, Japanese

After several weeks of rest and recuperation, the *Franklin*
raised her muddy anchor and set out to sea once again, to
resume her hunt for the valuable whale. Success once again
rewarded the efforts of the men of the *Franklin*. The pursuit
led to the waters of the East China Sea. Captain Davis
searched relentlessly for his prey, and his drive to fill his oil
casks became almost an obsession. The ship soon sailed very
close to the Ryukyu archipelagos. Knowing the Japanese isolationist policy toward foreigners, Captain Davis took care to
give the islands a wide berth.

One morning in the late summer of 1847, the *Franklin*
spotted a few Japanese fishing boats working feverishly in the
midst of a large school of bonito off the northern coast of
Japan. Captain Davis decided to take some of the tasty fish.
So plentiful and active were the frenzied bonito that the water
looked almost black. The whaleship's crewmen dropped the

main sail and released the anchor. The whalemen cast their
lines, and soon their backs were straining as they repeatedly
hauled onto the main deck nearly a hundred bonitos. This was
sufficient to take care of the crew's needs, and so Captain
Davis signaled the crew to weigh anchor. As they began to
execute his orders, several of the smaller Japanese fishing
boats drifted close to the *Franklin,* as if to protest the American ship's having taken some of the schooling fish.

When John saw the men in the smaller craft, he realized
that he might be able to make conversation with them.
Quickly he raced below deck to get his old, tattered kimono.
He donned the shabby clothing hastily and began wrapping a
white piece of cloth around his forehead in Japanese fashion.
Using his native tongue for the first time since leaving his
friends in Honolulu, the young man from Nakanohama
shouted to the Japanese fishermen. At first they acknowledged his shouts, but they seemed apprehensive. Soon they
became mute and no longer responded to Mung. In a final
attempt, Mung tried to plead with or coerce the men in the
small boats by tugging at his weathered kimono and pointing
to his headband. The fishermen's only responses were empty,
indifferent looks.

The *Franklin's* windlass soon had the anchor securely in its
chock, and the ship drifted slowly away from the small boats.
Soon, amid the squealing blocks, large folds of canvas were
swelled by the prevailing breeze. John stood on the quarterdeck, dejected and disbelieving because his countrymen had
refused to communicate with him. He watched until the
smaller vessels were no longer visible. The failure weighed
heavily on his heart. His hope of returning to his people had
been dealt a severe blow. He remained where he was, staring
at the passing swells, until several of his shipmates came to his
side to offer words of hope and encouragement. They suggested that the men on the small boats were from a different
section of Japan and had not been able to understand Mung's
dialect. At first, Mung simply shrugged his shoulders, as if in
agreement with the suggestion, but later, his shipmates were
able to convince him that he would soon have another opportunity to establish contact with his fellow countrymen.

More than a year later, in September 1848, the New Bedford whaler arrived in Honolulu. Mung could hardly wait to

get ashore and seek out his old friends, whom he had neither seen nor heard from since leaving Honolulu nearly six years earlier. He thought of the Reverend Samuel Chenery Damon, whom he had met during his first visit to Hawaii, and started toward Damon's place to ask where his friends were. En route, however, he met an islander he knew and asked him instead. The islander directed him to a site where Toraemon was still working as a carpenter.

Looking up from his work, Toraemon shrieked with joy at the sight of his old companion. The two men embraced, and Toraemon offered his friend a place to sit, at the same time bubbling over with news of all that had happened during their separation. Toraemon told Manjiro that at first he and their former boatmates had done odd jobs of various kinds. Soon they had grown tired of living off the goodwill of the government and so had applied for more meaningful employment. Their valued friend Dr. Gerrit P. Judd had helped Toraemon to obtain work as a carpenter's apprentice and had also helped Denzo and Goemon to find employment.

In addition, since 1841, Jusuke, Goemon, and Toraemon had become citizens of the Hawaiian Islands, as attested to by the following citizenship document:

Government of the Hawaiian Islands

The undersigned a native of Nibona, residing in Pae Island of Japan being duly sworn upon the Holy Evangelists, upon his oath declares that he will support the constitution and laws of the Hawaiian Islands, and bear true allegiance to His Majesty Kamehameha III., the King, hereby renouncing all allegiance to every other Government and particularly of Japan.

[Signed by Jusuke's hand, in Hawaiian.]

Subscribed and sworn to, this 25th day of October, 1844.

Before me, M. Kekuanaoa.

This same document was signed by Goemon on January 10, 1845, and by Toraemon on February 13, 1847. (Whether or not Denzo, like the others, became a citizen of Hawaii, I have been unable to ascertain.)

Manjiro was happy as he listened with undivided attention to Toraemon's tales. Suddenly, however, Toraemon's voice lowered; in a somber tone he told Manjiro of the passing of their friend Jusuke. Toraemon explained that Jusuke's old leg wound, incurred at the time of their shipwreck on Torishima Island, had never healed properly. Jusuke had suffered much discomfort as a result. Many attempts had been made to have the wound properly attended to by the island's physician, as well as treatments by a doctor from a neighboring village. Toraemon said that Jusuke had finally been laid to rest in a cemetery at nearby Kaneohe. Manjiro listened in distress.

Toraemon's story continued. The time after Jusuke's death had passed very slowly. Denzo and Goemon had built a small house and had learned to plant and raise a variety of crops, which were Denzo's only means of support. Goemon had been befriended by an American missionary, the Reverend Benjamin Parker, and could often be found working at the missionary church.

Next Toraemon told Manjiro another piece of startling news. One day Captain Whitfield had returned to Honolulu and had helped Denzo and Goemon to obtain passage on an American whaleship, the *Florida*. The captain had made arrangements for Toraemon to sail on another ship, but the officers on board had not been kind to him. He had decided not to risk the venture, as he was frightened by the men on the strange ship.

In addition, he explained, he had been somewhat apprehensive about the plan from the beginning. Since he had learned carpentry, and because he feared that he might be executed for violating Japan's "no-leave" policy, he no longer wished to take the risk of returning to his native soil. Toraemon said, however, that neither Denzo nor Goemon shared his views on the no-leave policy. It was their belief that, if given the opportunity, they could convince the authorities that they were innocent of wrongdoing. Therefore, with the help of Captain Whitfield and Reverend Parker, Denzo and Goemon had left Honolulu aboard the *Florida*, which was bound for the Sea of China. They were hopeful that they could find a safe place to land on Japanese soil.

When he heard this news about his friends, Manjiro became very upset. He angrily told Toraemon that their former boatmates should have waited for his return, so that, when conditions were right, they could have attempted the dangerous return together. Toraemon, also angry, responded that he had attempted to persuade Denzo and Goemon to wait but had been unsuccessful. Manjiro continued to ask about his friends, wanting to know how long they had been gone. Toraemon said it had been nearly a year since they left. Shaking his head in disapproval, Manjiro returned to the *Franklin.*

Coincidentally, it was only a few weeks later that Manjiro heard that Denzo and Goemon had returned. He went immediately to seek them out, and when he saw them, he rushed to embrace them. They described the circumstances of the failure of their attempt, which had forced them to return to Hawaii. Manjiro listened intently as Denzo explained the details—how they had landed at Ezo, and they and the captain had gone ashore, but the people had fled at their approach. Denzo had been satisfied, however, that the inhabitants of Ezo were Japanese, because he had seen Japanese implements and furnishings in the small huts of the village.

Denzo continued to explain that they were unable to communicate with the people, who were in hiding. The captain argued that the people were probably frightened at the sight of such a large vessel anchored offshore. After waiting in the village for several hours hoping that the inhabitants would return, the captain ordered the Japanese to return to the waiting ship.

Manjiro agreed with Denzo and Goemon that the captain of the *Florida* should have left them to their own fate. He told his friends, however, that he too had a plan. His plan would take them to a landing site at the Ryukyu Islands. He believed that the people of the Ryukyus might be more receptive and understanding than those of Ezo. He had heard many stories about the Ryukyu people, who were reputed to be kind and gentle. He had also heard that the Ryukyus contained no samurai. Another consideration involved in his selection of these islands as a landing site was that sailing home from them should be comparatively less difficult. In conclusion, however, Manjiro said that he was not prepared at this time to attempt the landing. He assured them that he would return to Honolulu soon, better prepared to execute his plan. He reminded his friends of his written commitment to the owners of the *Franklin*, by virtue of his signature, to complete the whaling expedition. He further reminded them that upon conclusion of the voyage, he would be paid a good sum of money, which would help to underwrite the costs involved in their return trip home. Denzo and Goemon promised that they would wait for Manjiro and would not make any more attempts to return home without him.

Manjiro felt sure that, with a good plan, he and his Japanese friends would be successful in their mutual attempt. Returning to Honolulu, he visited some of his old Hawaiian friends, including the Reverend Damon and Dr. Judd. He saw that marked changes had been made in the port city since his last visit. Many new buildings had been constructed and roadways laid out.

The Reverend Damon, the port's chaplain, provided much advice and comfort to the seamen who frequented the port. A mild-mannered man with sympathetic ways, he was a popular figure in Honolulu. Besides his Christian vocation, Reverend Damon was the founder and publisher of a tabloid newspaper, *The Friend*. Since 1843, the newspaper had been providing mariners with news of Honolulu and the surrounding islands. He also printed announcements of ship arrivals and departures, as well as the latest available prices of oil in U.S. port cities such as New Bedford. Although the prices listed in *The Friend* were as much as a year old, since Reverend Damon obtained them from ships arriving in Honolulu, they were an interesting barometer for the masters of whaling vessels. *The Friend* was without question the reading material most sought after by the men who worked the fishing grounds of the Pacific and Indian oceans. Through his newspaper, Reverend Damon was able to reach nearly every port throughout the Pacific.

The reverend listened patiently to Manjiro's stories of his escapades since they had last met, in 1841. Damon was captivated and amazed by the changes in his young friend from Japan, and by his determination. At this meeting, the missionary and the Japanese fishermen from Shikoku formed a friendship that would continue for the rest of their lives.

During his stay in Honolulu, Mung decided to write another letter to Captain Whitfield.

> Honolulu
> October 30, 1848

Kind Friend:

I went to see Mr. Damon's and Mr. Smith's family. They all glad to see me and told me you are a good friend to them and wanted me to write to you and give best respects to you and your wife. Mr. Damon gave me paper and semimonthly journal which contained some of your writing.

O captain how can I forget your kindness, when can I pay for your fatherly treatment? THANK GOD ten thousand times and never will forget your name. . . . I was sorry to hear that your ship being leaky and obliging you into port before the season. The GOD will direct you into the straightest and clearest path of the sea. . . . We are lying with 700 bbls. of sperm oil and have to go to another season on line. . . . Give my best respects to all your friends and your kind neighbors and my affectionate regards to your wife, Aunt Amelia and Mr. Bonney family. Tell them what quarter of the world I am in. I can never forget kindness they have done to me. It is hard for me to join words together and therefore come to close.

> John Mung

Several days later, Manjiro also wrote to his former teacher, Jane Allen, who had devoted much time to helping him with his American studies. It reads as follows:

> Honolulu
> November 2, 1848

Respected Friend:

I take pen with pleasure this day to inform you that I am in good health and spirits, and hope most sincerely that these few lines will find you and all your friends enjoying health and happiness. I have received your affectionate letter by my friend and now return to you my warmest thanks for your kind wishes, and hope you will always find that I pay a proper degree of respect to the advice you are so frequently kind enough to give me, that my conduct may evidence the truth of the assertion, for believe me I shall always feel truly gratified of having the good opinion of friends. We are lying with 700 bbls. of sp-oil and have to go another season on line. I had a couple of chances to getting

home, but being wanted at the Nautical Instrument, and capt.
being unwilling to let me go I could not.
    Capt. unites with me in love to you all.

                                                    John Mung

John Mung's letters were evidence that he never forgot
those who showed him kindness. Captain Whitfield must have
sensed the young boy's fine qualities when he offered to take
him home to Fairhaven and make him a member of his family.
As always, the fire in Manjiro's heart was kindled by his
driving desire to return home to his widowed mother.

After several weeks in port, the ship's supplies had been
replenished and the crewmen were rested. On November 28,
1848, it was time for the *Franklin* to set out to sea once again.
In the latitudes of the south seas, the men of the New Bedford
ship took an ample share of sperm. The killing continued until
Captain Davis decided to put in once again to the port of
Guam. Following a brief stay in the sheltered harbor, the
heavily laden vessel returned to her mission.

After the ship left Guam, Captain Davis's obsession with
the finding and killing of whale became worse, and soon
began to cause a loss of harmony between him and the men
aboard his ship. Life on the *Franklin* was unbearable, and the
men were terribly upset about the captain, who was becoming increasingly irrational. The slightest provocation would
set him off. His behavior was strange, and he developed a
confused state of mind. Before long, Captain Davis was in a
complete state of mental disorder. Initially, the crewmen
were reluctant to speak or act in a way which might imply
sedition or mutiny, for they were fully aware of the strict
regulations of maritime laws and the penalties for such an act.
Eventually, however, conditions aboard the ship could no
longer be tolerated; the entire crew agreed that they could
not serve an insane master. A vote was taken, and it was
agreed unanimously that Captain Davis would be placed in
protective custody and that the ship's first mate, Issachar H.
Akin, would be recognized as the new captain of the ship.
This was indeed a bold yet terrifying act by the crewmen of
the *Franklin*. Each and every man knew that he personally
would suffer severe consequences if the authorities back in
New Bedford decided that the crew's judgment had been in

error. Captain Davis was placed in irons and kept as comfortable as possible until he could be safely placed in the custody of the American Consul at Manila in the Philippine Islands. Once the *Franklin*'s new master was in command, the whaleship returned "on line" and continued taking whales. One problem, however, still had to be dealt with: the vacancy created when Captain Akin moved from his position as first mate to master of the vessel had to be filled. Captain Akin reassigned the second and third mates as first and second mates, respectively, which left the position of third mate vacant.

The captain and officers called a meeting with the ship's company to discuss the vacancy. The *Franklin*'s crew numbered twenty-three men. Of these, three were officers, three were boat steerers, five were ordinary seamen and lacked the necessary skills for the position of third mate, one was cooper, one was cook, seven were green hands, one was steward, and two were boys. Mung, who had signed on as a steward, stood out as the only likely candidate. Following some discussion, his name was suggested. This suggestion was predicated on several well-known facts. Mung had an education in navigation and was a seasoned whaler. He had served with Captain Whitfield on the *John Howland*, besides the two years before the mast he had had aboard the *Franklin*. In addition, he had proved his personal courage to the men of the ship several times over. Hence, the young fisherman from Nakanohama was selected to serve as third mate for the remainder of the voyage.

When the whaling season began to wane in June 1849, the *Franklin* set her course for home. As always, the crewmen were eager to be reunited with their families and loved ones. Soon the *Franklin* sailed past the Cape of Good Hope at the southernmost tip of Africa, and in September 1849 she arrived in the harbor of New Bedford. An entry in the New Bedford Whaling Records reads as follows:

BARK *FRANKLIN* of New Bedford . . . West & Paine

Enlarged in 1846 to $273^{26}/_{95}$ tons

DAVIS MASTER   Sailed May 16, 1846 for the In. & Pacific Oceans, Fayal June 16, sailed 17th for south seas. Landed 55 bbls sperm oil.

10 months out. 200 bbls. a letter from Capt. Davis reports him
at Guam March 13, 1847 180 bbls. on board. Bound to Japan. At
Manilla Nov. 28, oil not stated. At ditto Decem 16. getting
supplies at Guam Oct. 14, 450 bbls. reports sail for Manila Nov
7, for medical assistance Capt. Davis being sick. Sailed from
ditto previous to January 19, 1848 to cruise. *Akin Master,* Capt.
Davis would return home in consequence of ill health. At
Honolulu Oct. 17, 700 sperm. Sailed from ditto about Nov. 1 to
cruise. Arrived Sept. 23, 1849 with 750 bbls Sperm Oil in 40
Months & 7 days. Turned out 815 Bbls Sperm Oil

As the large vessel glided past the old fortress on the Fairhaven bank, Mung recalled his first sighting of the fort from
the *John Howland.* He was much more mature now, and this
return was one of triumph and satisfaction, especially because
he had attained the status of an officer. No longer was he a
lowly assistant who was assigned such tasks as unhooking fish.
Instead, he was an accomplished whaling man. John was
anxious to learn what his share of the profit would be. He
hoped that it would be enough to enable him to underwrite
the costs of returning to Japan, both for himself and for his
friends.

When the settlement was established, however, Mung's
share was determined to be $350—a tidy sum but not, in
Mung's estimation, enough to totally fund his plan. He had to
console himself with the thought that his experiences on
board the *Franklin* had enabled him to make the transition
from an inexperienced adolescent into a man.

Prior to leaving the ship, Mung reported to Captain Akin to
thank him for his kindness and confidence in appointing him
as third mate following the unfortunate incident with Captain
Davis. Meanwhile, the owners of the *Franklin,* after investi-
gating the circumstances surrounding the relieving of Captain
Davis, had decided that the action of the crew in taking command of the vessel was appropriate and correct. No charges
were brought against the *Franklin*'s crew.

John Mung, leaving the experiences of the *Franklin* behind,
headed directly for the Whitfield farm in Fairhaven.

6
Mung the
Prospector

On September 23, 1849, as Manjiro crossed the bridge from New Bedford into Fairhaven, he noticed a sight that had become familiar to him in the Massachusetts landscape: the leaves were changing color and had already begun to fall. Thus he was reminded that another season was passing. He was still determined to fulfill his promise to find a way to return to Japan with his friends, but his first obligation was to visit the Whitfields and tell them about his whaling cruise on board the *Franklin*.

As he walked again along the roadways he had come to know during his school years, he felt somewhat subdued and sad. He was remembering a time on the *Franklin* when he had received some dreadful news. Young William Henry, the Whitfield's only son, had died. Despite this sadness, he could hardly contain his eagerness to be reunited with his American family. His recollections of his stay in Fairhaven were revived as he walked along the road to the Whitfield farm, taking care as always to avoid puddles. It was late in the day when Manjiro reached the Whitfield home. Both Captain and Mrs. Whitfield were delighted to see their young stepson, now of a more manly stature than when they had seen him last. The three cordially embraced, their eyes damp with emotion.

The young subordinate officer of the *Franklin* spent the next several hours relating his experiences and revelations in minute detail, searching for signs of approval from his mentor. In the course of his report, Mung talked about his reunion with his shipwrecked friends and about their aborted attempt to return home without him. The captain listened intently and nodded approvingly from time to time. When the theme shifted to the incident concerning Captain Davis of the *Franklin*, Whitfield's interest and attention were very much aroused. A reputable shipmaster himself, the captain agreed with the action taken by the crew. He especially praised Mung for accepting the responsibilities of the position of third mate. He also approved the decision by Captain Arthur Cox of the whaleship *Florida* not to allow Denzo and Goemon to remain on the small island near the Cape of Matsumae.

The conversation between the two men continued late into the evening, though Mrs. Whitfield retired earlier. Not until the living room clock struck did either of the men realize the lateness of the hour. Whitfield rose from his chair as a signal to John that it was time to end their discussion, at least for now. Placing his hand upon Mung's shoulder, Whitfield thanked his young friend for his open and frank conversation. The older man was very pleased with Mung's report. He felt proud and satisfied. He knew that the shipwrecked lad from Japan had, when he was rescued, been faced with a poverty-stricken and meaningless life, but his future prospects were now quite different. The education and skills Mung had obtained both in Massachusetts and on American ships had undoubtedly provided the young man from Nakanohama with brighter prospects. The Fairhaven master felt well rewarded for his efforts, because now he knew that they had not been in vain.

In the days that followed, Mung spent a great deal of time visiting friends and places which he had come to know in and around Fairhaven. He was warmly received, especially by those who had become aware of his accomplishments. Exaggerated stories about him had been spreading through the area, but the attention he received didn't seem to faze John in the least.

Just as the physical appearance of Fairhaven and of the section known as "Poverty Point," where his friends the Whitfields, as well as Jane and Charity Allen, lived, had changed since Manjiro's departure three years earlier, so had his own personal appearance. The Allen sisters were surprised to see a grown man instead of the adolescent boy whom Jane had taught. When they had a chance to talk with him, they discovered that he was mature and self-confident. He had, in fact, all the faculties, attributes, and sterling qualities of a young man with a promising future.

Mung was happy to see his old friends and relished the

warm reception he received in Fairhaven. Nevertheless, he was still troubled by thoughts of his mother and the other family members he had left behind in the village of Nakanohama.

The whaling era was reaching its peak. The winds of change would soon chill the economy of the flourishing port city of New Bedford. The once predominant whaling industry would begin a steady decline that would carry it into oblivion, even as a new textile industry began to flourish.

In addition, and by a strange coincidence, at about the same time that Mung returned from his whaling expedition on board the *Franklin,* news of the discovery of gold at Sutter's Mill, near Sacramento, California, was already sweeping the country, including New Bedford. This important find precipitated a frenzy not only in New Bedford but throughout the United States. Tabloids were replete with news of gold findings. People in every quarter quickly became captivated by the illusion that they could instantly become rich. The entire country was soon gripped by the gold fever. Many people sold their homes, farms, and businesses to finance what they saw as the chance of a lifetime. Countless thousands of "forty-niners," as they were called, converged upon the region where the gold had been discovered, hoping to find riches.

New Bedford and Fairhaven did not escape the craze that had taken over the country. Mung, like most, soon fell prey to the delirium. He thought that the discovery of gold might well provide a solution to his problem—the need to finance his return trip home to Japan.

With each passing day, more gossip about gold discoveries circulated. Men were said to be amassing fortunes by finding gold in and around the rivers and basins near Sacramento. At first, Mung only toyed with the idea of prospecting, but as the rumors persisted, he began to give it more serious consideration. Once again he sought Whitfield's counsel and advice. Whitfield listened patiently as his ward discussed the possibility of going to California to try his hand at prospecting and explained that he would be acting not only in his own behalf but also in the interests of his Japanese friends in Honolulu. He talked about his conviction that, if he were successful in the search for gold, he would be able to finance a return to Japan.

After listening to all that Mung wanted to tell him, Whitfield finally responded. His advice to his young friend was that, if he felt in his heart that prospecting for gold was the right course of action for him, then he should do it. Otherwise, Whitfield pointed out, the question might haunt him for many years, especially if they were not able to find other means of financing a return to Japan.

John accepted Whitfield's comments as encouragement, and therefore he decided to challenge fate. The next step was to find a means of reaching the Sutter Mill area. He was a man of the sea and not accustomed to land travel. The thought of traveling overland more than 3000 miles (4800 kilometers), including hundreds of miles across open plains and prairies, did not appeal to him. Thus he decided to seek passage by sea, hoping to sign on as a crew member on the first available ship bound for California so as not to compromise his earnings from the whaling expedition. He became alert for news of ships which would be sailing for the West Coast.

Many companies had been formed soon after the discovery of gold, which were made up of people from all walks of life who banded together in partnerships. Each such group would draft an agreement about the rules by which the partnership or company would be governed, and the company would usually contract with a shipowner to provide passage to California for the partners. After they reached the goldfields, the people who held shares in the company would work together to search for gold. All the gold which they found would become the collective property of the company. After a prescribed period of time, the outstanding debts incurred by the company would be satisfied and the company would declare a dividend to the shareholders. This approach provided individuals with protection from the numerous bandits who preyed upon solitary prospectors in the vicinity of the goldfields.

Mung had studied the possibilities carefully and was aware of company partnerships, but he chose not to enter into an association with so many people, especially people whom he did not know. His decision was to venture to the goldfields by himself.

In October 1849, the following advertisement appeared in *The New Bedford Mercury*.

Bound for San Francisco, California—

The fast sailing ship, superior ship *Stieglitz*, coppered and copper fastened, commanded by Captain Joseph Holley, will be dispatched about November 5th for the above place direct. Her accommodations will be superior for a limited number of passengers. Her freight is already engaged. The ship was built at Charlestown, Massachusetts, and is well known in this community. For passage, apply to the agents, on Commercial Wharf.

October 13   Chas. R. Tucker & Co.

Mung noted this announcement with great interest. On the following morning, he went to the Tucker Company office, on Commercial Wharf in New Bedford. After asking for additional information about the scheduled voyage, John offered to sign on as a member of the ship's crew, asking for no compensation other than passage and food. His proposal was immediately rejected by the company's agent, who retorted that the ship already had sufficient crew. John persisted in his proposal, explaining his dilemma. Again the agent rejected Mung's plan.

Disappointed, John returned to the Whitfield farm in Fairhaven and told Captain Whitfield about his unsuccessful attempt to secure a position on the California-bound vessel. Captain Whitfield offered to talk to the captain of the *Stieglitz* and to try to convince him to allow Mung to work out his passage as a crewman. After some negotiations with the master of the ship, which was already laden with lumber, Whitfield was able to secure a berth for Mung, with the provision that, in addition to serving as a crewman, he would also pay a small fee for his passage. After this fee had been paid, Mung left the remainder of the money he had earned while on board the *Franklin*, along with some personal belongings, in the care and safekeeping of the Whitfields.

As the day of sailing approached, John again experienced a feeling of sadness at the prospect of saying farewell to the Whitfields. Despite this hollow feeling, however, he was buoyed up by the thought of finding enough gold in California to finance a journey home for himself and his Japanese friends.

Leaving the port of New Bedford on the morning tide on November 5, 1849, the heavily laden lumber ship slowly commenced the long ocean voyage to San Francisco. A number of stops were scheduled along the way. The *Stieglitz* took a southerly course along the eastern coastline of the United States and through the Caribbean. She then sailed steadily southward along the coastline of South America, making her way toward the dangerous waters surrounding Cape Horn, the infamous graveyard of many ships. Once she had successfully negotiated the treacherous Horn, the *Stieglitz* set course for the city of Valparaiso, Chile. Arrival in Valparaiso was welcome to the passengers and crew. Manjiro, however, though he did go ashore, did not participate in the revelry normally practiced by men of the sea. He did not want to spend his money foolishly or to fall prey to unscrupulous strangers. After several days' stay in Valparaiso to replenish her stores, the ship set sail for her final destination, San Francisco.

The trip south from Boston, around Cape Horn, and back north to the port city of San Francisco could usually be accomplished in approximately fifty-five to eighty-five days, depending on circumstances. This trip by the *Stieglitz* was no exception, and she arrived in San Francisco after not quite three months of sailing.

About 300 sailing ships were anchored in the harbor. Slowly the *Stieglitz* maneuvered her way into the anchorage area, which was surrounded by the city itself, on sharply sloping hills. Manjiro's first impression confirmed the many tales he had heard about the crowded conditions of this city, which was being besieged by thousands of people in search of gold. A closer look at the city only confirmed that first impression. Manjiro soon realized that not everyone who had come to the city was willing to take pick in hand or risk the threat of bandits. Many others had decided that it would be far more lucrative to supply those who had contracted gold fever with food, equipment, and other essential needs. Besides its normal setting of houses and other buildings, San Francisco was strewn with many makeshift shacks and tents, which had been erected to accommodate the hordes who arrived daily. Travel about the city was difficult and dirty because of the muddy streets.

What made matters even worse was that, as the population had increased, so had living costs. Eggs, for instance, were selling for $1 apiece. The normal cost of every available commodity was doubled or tripled. Merchants profited more than did most of those who wracked their bodies in the search for gold. The horrible living conditions coupled with the outrageous prices created such pressure that men who had once been peaceable and decent became brutal. Overnight, the once pleasant city of San Francisco had become a haven for the greedy and the disappointed, as well as for robbers and murderers.

Manjiro was much disturbed by this volatile atmosphere of tension and sin. His first order of business was to find a place to stay. After much searching and bargaining, he was able to secure a room in a run-down transient hotel for $20 per week. The room was in deplorable condition, but Manjiro, not wishing to expend any unnecessary funds, decided to rent it anyhow.

The morning after his arrival, he set out to explore the city and to inquire about the best way to begin prospecting. During his travels about the city, he noticed many Orientals. At first sighting, he thought that they were Japanese, but his attempts to make conversation with some of them revealed that they were Chinese. He learned that they had been brought to San Francisco and the surrounding area to serve as a cheap labor force. Many Americans were exploiting them— especially railroad builders. The beginning of the construction of a railroad system which would eventually grid the entire United States was already requiring massive amounts of manpower. Hundreds of Chinese had been brought to California to serve the needs of the railroad builders.

The Chinese were a constant target for bandits, who thought nothing of brutalizing or killing them in order to rob them of any valuables or money they might be carrying. The Chinese were easy prey, and no one seemed to care about their sufferings. The tales Manjiro heard from the Chinese caused him much personal distress, for he was fearful that bandits might mistake him for a Chinese.

During his travels about San Francisco, Manjiro noticed a railroad, within the city limits, which was used to cart away sand and dirt that were being excavated from the hillside. This sight reminded him that he had once ridden on a railroad while living in Fairhaven (1843–1846), an experience he would never forget.

After spending several days in San Francisco, Manjiro

secured passage on a riverboat bound for Sacramento. The
boat was steam-powered, and Manjiro had never seen such a
vessel before. At first he was astonished that it had no masts
or sails. He found out that, instead, it was equipped with a
very large kettle, known as a "boiler." At the front of the
boiler was a compartment where wood was burned. As Manjiro continued to investigate this strange boat, he discovered
that the heat from the fire caused the water to boil, transforming it into a very hot air mass called "steam." The vapor
pressure was so strong that it could turn a huge paddle wheel
on the outside of the ship. The action of the wheel resembled
that of an oar as it moved a vessel forward. During the cruise
upriver to Sacramento, Manjiro continued to study the working mechanism of this strange-looking ship, which he later
described as an "air boat." The "air boat," he realized,
worked according to the same principles as a railroad train.
Both used the theory of burning wood in the large firebox of
a boiler in order to produce steam, which in turn provided the
necessary power to move the vessel in either a forward or a
reverse direction.

On reaching Sacramento, Manjiro purchased some supplies
and a pair of pack mules, paying approximately $8 for each
mule, which was the going rate for mules in the gold region.
Leading his pack mules, he continued his journey, climbing
the mountains that surrounded Sacramento in search of a
fortune in gold.

As he climbed, he admired the picturesque scenery. The
mountains had glittering crowns of snow and ice, which
trailed off to the greenery of the tree line below. The placid
serenity of the higher elevations brought back pleasant memories to the young man from Nakanohama, recalling the towering mountains of his cherished homeland. His journey
through the winding passes above Sacramento lasted through
nearly a week of steady plodding. His progress was delayed
by the frequent need to cross the fast-moving waters of the
many mountain streams which cascaded to the foothills
below.

As soon as he reached the outer fringes of the goldfield,
Manjiro saw a small shack which was identified by a large
sign as a field office for the U.S. Bureau of Mines and Assay.
Since he had no real knowledge of the procedures to be followed in searching for gold, he went at once to the shack, to

seek the assistance of the government agent. The agent was helpful and offered advice on the various ways of searching for this most malleable and ductile of all metals. His best advice was that Manjiro should seek employment with an established mining company and work for a flat rate, so that he could be sure of steady work and wages. This plan was not especially appealing to Manjiro, but because of his limited resources, he decided to follow it.

With little effort, he quickly found employment at a mine. The hours were long, and the work was exhausting. The cramped, brutal conditions were especially onerous to Manjiro because he was a seagoing man, accustomed to working in bright, spacious quarters. Even so, he labored in the dark, damp mine for several weeks. His enthusiasm soon diminished, and the meager earnings he received were discouraging. He felt that he was stagnating and was unlikely to achieve his goal.

Therefore, after a month of backbreaking work, he decided to leave the mines and to try his luck finding gold by panning. In this procedure, a small amount of soil, usually taken from the base of a mountain stream, would be placed in a small metal dish or pan, along with water either from a container or from the stream. The panner, using a circular motion, would gradually spill the water and the lighter bits of soil over the edge of the pan, until only the larger particles of dirt and minerals remained in the pan. The prospector would then examine this residue for any glimmer of gold.

Manjiro found this method more acceptable. At the end of each day he would carefully hide the valuable dust he had collected, keeping it out of sight of anyone whom he suspected of being a bandit. Besides bandits, he, like the other forty-niners, had to watch out for hostile Indians, who lurked about the mining sites and preyed on unsuspecting argonauts.

With each passing day, more and more prospectors arrived to join the thousands who were already engaged in the frantic search for gold. As their numbers steadily increased, so did the cost of living. Beatings and robberies became the rule, rather than the exception. Though Manjiro lived in constant fear for his life, he continued to work, clinging to the belief that he could amass enough money as a prospector to accomplish his ultimate goal of returning to his native soil.

Prospecting was strenuous work, and the days were long.

Manjiro was always careful not to be extravagant in what he spent for food, because the prices were outrageously high. He therefore confined his diet to basic necessities—a practice which soon took its toll. He began to lose first his strength and then his health. He decided that he couldn't continue working under such conditions. He promised himself that he would terminate his role as a prospector once he had accumulated $600, the amount he needed to underwrite his journey home to Japan.

One day, while working his claim, Manjiro uncovered a large nugget of gold—the largest he had ever seen. At first, in his excitement, he thought he had discovered a rich deposit similar to those in the inspiring stories that had drawn him and the other forty-niners to California. He dug frantically but soon realized that his nugget was only a token find. Even so, he was elated to have found such a valuable specimen. He was afraid to say anything about it, even to acquaintances he had come to know and trust, because if word of his discovery got out, it might create a stampede to the digging site. He carefully unstitched the lining of his coat, placed the nugget inside, and resewed it.

That night, when he wrapped himself in an old, dusty blanket in preparation for sleep, his thoughts returned to his mother, as they so often did. How wonderful it would be to embrace her once again. Then he began to think about the large nugget he had found. As his reflections about his mother and the gold nugget intertwined, he decided that, instead of selling the nugget for cash, he would keep it as a present for Shio, his beloved mother.

Though his health continued to fail, Manjiro pressed on, scratching and searching for the prized metal. He knew that, unless he soon reached his goal of $600 and left the mountains, he might well die there, never to see his mother or his homeland again.

After four months in the goldfield, Manjiro decided to return to San Francisco on the steam-driven riverboat that had taken him to Sacramento. It was satisfying to feel that he would soon fulfill his longtime dream of returning to his family in Nakanohama. Gathering as many of his belongings as he could comfortably carry, he told his friends about his premonition. He sold his equipment and the property that he was not

taking with him for less than he had paid. Manjiro said goodbye to his friends and thanked them for their companionship.

As the steamboat chugged through the crowded San Francisco harbor, Manjiro saw that the waterfront was still
crowded with so many ships that there was hardly enough
space for the steamboat to enter. Most of the vessels had
come there to bring the hordes of prospective gold seekers.
Once ashore, he learned that while he had been in the mountains searching for gold, the territory of California had been
accepted as the thirty-first state in the union of the United
States of America.

Manjiro quickly found himself a room to stay in while he
was working out arrangements for passage to Honolulu. In
the days that followed, he combed the waterfront, looking for
a ship that would be sailing to Honolulu, or near it.

While in San Francisco he purchased gifts, as well as some
equipment that he felt he, Denzo, and Goemon would need
for their return home. The gifts he purchased included sugar,
patent medicine, and coffee, all of which were unfamiliar to
the Japanese.

He wrapped his purchases carefully to protect them from
breakage during transit. The equipment he had purchased,
including a ship's clock, various navigational instruments, and
an assortment of small hand tools, received special attention
in packaging.

Meantime, his search for a means of passage to Honolulu
continued. One day he saw a new type of ship entering the
port. She was much larger than the ordinary American whaleships which he had once considered huge. This vessel, large
as she was, had no tall masts and no sails. Manjiro was excited
when he realized that, like the steamboat that ran between
San Francisco and Sacramento, the ship was powered by
steam. She emitted clouds of black smoke from a large tube
that rose high above the deck. Slowly, the vessel maneuvered
to a dockside berth. She was heavily laden with goods and
rode low in the water. Manjiro was captivated by this awesome sight. He watched with great interest as the crewmen
secured the ship to the pilings of the wharf.

When Manjiro sought out more information about the ship,
he was told that she was the *Eliza Warwick*, a steam merchant
ship arriving from New York with Captain G. C. Whiting as

master, and that, once relieved of her cargo, she would be reloaded with a new consignment and would head for Honolulu. Manjiro immediately went on board and requested permission to speak with the ship's captain. The officer at the quarterdeck directed Manjiro to wait while he relayed his request to the master. The officer soon reappeared, told Manjiro that Captain Whiting had agreed to see him, and led him to the captain's quarters.

Manjiro explained his story to the captain, who proved sympathetic and agreed to allow him to sail as a member of the ship's crew. In addition, Manjiro would be required to pay the sum of $25. Unquestionably, it was a need for experienced crewmen that led the captain to allow Manjiro to sail on the voyage to the Sandwich Islands.

Much encouraged, Manjiro hurriedly went to his hotel room to collect his belongings and settle his account. He quickly returned to the ship, carrying many packages. Even after he was securely on board the *Eliza Warwick*, Manjiro could hardly believe that he would soon be reunited with the shipwrecked friends who were waiting for him in Honolulu.

It was now October 1850. Nearly ten years had slipped by since that dreadful time when he and his companions had been shipwrecked and stranded on Torishima Island, off the eastern coast of Japan. At last, after much hardship, they would soon be able to start their journey home.

7

Preparations and the Dangerous Journey Home to Japan

On October 10, 1850, the 350-ton steam-powered merchant ship *Eliza Warwick*, with Captain G. C. Whiting as master, entered the harbor of Honolulu, in the Sandwich Islands. Her uneventful voyage from California had taken eighteen days. Manjiro went ashore and looked for his old acquaintance, the Reverend Samuel C. Damon of the Seaman's Friend Society of Honolulu.

The chaplain was glad to see Manjiro and was able to give him the news that Denzo, Goemon, and Toraemon were well. Manjiro talked about his good fortune in the goldfield and also about the illness that had forced him to leave the mountains prematurely. He expressed his eagerness to share his success with his Japanese friends. He told the Reverend Damon that he had already purchased some supplies and navigational equipment and was planning to use the rest of his money to buy other provisions for the long voyage home.

After a lengthy discussion with the chaplain, Manjiro said goodbye and set out to find his old Japanese comrades. The first he encountered was Goemon, who shrieked with glee upon seeing Manjiro. He told Manjiro that he and Denzo were doing well and that Toraemon was living several miles outside Honolulu. Denzo was living with the Parkers, and Goemon and his wife lived in a house owned by Puupun. Goemon offered to go with Manjiro to see Denzo and Toraemon. The reunion of the four shipwrecked fishermen from Usa was joyous. The others listened with much interest to Manjiro's description of his visit with the Whitfields following his successful voyage on the *Franklin,* as well as to a detailed account of his perilous search for gold in California.

Hearing Manjiro's tales was exciting for the other three, and rekindled the hope that Denzo and Goemon still cherished—the hope of returning to their native soil. Toraemon, however, was not eager to return to Japan. Since the time, nearly ten years previously, when Captain Whitfield had brought them to Honolulu, Toraemon had become adjusted. He was satisfied with his present life. Practicing the trade of carpentry enabled him to live comfortably, and he was not willing to risk losing all that he had labored for, especially because the attempt that Denzo and Goemon had made had failed. He warned that the Tokugawa regime would be likely to look upon their return with especial disfavor because so much time had elapsed since they had been shipwrecked on Torishima Island. He said that they ran the risk of losing their lives, and it would be foolish to take the chance.

Manjiro was optimistic. He countered Toraemon's arguments by asserting that, given an opportunity, he could convince the authorities of their complete innocence in this unfortunate matter. Toraemon, however, remained steadfast.

Goemon was in total agreement with Manjiro's views, but he suggested that, before making any attempt to return to Japan, they must formulate a careful plan. Manjiro quickly interjected that he had such a plan. They would make their landing in the Loo Choo Islands (now called the "Ryukyu Islands") off the southern coast of Japan. He explained that, although the Loo Choo Islands were considered a part of Japan, they were not directly ruled by a daimyo of the Tokugawa Bakufu and therefore might not be so closely guarded. Another consideration was that the Ryukyus were comparatively close to Shikoku, their home island. The journey home by boat from the Loo Choo Islands would be a short one. Toraemon reiterated his opposition, adding that he was now married to a Hawaiian woman who would not understand or accept such a foolish decision. He said again that he was satisfied and happy with his life on the island and could not commit himself to such an undertaking. He did add, however, that he would take some more time to consider the alternatives. On that note, the matter was put to rest—at least for the time being.

Manjiro was impressed by Honolulu's noticeable growth since his last visit there. The waterfront area reflected the advanced development of this thriving Pacific port. Wandering about and hoping to recognize familiar faces, he recalled many fond memories. Even so, he soon began to feel bored. His idleness frustrated him so much that he became deeply depressed. Reverend Damon noticed Manjiro's state and, in an attempt to console him and ease his pain, often drew him into conversation about the details of his daring plan. The clergyman utilized all his skills to point out the many reasons why Manjiro's plan was destined to failure and should be abandoned. Even in his depression, however, Mung was confident. He insisted that his scheme would succeed if only given the chance. Realizing that he would not be able to persuade Manjiro, the Reverend Damon soon stopped trying. It was Manjiro's strong will, then, that finally decided the matter.

The Reverend Damon, as has been previously mentioned, was the founder and publisher of a popular maritime newspaper, *The Friend*. Knowing that he could not change Manjiro's mind, he offered his assistance and asked how Manjiro intended to implement his plan. Manjiro responded that his first step would be to acquire a suitably strong whaleboat, a decent sextant and compass, a barrel of bread, and a sufficient supply of water. With these and the equipment and supplies he was already holding, he was sure he could successfully land on Japanese soil. First, however, he would have to find a ship's captain who was willing to take the Japanese men and their boat close enough to the Loo Choos to effect a landing there. The problem was that he did not have enough money to carry out the mission. The soft-spoken chaplain promised to make every effort to help Manjiro to overcome this troubling problem. Soon thereafter, he published the following announcement in *The Friend*.

December 14, 1850

Expedition to Japan

The public is aware that from time to time, shipwrecked Japanese have been brought to the Sandwich Islands. There are now three who were brought hither by Captain William H. Whitfield in 1841. One of them, John Manjiro, accompanied Capt. Whitfield to the United States, where he was educated in a good common school, besides having acquired the Cooper's trade. He has returned to the islands, and here finds his former shipmates, two of them propose to accompany him, and if possible, return to Japan.

To complete the outfit is wanted ... a compass, a good fowling
piece, a few articles of clothing, shoes, and a nautical almanac
for 1850. Will not some benevolent person aid forward the
enterprise? The subscriber will be responsible for the safe deliv-
ery of the articles referred to.

Signed: S. C. Damon

The response was an immediate and generous outpouring
of support. Among the contributions were used nautical
equipment and a copy of Nathaniel Bowditch's *The New
American Practical Navigator*, a book which Manjiro had
studied eagerly in Massachusetts and which had had a lasting
effect upon him. An "expedition fund" was created and soon
swelled to nearly $160. Adding these funds to the money he
had already set aside, Mung set out in search of a whaleboat
that would be capable of carrying him and his friends from the
Loo Choos to their homeland. He found that the price for a
new craft of the type he needed would far exceed the amount
of money he had. Reluctantly, he decided to try to purchase
a used boat that he had heard about. The fisherman who
owned it lived nearby and might be willing to sell it for the
right price. Manjiro carefully inspected the small craft and
found that it was still in usable condition and seaworthy
enough for its intended use. He made an offer. At first the
owner rejected his offer, saying that the boat was worth much
more. After some bartering and pleas, the fisherman finally
sold him the boat. Manjiro was left with some money in
reserve which could be utilized to refurbish the craft.

Now that they had a boat, Manjiro, Denzo, and Goemon
began to believe that they would, at long last, be able to go
home. They worked together to make some necessary repairs
and decided to name their boat *Adventurer*.

By this time, nearly two months had passed since Manjiro's return to Honolulu. One day, while working on the
Adventurer, he received news that an American ship with a
number of Japanese on board had entered the port. He
went immediately to the harbor, where he learned that the
ship, the 304-ton New Bedford whaleship *Henry Kneeland*,
with George H. Clark as master, had rescued some Japanese
from a junk on April 22, at 45 degree north latitude and 155
degree east longitude. The name of the junk was the *Teen-*

zumolly. It was commanded by Captain Kuski, a Mr. Kikujiro was first mate, and there was a total of thirteen men on board. When Manjiro arrived at the *Teenzumolly*, he found the Reverend Damon talking to Captain Clark. Reverend Damon asked if he would be kind enough to serve as the intermediary between the American captain and the Japanese. Manjiro agreed, and assumed the role of interpreter. Mr. Kikujiro provided Manjiro with certain details concerning the junk *Teenzumolly*, as well as other related information. He explained that the junk was owned by a nobleman, in a town situated on the southeast side of a small island, southwest from Nippon.

Mr. Kikujiro continued, "The town is twice the size of Honolulu. The people are farmers and fishermen. Only two junks were owned there, but plenty of fishing boats. Rice is the principal product besides all kinds of vegetable produce. Both junks were owned by the honorable Mr. Soumong."

According to Mr. Kikujiro, "The *Teenzumolly* had taken a cargo of rice to Yeddo, discharged the same, received payment, partly in silver and partly in paper money. The *Teenzumolly* started on her homeward passage, ordinarily taking only three days, but was overtaken by adverse winds. [Our] supply of water was exhausted at the end of sixteen days, and . . . rice at twenty-six. [We] were then reduced to some refuse fish scales and occasionally showers, but the merciful care of Divine Providence [sic] all were preserved until at the end of the sixty-days, [our] junk rudder-less and dismasted, [we] then fell in with the *Henry Kneeland*, Captain Clark, who took [us] all on board his vessel and supplied [our] wants. [We] [cherish] most greatful [sic] feelings toward Captain Clark and his ship's company. Subsequently Captain Clark delivered six of [us] to the Russian authorities at Petropaulaski, under the promise that [we] should be returned to Japan. Two were taken by Captain Sherman, of the 340-ton New Bedford whaleship *Nimrod*, and two by the 426-ton New Bedford whaleship *Marengo*, Captain Devoll, master."

The Reverend Damon and Captain Clark were under the impression that the Japanese, if taken back to their country, would be put to death. However, Mr. Kikujiro positively assured them, through Manjiro, that this was not a fact. Instead, he assured them "That should any vessel take [us] back to

[our] native village, the inhabitants would rejoice to hail the vessel and would put on board a supply of fresh recruits, without charge."

Mr. Kikujiro continued, "Seven of the men [are] married, and their families reside in the village where [our] junk was owned." He further explained much information regarding the Japanese islands and the customs of the people. In respect to his native village, Mr. Kikujiro said, "There [are] sixty idol temples which," according to his account, "are full of gods. Every temple is presided over by a priest who acts ex officio as a school teacher. The children are both rich and poor, attend school together, and nearly all the inhabitants can read and write. The people are taxed for the support of their temples. Every farmer paying about five bushels of rice per acre."

Damon asked Mr. Kikujiro, "How do laws punish the thief?"

Mr. Kikujiro replied, "For the first and second offense, the thief is imprisoned, but for the third, his head is cut straight off."

When asked, "How do they punish the murderer?" he replied, "His head is cut off direct. As for marriage," he went on, ". . . a man is allowed but one wife, but if she doesn't please her husband, he can send her back to her house, with the consent of the old people, otherwise the husband must support her."

Mr. Kikujiro also told his interrogators, ". . . Bad people are believed to go to a bad place, and the good people to a good place. When a person dies, a record is made of his name and it is hung up in the house of his friends, and the household have stated periods for praying to the spirit of the departed. In Japan, there are six principal sacred days, including New Year, which occurs in January."

After Reverend Damon and Captain Clark concluded their interview with the rescued Japanese, Damon thanked Manjiro for his assistance. Manjiro then invited Captain Kuski and Mr. Kikujiro to come with him to meet his friends Denzo and Goemon.

Manjiro, Denzo, and Goemon were delighted to meet Captain Kuski. Together they discussed their experiences and the difficulties they faced in returning to their homeland. Denzo suggested that Captain Kuski and his men consider going home to Japan on the *Adventurer* rather than sailing on the

American ship to China, but Captain Kuski declined the offer. He thanked Denzo but indicated that he would prefer to rejoin his shipmates in China. Several days later, the American merchant ship departed from Honolulu with the rescued Japanese on board.

On December 8, 1851, a large merchant ship appeared in the harbor. She was soon identified as the 343-ton barkentine merchant vessel *Sarah Boyd*, twenty-one days out of San Francisco, with Captain Jacob D. Whitmore as her master. The vessel, which had been built in Bath, Maine, in 1846, had arrived to exchange cargo. Once reloaded, she would be sailing toward the China Sea and stopping at several ports along the way, including Shanghai. When he heard this news, Manjiro decided once again to seek the aid of the Reverend Damon, hoping that he might intervene on their behalf. The Reverend Damon said that he had heard of Captain Whitmore but didn't know him personally. However, Damon agreed to ask Captain Whitmore whether he would be willing to help. He went with Manjiro, Denzo, Goemon, and Toraemon to the quarterdeck of the *Sarah Boyd* and requested permission to speak with her master. The Reverend Damon presented Manjiro's plan to Whitmore.

Captain Whitmore seemed somewhat sympathetic but expressed doubt about the kind of reception they might receive in the Loo Choo Islands. He warned them that he had heard many adverse stories regarding the fate of foreign vessels which sailed too close to Japanese shores. However, influenced by the urging and prodding of the Reverend Damon, Captain Whitmore did agree to assist the Japanese. He told them that they must be ready to sail no later than "the 17th instant" (meaning December 17).

Manjiro glowed with excitement. This was the opportunity they had long been waiting for. Toraemon, though, must now make his choice. He would have to decide whether to risk returning to Japan with the others or to remain in the Sandwich Islands with his Hawaiian wife. He knew that this might well be his last chance to return to his native land. Conversely, he also knew that, if the mission was successful, he would probably be able to return to Honolulu for his wife. After considerable thought, he decided not to accompany his friends.

Goemon also had married a Hawaiian woman. Although he

had told her that he had a dream of returning to his homeland someday, he had not mentioned Manjiro's plan to her, for fear that she would object. Now he was faced with the task of telling her about his decision to return to Japan. When he did tell her, in Manjiro's presence, she said that she had always known that his dream of returning to his homeland would one day become a reality. Much to his surprise, she was prepared to accept his decision. Manjiro realized that the tender moments that followed were private. He left Goemon and his wife alone to share their bittersweet parting, in which joy and sorrow mingled.

The next several days were spent preparing the *Adventurer* and their nautical equipment and supplies for the daring, desperate, uncertain journey. Each piece of equipment was packed carefully and placed on board with great solicitude, with the goal of securing it against injury during the journey. When all was in readiness, the three men paid a call to the Reverend Damon, to whom they owed so much. The chaplain welcomed his Japanese friends and presented Manjiro with a document signed by and bearing the seal of the Honorable Elisha H. Allen, Consul of the United States in Honolulu. It was Damon's feeling that the document might carry some influence and authority if the travelers needed to substantiate their story to the Japanese officials. The document reads as follows:

Consulate of the United States
Honolulu, Hawaiian Islands

To whom these presents shall, doth or may come; I Elisha H. Allen, Consul of the United States of America, for Honolulu Hawaiian Islands, send greetings:

Know ye, that satisfactory evidence has been produced to me that John Manjiro, Denzo and Goemon, left the southeast part of the island of Nippon, Japan, in a fishing vessel and were shipwrecked; and after remaining on an uninhabited island for about six months, they were taken off by Captain Whitfield of the American whale ship, *John Howland*, who brought them to the Sandwich Islands. Denzo and Goemon remained here; Manjiro went cruising for whales, and in the year eighteen hundred and forty four reached the United States where he was educated. Last October he arrived here again, after visiting California, the gold region of the United States of America.

Captain Whitmore has kindly consented to take this company in the bark *Sarah Boyd*, a vessel belonging to the United States of America, and leave them near the Loo Choo Islands. Some friends here aided them in making preparations for their voyage, and I trust they may be kindly treated by all persons whom they meet.

I am informed by the chaplain of the Seaman's Friend Society that Manjiro has sustained a good character and has improved in knowledge. He will tell his countrymen of Japan how happy the Americans would be to make their acquaintance, and visit them with their ships, and give gold and silver for their goods.

Given under my hand and seal of this Consulate at Honolulu this thirteenth day of December, in the year of our Lord, eighteen hundred and fifty.

Signed: Elisha H. Allen
U.S. Consul

The stage was now set for Manjiro, Denzo, and Goemon to initiate their daring plan. They hoped that Allen's letter of reference would help them to convince the officials of the Tokugawa regime of the truth of the story Manjiro planned to tell them.

The planned expedition to Japan excited much concern and interest among the people of Honolulu. Many islanders who had become friendly with the stranded Japanese came to the *Sarah Boyd* when they heard that Denzo, Goemon, and Manjiro were soon to depart, wanting to wish the Japanese sailors a safe and successful conclusion to their trip. The encouragement of the many well-wishers was a help to the three sons of Nippon in the trying moments just prior to their departure. Bolstered by the good wishes of their friends, they felt ready to accept their fateful challenge.

On December 16, Manjiro went to Damon's chapel to meditate. While living among the Americans, and especially through attending church services in Fairhaven with the Whitfields, he had acquired a strong religious sense and the ability to meditate. Now he meditated for a long while and prayed to the divine power for guidance and assistance during the perilous journey home. When he left the sanctuary, he went to the chapel library, where he sat at a corner table and wrote the following letter to Captain Whitfield:

Dear Friend:

I never forget your benevolence of bringing me up from a small boy to manhood. I have done nothing for your kindness until now. Now I am going to return with Denzo and Goemon to my

native country. My wrong doing is not to be excused, but I
believe good will come out of this changing world, and that we
will meet again. The gold and silver I left and also my clothing
please use for useful purposes. My books and stationary please
divide among my friends.

John Mung

Manjiro entrusted his letter and his Western money and
belongings to the care and reliability of the Reverend Damon,
who promised to send them to Captain Whitfield on the next
ship returning to the United States.

On the morning of December 17, 1851, the *Sarah Boyd*,
with Manjiro, Denzo, and Goemon on board, departed from
the friendly port of Honolulu. As the ship faded from view,
many of the well-wishers who had come to say farewell and
watch the ship leave wondered whether they would ever
again see the personable Japanese whom they had accepted
as neighbors and friends.

On board the ship, Manjiro and his friends realized that
their fateful hour was coming soon. Either their longtime
dream would soon become reality or they would fail forever
to reach their homeland. They could even lose their lives.

So that the reader may fully appreciate the perilous situation which Manjiro and his friends faced upon returning to
their native soil in 1851, we now digress to describe the historical background of Japan's political situation in the mid-nineteenth century, in relation to her international neighbors.

In 1603, after much fighting among the various clans, a
feudal lord named Iyeyasu had emerged victorious over all
other rival lords, had founded the Tokugawa Bakufu, and had
been recognized as the reigning shogun. As chief military
officer to the Emperor, the shogun ruled over all territories
and provinces under the Imperial domain. The tribunal seat
of the powerful shogun was in the ancient city of Edo (now
Tokyo). Here, rather than in the Imperial city of Kyoto (which
was located several hundred miles to the west), the strict rules
that regulated Japan were established. From Edo the shogun
exercised his political power and his duties as the supreme
ruler of Japan, enforcing his will upon the masses. The Emperor's authority was mostly confined to ceremonies.

By establishing the regime known as the Tokugawa Bakufu, of which he himself was the head, Iyeyasu ensured his complete sovereignty over all other lords and clans. As part of his network of authority, he created a governmental system composed of daimyos, barons or clan leaders who enforced the decrees and power of the shogun. Fearful of a surprise bodily attack from daimyo conspirators, the shogun, even when in close company with the daimyos, kept a careful distance between himself and the daimyos, and his personal samurai bodyguards were always close at hand.

The reign of terror that followed Iyeyasu's rise to power instilled his undisputed authority into the minds of the masses of Japanese people. They knew that any nonconformance with or challenge to the word of the shogun would bring extreme punishment or even death. The shogun also instituted a policy of isolation from outsiders, to discourage the Japanese people from fraternizing with foreigners. The Tokugawa Bakufu hoped, by maintaining a barrier, to prevent the Japanese people from becoming aware of the progress being enjoyed by those living outside Japan. Iyeyasu and his supporters were confident that isolation from the rest of the world would minimize threats to their political regime. Only three countries—England, Holland, and China—were allowed to frequent a limited number of ports in Japan. Soon even the English were barred. The Dutch, however, were allowed to establish a colony in the port city of Nagasaki, mainly for the purpose of trade.

Once the policy of isolation was securely in place, the Tokugawa Bakufu was able to maintain control over the Japanese people for several generations, during which the descendants of Iyeyasu reigned. The Tokugawa regime successfully suppressed all thoughts of conspiracy, insurrection, and political change. This reign of terror continued uninterrupted until 1854, when an American, Commodore Matthew C. Perry (1794–1858), successfully concluded negotiations with the Japanese which led to the opening of Japanese ports to world trade.

It is clear, then, that by returning to Japan in 1851, Manjiro and his friends were placing themselves totally at the mercy of the Tokugawa Bakufu. The Bakufu had posted warnings stating, in essence, "The sending of ships to any foreign country is hereby forbidden. Anyone who secretly enters into a ship and is later detected will be put to death. Any person who leaves the country to go to another and later returns, then he too shall meet with the same fate."

Manjiro, Denzo, and Goemon were fully aware of these warnings when they boarded the American ship *Sarah Boyd*. The voyage from Honolulu was slow because heavy running seas and windswept tides retarded the forward speed of the *Boyd*. It took nearly three weeks to reach their destination, Mabuni, which was located on a point of land known as "Okinawa" on the largest of the Loo Choo Islands.

As they approached Okinawa, the ship was still yawing and rolling in an enraged sea. Captain Whitmore summoned Manjiro to his side. Cold rain pelted their faces while Whitmore tried once again to discourage Manjiro from the dangerous undertaking. Manjiro could not be persuaded. Instead, he once again thanked Whitmore for his assistance.

The ship's helmsman was fighting desperately to maintain control of the huge vessel. Concerned about the safety of his ship, Captain Whitmore ordered her to be brought about and sailed her skillfully through pounding swells toward the lee of a point of land on a protruding peninsula. Using the landfall as a natural barrier against the infuriated sea, they stayed for the night, which gave Whitmore still another opportunity to discuss with Manjiro the planned landing. He also mentioned that he had been observing the skills of his Japanese passengers since the ship left Honolulu. He told Manjiro that he would prefer them to remain on board as members of the ship's company and to sail to the United States instead of attempting the suicidal landing. Manjiro declined the offer, thanking Whitmore for his kindness and concern but reiterating that he was certain his plan would succeed if it was executed properly. He begged the captain to try to understand the emotional torment that he and his Japanese boatmates had experienced since their shipwreck more than ten years earlier. Finally, nodding his head in a discouraged manner, Captain Whitmore conceded that he truly understood their position. The two men shook hands and retired to their respective quarters for the night.

The three Japanese were up at first light on the following morning, checking their small boat and its supplies. They anxiously awaited permission from the ship's master to lower the *Adventurer* over the side of the ship. Although it was still raining, the sea had subsided somewhat overnight; yet it still possessed an angry aspect and offered cause for concern about the landing. Shortly after sunrise, a drop in temperature converted the rain into wind-driven hail.

Captain Whitmore told Manjiro that he would take the ship in as close to land as safety would allow but that, from that point on, it would be entirely up to the Japanese to make their landing. However, he further advised Manjiro that he would maintain the ship's position until he received a signal from Manjiro that the landing party were safely on shore.

The large ship slowly proceeded toward the selected landing area. Master Whitmore guided his vessel skillfully through the treacherous waters until she was as close to shore as the captain thought was possible without endangering his ship. He bellowed several orders to his crew, who brought the craft about into the biting wind. Holding the bow of his ship into the strong breeze, Captain Whitmore signaled that Manjiro's boat should be lowered into the lashing waters. With the help of some of the crew of the *Boyd*, Manjiro, Denzo, and Goemon gingerly lowered the *Adventurer* into the sea.

As Denzo and Goemon scaled down into the bobbing craft, Manjiro handed Captain Whitmore a letter, asking him to have it delivered to Toraemon, in Honolulu. Hurriedly, he again thanked Whitmore for this kindness, bowed respectfully, and shook hands with Whitmore. Then he lowered himself into the pitching whaleboat. As the smaller craft slid away from the American ship, the three Japanese waved farewell to the *Boyd*'s crew, who had gathered along the rail to witness their departure.

Once clear of the *Boyd*, the *Adventurer* was at the mercy of the turbulent waters. Manjiro attempted to hoist a sail instead of rowing into the brutal waves but was unable to do so because of the gale-force winds. He then ordered the others to take up the oars as a means of bringing their boat under control. Using all their strength, the men pulled strenuously on the oars, battling the elements. Inevitably, they were reminded of a similar struggle, when they had landed on Torishima Island a decade earlier.

The task of rowing the craft to the landing point used up the better part of the day. Exhausted, the men dragged the boat beyond the tide mark. Dropping onto the cold wet sand, Manjiro signaled the ship by waving a piece of his clothing, indicating that they were safely on shore. As the three destitute fishermen watched, the *Boyd* added more canvas to her yards and got underway. Soon she disappeared over the horizon, leaving the worn-out crew of the *Adventurer* to their fate.

Before long, darkness encroached. The fishermen from Usa lay close together, trying to warm themselves. At last the three destitute sons of Nippon were on Japanese soil.

8

Tribulations
and the Persecution

With the new dawn, Manjiro, Denzo, and Goemon began to feel a new confidence. The raging tempest of the previous day had stilled. The sky was clear, and the sun shone brightly on Okinawa, the one of the Loo Choo Islands on which they had landed, and glistened on the water. Denzo offered to go and search for people. Manjiro and Goemon agreed, with the understanding that if he saw anyone, he was to return immediately to the *Adventurer*.

Denzo walked only a short distance before he came upon a small cluster of primitive huts. As he cautiously approached, the startled islanders shrieked in fright and fled in all directions. He called to them, stretched out his arms, and attempted to quell their fears, but was unsuccessful. They were frightened, and they insisted upon avoiding the stranger. Denzo returned to the beach and told Goemon and Manjiro what had happened. Manjiro thought for a moment and then suggested that the islanders might be apprehensive either because of Denzo's American-style clothes or because they did not understand Japanese. He decided to investigate this matter himself. Armed with a pistol he had acquired in Honolulu, he followed Denzo back to the huts, accompanied by Goemon.

As they approached the village, which they were later to learn was called "Mabuni," they saw that the frightened inhabitants were half hiding behind their huts. They stood motionless, watching the cautious approach of the three strangers with great concern. Denzo again called out to them, but they withdrew behind the dwellings. Manjiro decided to try a different approach. He beckoned to them, inviting them by gestures to come closer to him. At first the islanders showed no response, but then they began to edge cautiously toward the three strangers.

Once they were close enough, Manjiro began to panto-
mime the acts of eating rice from a bowl with chopsticks and
drinking from a cup. They watched unresponsively at first,
but when Manjiro stopped to think for a moment, one of the
islanders gestured for them to follow him. He led them to a
nearby hut and motioned to them to remain outside. He entered the hut, and a few moments later, another man, very
authoritative-looking, came out of the hut. He said not a
word, merely stood and looked at the strangers, as though
trying to assess their character. To interrupt the prolonged
silence, Denzo directed several questions to the man, who
responded in a dialect of Japanese that was somewhat confus-
ing to the fishermen. Denzo repeated what he had said, but
they were still bewildered. However, at least now they knew
that these islanders were Japanese and that they themselves
had indeed landed on Japanese soil.

The awkward conversation continued, with each side trying to decipher the meanings of the other. Manjiro was able
to determine that the man in charge was a village official. For
his part, the man monitored every move made by the intruders, watchful for any sign of skulduggery.

The attempts to communicate continued for several hours,
during which the islanders provided the trespassers with
some welcome food and water, as well as with firewood.
Manjiro and his friends made a small fire and sat by it to eat.
The food they had been given included rice, and the opportunity to eat with chopsticks once again was pleasing. The village inhabitants watched curiously as they ate.

Once their hunger pangs were satisfied, the three travelers
discussed their next move. Their plan was to sail north along
the seaboard of the Loo Choos and then across the open
stretch of water between the Loo Choo archipelagos and the
large Japanese island of Kyushu. Once reaching landfall on
Kyushu, they would sail northeast toward the smaller island
known as "Tanega-Shima." (Tanega-Shima was the place
where Europeans were first known to have set foot on Japan.
These first Europeans were three Portuguese who were shipwrecked in 1543.) Manjiro would employ his skills as a navigator to guide the boat.

Before they were able to begin the second phase of their
plan, three men rode into the village on horseback. They rode

straight to the house where the official-looking man had questioned the strangers earlier, and one of the villagers pointed out Manjiro and his friends. The mounted men rode cautiously toward the travelers from Usa. They said nothing, simply dismounted and walked in a circle around the trespassers, as if trying to determine the reason for their sudden appearance on the island.

There was no question that the horsemen were in the service of a high authority. Manjiro later discovered that the three horsemen had been dispatched to Mabuni village by an authority called the "Bugyosho," who had been informed of the intrusion by the villagers. Finally, one of them sternly ordered Manjiro and his companions to lay out all their belongings, and the other two men began to examine their possessions. Soon afterward, the man in charge motioned to Manjiro, Denzo, and Goemon to follow him. He led them to a nearby house, where they were placed in a small room under guard. The three horsemen carried away all the possessions of their prisoners.

Later in the day, the three Bugyosho officials returned, and the one in charge began questioning the intruders. He was especially interested to know their names and where they came from, as well as why they had come to this place. Soon after the questioning began, Manjiro rose to his feet and bowed respectfully, offering himself as spokesman. He explained courteously that they were Japanese fishermen from Tosa Province on the island of Shikoku. He told the story of how they had been swept away by the Kuroshio Current and then had lost their small boat on a coral island in the Pacific Ocean. He said that, after spending many months on the island with little food and water, they had been rescued by an American whaleship that had been searching for turtles in the waters close to the island. He explained that they had been taken to the Sandwich Islands only with the intention of making arrangements to return them to their homeland.

As before, communication was difficult because of the differences between Manjiro's dialect and that of the investigators. Even so, Manjiro's tale was convincing, as he told of having been taken on the whaleship to a place far away in America, called "Massachusetts," solely for the purpose of being educated. He asserted that it had always been his intention to return to his home, the village of Nakanohama in the province of Tosa, as soon as possible. He assured the officials that he was telling them the truth, and pointed out that otherwise they would not have landed on the island.

The officials were persistent and took a great deal of time, skillfully phrasing and rephrasing each question in an attempt to overcome the language problem. They had inspected the American whaleboat, and it had captured their attention. They appeared to be impressed by its sturdiness and its contents. They were interested to know how far Manjiro and his companions had sailed in the boat prior to landing. Manjiro explained in detail that they had been brought close to the island by another large American ship and had sailed the rest of the way in their small craft.

Before long, Manjiro and his compatriots learned that the person conducting the questioning was a local council official acting under the auspices of the Satsuma dynasty, which was headed by the powerful daimyo family of Shimazu. This feudal family had been established early in the Edo period (1603–1868), and the reigning leader was Lord Nariakira, who was, in fact, the ruler of the entire domain of the Loo Choo Islands. So powerful was this feudal family that the Tokugawa shogunate itself respected Shimazu power among the daimyo clans.

Nariakira was possessed with great wisdom in the ruling of his domain. Among other things, he kept himself well informed about the increasing number of sightings of foreign ships in and around the territorial waters of Japan, and he had their activities and movements tracked. It was Lord Nariakira's belief that Japan could not continue much longer to maintain its policy of absolute isolation from the world community. He expected that Japan would soon be forced to open her ports to foreigners, and hence, as a great ruler, he had become an open advocate of reform.

While Manjiro and his friends were being questioned by the local official in Mabuni village, messengers had been dispatched to the magistrate's office of the Bugyosho, in nearby Naha, the provincial seat, in order to apprise the officials of the presence of the three unidentified intruders. The Bugyosho was a subordinate authority of the Satsuma, and it had its main headquarters in the port city of Kagoshima on the large, southernmost Japanese island of Kyushu. (In 1549, a Jesuit mission headed by St. Francis Xavier had landed in Kagoshima and received permission to preach. By 1614, Christian missionaries could claim 300,000 followers throughout Japan.) The three intruders were informed that all their belongings, including their boat, would be examined more closely. In addition, they were to be taken to another place for further questioning. They were then returned to confinement.

In the evening, the three emissaries of the Bugyosho returned and ordered the confined men to proceed with them to Naha. The journey, however, was interrupted by a foot messenger, who said that they should go to the small village of Onaga, located near Naha, instead of going to Naha itself.

Very late in the evening of February 3, 1852, the bewildered fishermen were led to a large house in Onaga, where they were again placed in confinement. The next day the officials of the Bugyosho resumed their persistent questioning. The same questions were repeated over and over. Manjiro answered each question in a deliberate and consistent manner, but Denzo and Goemon became confused and shaken, because they were fearful of the consequences if their answers were found unacceptable. Ironically, it was because of the inconsistency of their answers that the interrogation was prolonged.

The days became weeks and the weeks months, and still the interrogation continued. The officials of the Bugyosho purposely induced constant mental pressure. As one interrogator grew tired during the long sessions of questioning, he would be relieved by another, in order to maintain a burden of stress upon the men under suspicion. Soon the anguish and monotony of this constant stress began to take a toll upon the prisoners, and their fortitude began to show signs of erosion. Despite everything, Manjiro somehow managed to remain steadfast.

At the end of each probing session, the aggrieved men from Usa were allowed to return to their house of confinement. There they were treated well and kindly, and they were also allowed to mingle with the villagers. Denzo and Goemon elected to remain by themselves, but Manjiro was able to make the most of the liberties that were allowed. He freely fraternized with the natives of Onaga, and this intercourse allowed him to learn to speak the dialect of the Loo Choos more fluently.

Finally, after nearly six months of intense cross examination, the three men from Usa were informed that they would soon be transferred to Kagoshima, on the island of Kyushu, where they would be interviewed by high-ranking officials from the main office of the Satsuma regime. Soon afterward, Denzo, Goemon, and Manjiro were put aboard a transport vessel, along with their small boat, and taken to the port city of Kagoshima, where Lord Nariakira resided.

As mentioned previously, Nariakira was well aware of the winds of change that were blowing toward Japan from all points of the compass. Not only did he support a relaxation of the closed-door policy, but also he encouraged the return of supreme divinity to the Emperor, where it had resided prior to the rise of power of the Tokugawa shogunate. Lord Nariakira had decided to question Manjiro himself because he hoped to learn more about the ways of the Americans.

Before he summoned Manjiro, however, he ordered that the intruders be properly fed and nourished according to their wishes, so as to ease their fears and create in them a more trusting attitude.

After he had been fed and rested, Manjiro was summoned by Lord Nariakira. Manjiro readily answered the ruler's questions and even volunteered his own opinions, especially on matters which were contrary to accepted policies of Japan. Manjiro told the inquisitive lord stories that revealed much about the life and customs of people in America. Lord Nariakira was especially interested in hearing about industrial technology—such things as steam engines, locomotives, the telegraph, photography, and scientific studies of natural phenomena. He admitted that he had heard of such things but had never witnessed them.

Apparently, the influential leader of the Shimazu was not interested in questioning either Denzo or Goemon, leaving that chore to his subordinates. He regarded Manjiro as a more valuable source of information on technology because he had spent so many years living among the Americans.

Nariakira prompted Manjiro to tell him about the chasing and capturing of whales. The fisherman described the methods employed by the Americans and their great success in this profitable venture. He emphasized the extreme importance of using small whaleboats and described the procedure in which, after a whale had been sighted, several of these small boats would be lowered into the water. The boats, each manned by a crew of six, would pursue the great sea mammal. The master ship, much greater in size than the whaleboats, would stand off in the distance until signaled by the smaller craft. These details fascinated the silk-robed clan leader.

After several such sessions, Lord Nariakira ordered Manjiro to build a scaled-down model of an American whaleship so that he could assess the reliability of such a craft. Manjiro respectfully explained that, although he admittedly was familiar with such vessels, he was not a qualified carpenter. American whaleships were built by skilled carpenters known as shipwrights. He did say, however, that he would be willing to try. The leader assured Manjiro that he would provide local boat builders who would be capable of constructing the vessel, with proper direction. Manjiro promised to do his best. Constructing the diminutive replica took approximately seven weeks, during which Manjiro and the builders worked each day from sunrise until the light faded after sunset.

The ship, when finished, was capable not only of sailing but also of carrying a substantial load of cargo. Nariakira was pleased, and Manjiro had a strong sense of accomplishment and satisfaction. The islanders flocked to the shoreline to see the startling new boat, and received it with great enthusiasm.

During the time of the interrogations at Kagoshima, many messages regarding the outcasts were being exchanged between the offices of the Bugyosho and the magistrate in Nagasaki, some 94 miles (151 kilometers) to the northwest. The magistrate's office was under the direct control of the Tokugawa shogunate. Eventually, the decision was made that any additional questioning would be undertaken by representatives of the shogun. The port city of Nagasaki had at one time been a Christian stronghold, and it was the only port in all of Japan that received foreigners (Dutch and Chinese traders) between 1639 and 1854.

Having satisfied his own curiosity about the circumstances of the three outcasts, Nariakira wrote to the ranking official of the Tokugawa Bakufu in Nagasaki. His letter related the almost incredible story of the three shipwrecked fishermen.

He noted that Manjiro, Denzo, and Goemon had sworn, under oath, that their story was wholly true and free of deceit. They had further sworn that it had always been their most earnest intention, throughout their many years of absence, to return to their rightful home in Tosa province. The letter also included the details of Jusuke's death and of Toraemon's decision to remain in Honolulu.

Lord Nariakira also wrote about the testimony offered by the three outcasts, asserting that at no point during the interrogation had he been able to establish any evidence of wrongdoing on their part. His letter concluded with a declaration that the three outcasts would be afforded complete and continued protection until the authorities in Nagasaki called for them.

In September 1852 Manjiro and his two companions were ordered to gather their belongings and prepare themselves to leave Kagoshima. Escorted by several guards, they were quietly placed aboard a large pavilion-styled vessel which was obviously designed to carry high-ranking officials. Their small landing boat was also placed aboard the distinctive-looking craft.

The weather was inclement, causing some delay, but that night the ship finally slipped out of the harbor, which was by that time completely dark. The sea journey to the port city of Nagasaki took two days. The harbor of Nagasaki was bustling with activity. As the majestic ship advanced, the smaller tribal boats hastily moved out of its path, assuming that the ship was carrying persons of notable authority and power.

Once the ship was made fast, the three fishermen were quickly led to the building in which the governor had his office. They were sent into a large room crowded with many stern-looking men and ordered to sit on the floor before a long, low table. Seated at the table were several silk-clad men, obviously of high status, who stared curiously at the three low-class fishermen. Soon the governor of Nagasaki, whose name was Maki Shima, entered the room, escorted by several aides. He sat down at the center of the low table. Manjiro, Denzo, and Goemon, realizing that they were in the presence of a high-ranking personage, assumed the traditional prostrate position before him. None of the three had ever before been in the presence of such a prestigious Japanese official.

The governor signaled one of the house guards to move the three men closer to him so that he might hear their comments without distraction. Then one of the distinguished men of the tribunal began the questioning; he was followed by another, and then another. The questions were a repetitious, persistent, punishing assault, and the vigor and intensity of the interrogation rapidly approached unbearable levels. Whereas Lord Nariakira had been rather low-keyed, the shogunate interrogators were harsh and relentless in their pursuit of acceptable answers.

Frantic but still respectful, the fishermen pleaded to be let off, pointing out that they had already answered the same inquiries many times and asserting that their sworn statements were true. The Tokugawa prosecutors replied that they, and only they, would decide upon the sequence of questioning and whether the answers were satisfactory. The fishermen were again ordered to reiterate the details of their story. The first session of the brutal inquisition continued for several hours and was followed by seventeen more sessions, all equally punishing. Throughout the eighteen sessions, most questions were directed to Manjiro, as he had shown himself to be the most articulate and best informed of the three.

At the second session, one of the first points of interest and concern was Christianity. Because the three prisoners had lived in harmony with the foreigners, the tribunal questioned whether they had accepted Christian religious teachings, either in part or wholly. They vowed that they were innocent and were asked to prove it by tramping barefoot upon several brass plates bearing Christian symbols—a test known as *fumi*. Trampling upon the plates signified renunciation of any involvement in the Christian religion, whereas a refusal to participate in *fumi* would be cause for the death sentence. All three submitted to the test, trampling upon the brass plates without hesitation. The tribunal nodded approvingly. (Although Manjiro did trample on the plates and thus passed the *fumi* test, he did it without sincerity and only because he knew that if he didn't conform to the expectations of his interrogators, all would be lost.)

When questioned further regarding Christianity, Manjiro described some of the numerous temples he had seen in America. He said that the structures, which contained many sacred images, were very large and had clock towers reaching as high as 200 to 300 feet (61 to 91 meters) into the sky. He further explained that the temples, rather than containing a Buddha, displayed likenesses of a man who had made the world in seven days and then rested. He said also that the temples contained many seats and that ceremonies called "Sunday services" were conducted in the temples on the seventh day of each week. The people took small books called "prayer books" to the Sunday services. The head man talked to the people, and soon afterward, they all left.

He explained that American funeral procedures were much like those in Japan. The dead person was placed in a wooden box and buried in the ground, in a place where other dead persons also lay. The head religious man spoke words from the small book, and when he was finished, all in attendance left.

In yet another session, the chief magistrate directed Manjiro to describe the Sandwich Islands, which had been mentioned repeatedly in previous testimony. Manjiro explained the status and collective sovereignty of the Sandwich Islands, especially Honolulu. He made it clear that Honolulu was a port of major importance and interest, not only to the ships of the United States but also to those of other countries, such as England and Spain. He talked about the many ships that would stop at this port for food, water, and other commodities. In addition, he said, since many of the ships were at a great distance from their home ports, any necessary repairs t the ships could be made at Honolulu. He told the tribunal tha the head man of the Sandwich Islands, who lived in Honolulu would collect a tax from each ship for the use of the harbor He said further that seven separate islands made up the Sandwich Islands, all of them very mountainous. The soil was sandy and could not support most crops other than potatoes, onions, and certain fruits. He had not seen any grain crops and doubted that the soil could support grains.

In still another session, Manjiro was ordered to discuss America. In response to questions about the American government, he said that the head of the government was a man of great knowledge and ability. He was elected "king" and remained in office for four years before being succeeded by another. This individual lived a very simple life and would go out on horseback accompanied by only one servant. He said that the "king" who had been in office when he was in America had been Zachary Taylor and that he had been a hero in a recent war between the United States and Mexico.

When he was questioned about the control of criminals in America, Manjiro said that, when prisoners were found guilty of wrongdoing, they were given sentences of different lengths, according to the seriousness of their crimes. Prisoners were confined in large open areas called "cells" and were not chained but allowed to move about freely within the cells. While in confinement, they were taught new skills, including how to make various items. Many were released before serving their full terms, if they behaved well during the confinement.

In another session of intense interrogation by Tokugawa officials, Manjiro explained that young people in America decided for themselves whom they would marry, rather than relying on a third party to make such arrangements, as was customary in Japan. When they were between thirteen and seventeen years of age, they would begin to seek mates by mingling with groups of people of their own age. When two people found one another desirable, they would exchange letters expressing their personal feelings. (This statement might reflect the time when Manjiro had sent a May basket with a note to a classmate, while he was attending the school on Sconticut Neck that abutted the Whitfield farm in Fairhaven.)

When two people wished to be married, they would seek their parents' approval. If successful, they would then inform other family members. Occasionally, if their parents refused to approve the match, the couple would marry anyway, though this would cause great problems, sometimes leading to their separation from other members of their families. Manjiro explained also that, in America, each man could have only one woman as his wife. If a man were found guilty of violating this rule, he would be punished.

America and the living habits of its populace seemed to be extremely important to Lord Shima, and he encouraged Manjiro to speak freely about all his experiences among the Americans. Manjiro responded by talking eagerly about American technology. Although he was not really qualified to explain the technical bases and details of all that he had seen, he

nevertheless seized this opportunity to tell the ruler how advanced the Americans were in comparison to the Japanese.
He believed firmly that adoption of American technology
would make life in Japan less burdensome for his fellow countrymen.

He told Maki Shima about the telegraph, which he had
already explained many times to other interrogators. He explained that Americans would string two wires above the
roadways and would then use an instrument he labeled a
"magnet" to dispatch letters from one point to another without a human messenger. They would attach a letter to one
wire and send it, and soon another letter would be returned
on the second wire to the point of the sender.

Manjiro knew that this simple analogy of the principles of
the telegraph was inaccurate, but he decided to use it to try
to make his superiors understand and to convince them of the
importance of this type of technology. He was certain that
they would not be able to comprehend a more detailed, technical explanation of the telegraph, since they lacked both
mechanical and scientific knowledge. In response to this incredible explanation, the tribunal merely shook their heads in
disbelief and grumbled among themselves about the prepos-
terous story they had just heard.

The story of the telegraph was not the only report that
startled the imaginations of the tribunal. Manjiro also told
them about great "iron boxes" called "railroad trains" and
"steamboats." He said that twenty or thirty people could be
placed inside one of these iron boxes and taken from one place
to another without any exertion on their part. He explained
that both the train and the steamboat employed the same
principle. In each, wood was fed into a furnace under a large
kettle called a "boiler." When the wood was fired, water
within the kettle boiled and gave off a mass of hot air called
"steam." The steam, because it was confined and not allowed
to escape, created a great pressure that was capable of exert-
ing a tremendous force, equal to the strength of many men.
This confined pressure was able to move a metal train forward on two iron rails called "tracks," with many people
inside.

Manjiro's enthusiastic manner and his confidence in the
stories he told awed his superiors. He told them about an idea

he had heard of—connecting the Atlantic Ocean with the
Pacific Ocean at a point of land called an "isthmus." An
isthmus, he explained, was a narrow strip of land between
two larger bodies of land. There was an isthmus between
North America and South America. Digging a canal across the
isthmus would enable water to flow from one ocean to the
other, thereby creating a waterway through which ships could
pass. This suggestion only further confused the interrogators,
who were nevertheless impressed by Manjiro's vast knowledge, encompassing many subjects.

In another session, the young man from Nakanohama spoke
openly of his awareness that American ships were denied
access to Japanese ports. He asked the interrogators to believe that American ships' attempts to enter Japanese ports
were honorable in nature and to trust that Japan would have
nothing to fear as a result of allowing them in. He pointed out
that, because of the vastness of the oceans, it was sometimes
necessary to enter foreign harbors in order to have a ship that
had been damaged in adverse weather repaired. In addition,
he said, ships' crews required fresh provisions and water.

He concluded his speech on this matter by pleading with
the authorities to reexamine their policy of denying foreign
ships the use of their harbors. Allowing foreign ships to enter
Japanese ports, he said, would help to create a basis for good
trade relations between countries.

Lord Shima and his board of inquiry continued the inquisition by asking Manjiro to expound upon various facets of life
in America, as compared to life in Japan. In one session, for
instance, Manjiro was asked about hairstyles in America. He
responded that neither men nor women, from youth into old
age, particularly concerned themselves about changing their
hairstyles. The men contained their hair under a hat, while
the women allowed theirs to fall straight down over their
shoulders and cover their ears. Women would sometimes
wear their hair in a ball called a "bun" and would sometimes
cover it with a hat called a "bonnet."

In one of the concluding interrogations, Manjiro was prod-
ded by Lord Shima to talk about music in America. Manjiro
spoke about the many different types of musical instruments
which were plentiful in the United States, including the banjo,
the piano, the cello, and the violin. He said that the Ameri-

cans greatly enjoyed singing and knew many songs, and that
they also made music with their instruments.

In the final convocation of the trials at Nagasaki, Lord
Shima again raised the subject of Christianity. The tribunal
still harbored some doubts about the fishermen's innocence in
regard to this important matter. Once again the three outcasts
were ordered to trample barefoot on the *fumi,* or brass plates
bearing Christian images. The three complied without hesitation, as they had before. Though Manjiro had participated in
religious services as a member of the Whitfield family, and
though he had attended services aboard the American ships,
he did not consider himself a convert. As for Goemon, though
he had served the household of the American missionary in
Honolulu, he too was not a convert. None of the three, in fact,
harbored thoughts of renouncing the religious beliefs of their
country. Their willingness to comply once again with Lord
Shima's order obviously pleased the interrogators. Lord
Shima asked Manjiro how he felt about what he had just
done. Manjiro replied that his feet were cold, as he was no
longer used to going without shoes—an answer that seemed
to be satisfactory.

The three men from Usa were informed that, although the
interrogation was formally concluded, they would still be subject to further questioning if necessary. They were to remain
in confinement until a final decision was made regarding their
future. None of their belongings, including their boat and
Manjiro's gold nugget, would be returned; instead, everything would remain in the hands of the Bakufu. Manjiro was
so infuriated by this decision that Denzo had to intervene in
order to calm him down and soothe his outraged feelings.

Throughout the difficult period of the trials at Nagasaki,
Manjiro and his shipmates had been confined in a local prison.
However, they had not been treated as common prisoners but
had been allowed many privileges and treated well. Their
hope throughout this time was that they would be judged
innocent of all charges and allowed to return to their homes
in Usa on Shikoku Island.

9

The Repatriation
of Manjiro

Following the agonizing trials at Nagasaki, the three fishermen remained in confinement until June 1853. Nine months had passed since their arrival in Nagasaki. Finally, word came that they had been given permission to return to their home province.

They were again brought before the Tokugawa functionary, who told them that they were being transferred and would be under the control of the Tosa daimyo. He issued a stern warning that they were not to speak to anyone without the permission of the Tosa officials. In addition, he reminded them that all their personal belongings, which had been previously confiscated, would remain with the Bakufu in Nagasaki. This included Manjiro's prized gold nugget as well as their landing boat, the *Adventurer*. Each of them was issued a pittance to live on until more permanent arrangements could be made.

Several retainers had already been sent to Nagasaki by the Tosa daimyo, to escort the three outcasts to Shikoku Island. They were taken on board a government guard boat, which had also been sent by the daimyo. The vessel was constructed of unpainted wood and had a very sharp bow, a broad beam, a slightly tapered stern, and a clean run. The vessel could be sailed swiftly through the water, and seemed to skim upon its surface rather than to divide it. The crewman were rather tall, muscular, and tawny, and were naked except for loincloths.

Leaving Nagasaki in June 1853, the boat set a course for Kochi, the capital city of Shikoku Island, arriving there in the second week of July. Manjiro and his friends were escorted to an inn, as previously arranged by the daimyo. They waited at the inn for several days and were not allowed to wander

about. Then they were summoned to appear before the daimyo of the province, Lord Yamanouchi Yodo (1827–1872).

The three fishermen were conveyed through the streets of
the city to the castle of Kochi. Lord Yamanouchi had arranged
to have the outcasts interviewed by his retainers. The people
of this castle town had been told that the three fishermen had
returned from the dead, and they patiently waited along the
roadways hoping to catch a glimpse of them. It was known
that more than eleven years had elapsed since the fishermen
had left the port of Usa, and a fever of curiosity had spread
through the city.

Kochi Castle, an impenetrable stronghold, had been constructed in 1603 by order of Yamanouchi Kazutoyo, Lord of
Tosa Province. When they reached the castle, Manjiro,
Denzo, and Goemon were hurriedly taken through the main
gate of the castle, Ote-mon Gate, which was designed in such
a way that enemies advancing toward the castle could be
attacked from three sides. If an enemy host, even so, were
able to penetrate Ote-mon Gate, they would be confronted
with another obstacle—more than a hundred stone steps built
with alternating long and short depths, which made rapid
ascent very difficult. In addition to these built-in defensive
measures, the castle was defended by many samurai, who
lived high above the approaches to the castle. It has been
reported that construction of the castle took approximately
ten years, with 1300 people working every day.

The fishermen were summoned daily to the castle, where
the retainers of Lord Yamanouchi subjected them to a relentless siege of questioning. Many of the questions had already
been asked many times before by officials at Kagoshima and
Nagasaki. The tedium and monotony of the repeated interrogation caused great anxiety to the captives. The main concern
of the Tosa officials seemed to be the experiences the fishermen had had abroad, rather than their innocence or guilt
about having left their country.

After many sessions, lasting from July through September
of 1853, Lord Yamanouchi was satisfied and brought the interrogation to a close. The fishermen had endured many inten-
sive examinations, starting in January 1852 and the end of the
interrogations was an immense relief.

The three former fishermen were told that they could no

longer set sail to earn a living. They were given a small stipend, just enough to enable them to subsist. They respectfully thanked the officials of the Tosa daimyo for their generosity and understanding. On October 1, 1853, they were escorted out of the castle and set free to return to their respective homes.

Nearly overcome by their feelings about having finally attained their release, the three men immediately set off for their homes in Usa and Nakanohama. They were thankful that they had finally been able to convince their interrogators that they had not purposely violated the Japanese doctrine prohibiting departure from the country. Much of the credit for this success must be attributed to Manjiro's high-spirited tales about the Americans. Their captors had been so engrossed by these tales that they had decided that the fishermen were innocent.

Manjiro offered to accompany the two brothers, Denzo and Goemon, to their home in Usa, a distance of approximately 10 miles (16 kilometers). From there he would go to his home village of Nakanohama, nearly 90 miles (145 kilometers) from the port of Usa, from which they had departed so many years earlier.

The journey home from Kochi was uneventful, but when they arrived in the village of Usa, Denzo and Goemon were unable to locate their home, for it no longer existed. They were expected, however, for the news of their miraculous survival had preceded them. They were greeted by many old friends and relatives, and they were elated by the reception they received. One of the relatives offered shelter to the brothers and also to their friend Manjiro.

The following morning, Manjiro had to say farewell to his trusted friends. This task was difficult because his feelings were strong and yet, in Japanese culture, outward signs of emotion at such a time might be interpreted as weakness. He bowed solemnly before the two brothers, and they responded with equally solemn bows.

Carrying a small bundle containing the few personal belongings that the officials had allowed him to keep, Manjiro set off on foot for Nakanohama. He turned and waved a final farewell to his old comrades.

Legend has it that, as Manjiro's status grew in the years

that followed, Denzo became bitter because Manjiro the samurai never took time to associate with or visit his old comrades. Denzo believed that he had always been a friend to Manjiro. It was he who had found Manjiro alone and hungry on the beach in Usa and befriended him. It was he who had taken Manjiro into his home and fed him. It was he who had spoken on Manjiro's behalf when he needed a job. Denzo became disheartened to such a degree that he turned to alcohol and became a recluse. He died a lonely, broken man, and was buried in the port city of Usa.

The two-day journey from Usa to the village of Nakanohama seemed long. Manjiro had ample time in which to gather his thoughts in preparation for the much anticipated reunion with his family, especially his mother.

The sights along the rutted roadway leading to his birthplace were by now quite unfamiliar. His years of absence had snatched those remembrances from his mind. After nearly two days of walking, he finally, for the first time in over a decade, caught a glimpse of his childhood home. As he approached the outskirts of the village, he saw a small group of people waiting and watching. Obviously, word of his return had preceded him.

When the group recognized Manjiro, several people shrieked in disbelief. Others cheered, and the group began to chant a welcome. This reception caused Manjiro to straighten his lean frame and smile. He continued to walk toward the assemblage nodding, as if in approval, to some faces which were familiar. His eyes alertly searched the gathering for one face in particular—that of his dear mother.

The autumn day was warm and sunny, and the atmosphere was festive. As Manjiro walked along the narrow walkway toward the house of his birth, his heart began to pound with excitement. The crowd of villagers surrounded him and made his progress slow. When he reached an ancient well across from his home, Manjiro was reminded of the many times when he, as a small boy, had fetched water from the well in an old wooden bucket, for his family's use.

Suddenly, the crowd of well-wishers grew silent. Manjiro's eyes began to sparkle. A woman was standing with her hands near her lips. She too showed signs of being visibly shaken. After staring for a moment, Manjiro walked slowly toward her. He was deeply moved but somehow managed to retain his composure. The dream of being reunited with his mother, which had haunted him for so long, had at last become a reality. Manjiro bowed before his mother in a respectful manner and then rushed forward to embrace her. His act of veneration was much approved by the onlookers.

Standing close behind Shio, Manjiro's mother, were his sisters Seki and Shin with a young man whose face was unfamiliar to Manjiro. He was introduced as Etsuske, Seki's husband. When Manjiro had disappeared more than a decade before, the family had been left not only fatherless but without a son to carry on the family name and responsibilities. According to Japanese custom, if a family has no male offspring to carry on the family name, any man who marries into the family may assume the family name of the bride. Thus any children resulting from the union will carry on the family name. Lower-class Japanese in the nineteenth century were not allowed to use family surnames, but were simply known by the names given them at birth. Therefore, when Manjiro's sister Seki had reached marrying age and married a young man called Tokizoo, it had been agreed that he would assume the name Etsuske, which was Seki's father's name.

After the initial excitement subsided, Manjiro and his family retired into their small house. In the privacy of home, Manjiro again embraced his mother, unashamedly burying his face in her bosom and weeping with joy, ridding himself once and for all the heavy burden of longing he had borne for over eleven years.

The entire village of Nakanohama was electrified by the news of Manjiro's return. Soon neighbors began to visit Manjiro's home, bringing many special dishes that they had prepared for the joyous occasion. So much food was brought that the family and their friends dined upon a virtual banquet.

The throng of happy well-wishers showered Manjiro with questions. They were eager to hear from his own lips the details of his exciting adventures and experiences abroad. Many rumors had preceded him, and the villagers had never before heard such strange and exotic stories. What most interested them was the fact that a poor, innocent boy from Nakanohama had traveled clear around the world, visited wondrous places, and done many things which were totally outside their experience. They were very proud that Manjiro, the uneducated son of a lowly fisherman from their small, obscure fishing hamlet, had risen to such importance and acclaim that he had captured the attention of the Tosa daimyo.

As darkness slowly engulfed the village and the jubilation subsided, Manjiro and his mother sat together and talked about many things that had taken place since his unexpected departure more than eleven years before. Despite the difficult and sad times they had each been through, the reunion between Manjiro and his mother was a happy one. Shio, however, told her son that she had had a small memorial stone erected for him in his memory in the nearby hillside cemetery. Both had mixed feelings about this revelation.

The next morning, Manjiro's sisters took him to the cemetery on the grounds of the Daikakuji Temple and showed him the memorial stone. Manjiro said nothing at first but soon admitted that it was awkward and eerie to see his own memorial stone. Yet he was comforted and proud to know that his family had not forgotten him.

During the next two days, Manjiro told the villagers many tales about his experiences, including his adventures aboard the whaleships *John Howland* and *Franklin*. He talked about Fairhaven and about the many kind people he had encountered there. Of even greater importance and interest to his people, especially the village fishermen, were the young man's stories of learning to navigate a ship—starting from any given point and sailing out of sight of land, and then, using special instruments, returning to the point from which he had started, even if it was dark. This tale of sailing by use of instruments seemed dubious to the fishermen of the village. To prove his point, Manjiro made an offer to the fishermen who would listen: he said that, if he could get permission from the Bakufu, he would teach them to navigate.

On the third day after Manjiro's return to his village, a messenger arrived from Lord Yamanouchi of Kochi, to summon Manjiro back to the castle. Manjiro reacted to this unexpected news by becoming numb and apprehensive. He feared that the interrogation was to be resumed. Reluctantly, he told his mother the distressing news and promised to return as soon as he could.

When he arrived at the castle in Kochi, Lord Yamanouchi received him immediately and asked about his well-being and disposition since their last meeting. Manjiro said that all was well with him and that he had had a joyous reunion with his family. Then, the feudal authority began to speak, rambling on about many topics, most of them related to Manjiro's experiences abroad. Manjiro listened attentively. Summing up his lengthy oration, Lord Yamanouchi, a young man himself, offered Manjiro an assignment as instructor of navigation and whaling to the students of the Kyojukan School in Kochi, which was conducted under the ever-watchful eyes of the daimyo. Lord Yamanouchi pointed out that the scientific information that Manjiro had learned in America would be of special interest to the students of the Kyojukan School. He said that Manjiro should also share with his new students his knowledge of other matters in the outside world. He told the world traveler that he should remain in Kochi rather than returning to his native village.

Manjiro dared not refuse, for fear of seeming disrespectful toward the ruler. The rank of "Retainer to Lord Yamanouchi" was bestowed upon him, which gave him the privilege of wearing a single sword. He was expected to wear the sword at all times, as he was now a samurai. Manjiro found the wearing of the weapon distasteful, for he did not consider himself a warrior or a man of violence. Instead, he was a man of peace, committed to the teaching of modern technologies. However, rather than offend his patron lord, Manjiro wore the weapon.

Manjiro entered upon his duties at the Kyojukan School with some apprehension, for he knew that he would be watched with suspicion. Soon, however, his fears were diminished, and ultimately they were dispelled, as Manjiro became accepted as a teacher of goodwill. He became known as "the Honorable Teacher" and was very effective as a *sensei*, or teacher. His knowledge of many subjects was unmatched among his colleagues. He taught his students the English alphabet, explained the techniques and art of barrel making, and showed them various fishing methods used by the Americans, among other subjects.

While he was teaching at the Kyojukan School, Manjiro began thinking about the future of Japan. He was convinced

that Japan would soon be opening her harbors to other countries. He therefore took it upon himself to propound his theories at every opportunity, so as to prepare his students for the
destined shift in Japanese policies. For Manjiro, the risk of
this approach was great, and he could expect little or no
personal advantage or reward. He saw what he was doing as
beneficial to his country and its people, and so he risked losing
all that he had gained, or even losing his life, if the authorities
disapproved of what he was doing.

The students of the Kyojukan School were unaware that
they were being prepared for a change in their country's
policy of isolation. They accepted Manjiro's teachings with
great enthusiasm and respect.

While at the Kyojukan School, Manjiro painstakingly made
drawings of the twenty-six letters of the English alphabet. He
labored diligently to teach his students how to correctly use
and pronounce each character by using the song about the
ABCs that he had learned while attending school in Fairhaven. Another subject upon which he placed great importance was geography, and this subject interested his students
even more than English. Using a chart that he had brought
back to Japan, which had been drawn in England in 1846,
Manjiro was able to show his students exactly where Japan
was located in respect to other important countries.

Even Lord Yamanouchi took a great interest in this nautical
document. The powerful leader, like Manjiro and others,
knew that the world was changing and that it was only a
matter of time before the policy of isolation would end.
Therefore, the Tosa lord seized this opportunity to learn
about other lands from Manjiro. Lord Yamanouchi instructed
a brilliant young artist, Kawada Shoryru, to make a copy of
the English chart that Manjiro had brought back and to in-
scribe upon it in Japanese the names of the countries which
Manjiro of Nakanohama so often spoke of.

The news of this undertaking by Kawada Shoryru could not
be kept secret. Before long, many scholars began arriving in
Kochi in order to see the chart. The feudalistic dynasty would
soon end, and Manjiro's nautical chart, along with the information about navigation and technology which he supplied,
was an important impetus to changes that would profoundly
affect the policies of Japan.

10

Commodore Perry and the Black Ships

For more than 200 years, Japan had existed in an unprecedented state of isolation, mystery, and ignorance. The commercial nations of what Westerners called "the civilized
world" knew very little about Japan. What was known about
Japan was in fact very much less than what was unknown.

In 1831, a Japanese fishing junk was blown far off course in
the Pacific Ocean and landed on the coast of America. The
survivors were taken to the port of Macao and left in the care
of some Americans there. Several years later, despite the
well-known closed-door policy of Japan, it was decided that
the shipwrecked men would be put on board an American
merchant ship, the *Morrison*, and returned to their country.

All the guns and armaments of the *Morrison* were
removed, to avoid any appearance of hostile intentions. When
the ship reached the Bay of Yedo, the local Japanese soon
noticed that she was unarmed, and the next morning they
fired upon her from shore batteries. The *Morrison* quickly
weighed anchor and made a run to Kagoshima, the principal
town of Kyushu Island. However, as soon as the *Morrison*
anchored in Kagoshima, Japanese shore batteries again
opened fire. With no armament on board, the *Morrison* had
no choice. She quickly got under way and returned to macao
with the distressed Japanese still on board.

In 1846, an expedition was sent from the United States to
Japan on a definite mission to try to open negotiations. The
American ships were the *Columbus*, with ninety guns, and
the corvette *Vincennes*, under the command of Commodore
James Biddle (1783–1848). When they entered the Bay of
Yedo in July, they were immediately confronted and sur-
rounded by lines of guard boats. The *Vincennes* was boarded
by a party of Japanese, including soldiers, who placed wooden

figures on the bow and the stern. The Americans did not know what the wooden figures meant, and after a great deal of confusion about how to interpret them, they ordered the Japanese off the ship. The American ships delivered a letter to the Emperor and then lay at anchor for more than ten days. Finally, the *Columbus* received a reply from the Emperor, quite brief and to the point: "No trade can be allowed with any foreign nation except Holland."

In February 1848, the United States ship *Preble*, under Commander Glynn, was part of an American squadron in the China Sea. Word was received that sixteen American seamen had been shipwrecked off the coast of Japan and taken prisoner. The *Preble* was immediately dispatched to secure their release. As the American warship approached the Japanese coast near Nagasaki, many guns began thundering from the highlands, signaling the approach of a strange, unwanted vessel. Nevertheless, the *Preble* entered the harbor of Nagasaki. She was immediately besieged by hordes of guard boats filled with soldiers and was ordered away. The *Preble* defied the order and dropped anchor. Many more guard boats arrived, and many heavy artillery guns were being trained upon the *Preble* from the elevated shoreline surrounding the harbor. Commander Glynn vigorously commenced negotiations for the release of the captured American seamen.

Following their capture, these men had been forced to trample upon a crucifix and told that it was "the devil of Japan." They had been threatened with death if they refused, and so they had done as they were told.

The Japanese were unresponsive to Glynn's initial overtures. He then told them in no uncertain terms that if they did not voluntarily release the American prisoners, they would be forced to do so. He backed up his threat by stating that the U.S. government had the power and will to protect each of its citizens. Intimidated, the feudal authorities reassessed their actions and promised that the American prisoners would be handed over to the *Preble* within two days. The American prisoners were released on time, ending the incident peacefully.

An urgent concern about such cases was what caused the American government to seek to influence Japan to open her sealed harbors for trade with all countries of the civilized world.

When Japan had first imposed its policy of isolation in 1603, Portugal, Spain, Holland, England, France, and Russia had all tried to reestablish commercial relationships with her. Portugal, Holland, and England were successful at first, but England was later expelled and Portugal voluntarily abandoned the field, leaving Holland as the only Christian nation that had traffic with Japan.

The Dutch paid a high price for the privilege, including humiliation for the nation and imprisonment for some of its citizens. Dutch representatives at the shogun's court in Yedo (now Tokyo) were made to perform embarrassing acts before the court prior to their audience with the shogun's emissaries. In addition, they were kept in perpetual imprisonment on the island of Dezima. They were prohibited from conducting divine services on Sundays and solemn festivals and were not allowed to pray or sing psalms. They were required to avoid the sign of the cross and all outer signs of Christianity, including calling upon the name of Christ, in the presence of Japanese. The last humiliation was that they must patiently and submissively bear the abusive and injurious behavior of the proud Japanese. Even though the profits of barter with Japan seemed to be inadequate compensation, they bore the humiliation rather than give up their lust for gold.

The rest of the world was chiefly indebted to the Dutch for any knowledge of Japan it received. It was people like Engelbert Kaenpfer, Carl Peter Thunberg, Isaac Titsingh, Hendrick Doeff, J. F. Van Overmeir Fischer, G. F. Meijlan Meylan, and Philip Frank Siebold, all connected with a factory on the island of Dezima, near Nagasaki, who were responsible for informing the world about Japan. The Dutch were confined to the island, and all their trade with the Japanese took place on the island. (The fragmentary remains of the factory at Dezima may be seen in the harbor of Nagasaki even today.) The Dutch were under suspicion and were closely watched. Their only opportunities for seeing anything beyond the limits of Nagasaki occurred during periodic visits to the imperial court at Yedo.

In 1852, the U.S. government resolved to send an expedition to Japan. It was initially planned that the squadron would be composed of the following vessels: The *Mississippi*, the steamer which had been the flagship of Commodore Matthew C. Perry in the Gulf of Mexico during the Mexican War and was his favorite vessel; the *Princeton* and the *Allegheny*, both steamers; and three sloops of war, the *Vermont*, the *Vandalia*, and the *Macedonia*. The frigate *Susquehanna*, a steam-driven vessel, and the sloops of war *Saratoga*, *Plymouth*, and *Caprice* were waiting at the East India Station (which comprised the areas of operations of U.S. warships in the vicinity of Shanghai, China) to join the squadron. The armed store ships *Supply*, *Lexington*, and *Southampton* were also attached to the expedition. Of these vessels, only the *Princeton*, which proved to have imperfections in her boilers, never joined the squadron. The *Powhatan* was substituted.

This "East India Squadron," as it was called, was awesome not only in firepower but in appearance as well. The hulls of the American warships were painted the traditional black, and the gunports were outlined in white. The Japanese termed this array of warships the "Black Ships."

The mission to Japan was carefully planned and calculated on the basis that the Japanese might be expected to behave in certain ways. In making their plans, the Americans relied upon information provided by the Dutch, for they had no in-depth knowledge of Japanese culture, habits, religious doctrines, or military strength.

In the service of the commodore on board the *Susquehanna* were several interpreters, including Dr. Wells Williams of Canton, China, the Chinese interpreter, and A. L. C. Portman, the Dutch interpreter.

Commodore Perry's instructions included prohibiting those under his command from communicating with newspapers or other publications about either the squadron as a whole or the discipline and internal regulations of the individual vessels. Further, no mention of the proposed mission was allowed even in private correspondence with friends and family. All journals and private notes kept by the members of the expedition were to be considered government property until the U.S. Navy gave its permission to publish them. The object of these regulations was to withhold information that might jeopardize the success of the mission.

On November 24, 1852, Commodore Perry departed from Norfolk, Virginia, on the *Mississippi*, to begin the highly secret mission to Japan. The commodore's intention was to steam to the island of Madeira in the Canary Islands to pick up a supply of coal and provisions. The schedule called for the ship to arrive at Madeira on December 14 and then proceed to the Cape of Good Hope, Mauritius, and Singapore.

The State Department recommended that, for the safety of the East India Squadron, Commodore Perry make every effort to secure one or more ports of refuge in the islands of Japan. If this was not possible, the commodore was to try to find such a haven in the Loo Choo (pronounced "Doo Choo" locally) Islands, where the people were friendly and peaceful. Perry was also advised to take no supplies from the islanders without equal and fair payment, and to forbid all acts of plunder and violence by the men under his command. He was further ordered to make no use of force, except for defense if attacked, and then only as a last resort. The intention was to influence the Japanese to perceive the squadron's coming as a benefit, not as an evil threat.

The *Mississippi* arrived at Shanghai on May 4, 1853. Between that date and May 17, the commodore transferred to the *Susquehanna*, which then became his flagship, and the ships took on the usual supplies of coal and provisions for the voyage. On Monday morning, May 16, the *Mississippi* moved down the river. It was followed the next day by the *Susquehanna*. The squadron which now prepared to sail for the Loo Choos was composed of the *Susquehanna*, the *Mississippi*, the *Supply*, and the *Caprice*.

On Thursday, May 26, six months after Commodore Perry left the United States, the East India Squadron touched on Japanese territory at the harbor of Naha, the principal port of Okinawa, which is also called "the Great Loo Choo Island."

Several junks were immediately dispatched to Japan to carry the news of the arrival of the American Black Ships. On the next day, May 27, Commodore Perry gave the master mate permission to lower a gig and pull about the harbor, but he warned against attempting to land or communicate with the islanders.

The East India Squadron eventually made contact with the islanders and remained in Naha for more than a month. The Americans were warmly received and taken before the chief magistrate of the Loo Choos, who was also the mayor of Naha. The Americans surveyed the island and recorded information on the island itself and its natural resources, as well as its people and their habits.

On July 2, Commodore Perry transferred his flag to the

steamer *Susquehanna* and ordered the squadron to depart from Naha, leaving the *Supply* at anchor. The *Caprice* was dispatched to Shanghai for needed repairs. The destination of the balance of the squadron was the Bay of Yedo.

While steaming northward along the eastern coast of Japan, the squadron was under constant surveillance by many coast watchers. The squadron reached Yedo Bay on Thursday, July 7, and continued advancing up Yedo Bay on Friday, July 8, until about five o'clock in the afternoon when the squadron came to anchor at the city of Uraga. Even as the ships came to anchor at Uraga, Japanese boarding parties arrived, but they were refused permission to board. A Japanese member of one of the boarding parties said, in good English, "I can speak Dutch." Portman then held a lengthy discussion with this Japanese interpreter, who asked whether the ships were from America and said that they had been expected.

After making numerous attempts to send the Japanese parties away, the Americans finally told them that the American officer on board the *Susquehanna* was of very high rank and would confer only with the highest-ranking official of Uraga. The interpreter pointed to one of the Japanese officials in the boat and said that he was the vice-governor of Uraga, the highest official available, and that he should therefore be received. The Americans asked why the governor himself did not appear, and the Japanese interpreter replied that the governor was prohibited by law from going on board ships in the harbor. He advised that the commodore should appoint an official equal in rank to the vice-governor to conduct a conference. He added that the vice-governor was particularly interested in knowing the objectives of the squadron.

Commodore Perry purposely delayed for a while but then appointed his aide, Lieutenant John Contee, to receive the Uragaian official and allowed the Japanese interpreter and the vice-governor to board the ship. The interpreter introduced himself as Hori Tatsnoske and the vice-governor as Nagazima Saboroske. Commodore Perry remained secluded in his cabin throughout the lengthy conference between Lieutenant Contee and the vice-governor.

Lieutenant Contee told Vice-Governor Saboroske that Perry was bearing a letter from the President of the United

States to the Emperor of Japan and that he hoped to arrange for the commodore to deliver the letter and some other documents in person. The vice-governor was puzzled, but he immediately replied that Nagasaki was the only place where negotiations concerning foreign business could be conducted, according to Japanese law. He suggested that Perry go to Nagasaki to deliver the letter. Contee replied that Uraga had been chosen because of its proximity to Yedo. He added that the commodore would accept no form of indignity and that unless all the guard boats surrounding the ships of the squadron were dispersed at once, he would use force to remove them.

The Japanese official immediately rose to his feet and went to the ship's rail. He ordered most of the guard boats to leave, but a few remained in place. The Americans sent an armed cutter to warn the remaining boats away, taking the opportunity to show a force of arms. This action proved effective. The remaining guard boats moved away from the ships and did not return. All the while, the *Susquehanna* remained at anchor.

When the conference was concluded, on Friday, July 8, the vice-governor departed, after suggesting that a higher-ranking official might return on the following day, perhaps with more information for the Americans. He insisted, however, that he was doubtful that the answers sought by the Americans would be made available at Uraga. He again suggested that the squadron proceed to Nagasaki. Lieutenant Contee insisted that the commodore would never consent to such an arrangement, for Perry was determined to deliver the letter from the Bay of Yedo. He warned that if the Japanese government did not appoint a suitable person to receive the documents, the commodore would deliver them to the Emperor in person, no matter what the consequences.

On Saturday morning, July 9, at sunrise, a boat containing a corps of artists came close to the ship. The artists, however, made no attempt to come aboard but instead busied themselves taking sketches of the strange vessels. The important visit of the day occurred at seven o'clock in the morning, when two large boats rowed alongside, one of which contained a half dozen officials. The interpreter who spoke Dutch was with them, and announced that the personage of the highest authority of the city was present, and desired to come aboard. This personage was Kayama Yezaiman, the governor and highest functionary of Uraga. A long discussion ensued, on board the *Susquehanna*, during which the governor more than once declared that Japanese laws made it impossible to receive the President's letter at Uraga. He said that, even if it were received at Uraga, the answer would be sent to Nagasaki, and he added that the squadron must go to Nagasaki. Lieutenant Contee, on Commodore Perry's instructions, stood fast.

Intimidated, the governor said that he would immediately send to Yedo for further instructions but that it would take about four days to obtain an answer. Fully aware that Yedo was only an hour away, Perry instructed Lieutenant Contee to tell the governor that Commodore Perry would wait only three days, until Tuesday, July 12, for an answer. If none was received in that time, he would leave, but in the spring he would return with a larger force, in order to complete his mission.

During the negotiations on board the American warship *Susquehanna*, each ship of the squadron lowered small armed cutters to survey the harbor and to be prepared for any trouble which might develop. The governor inquired what the smaller boats were doing, and Lieutenant Contee said they were surveying the harbor. The Japanese official became angry and told Lieutenant Contee that Japanese law did not allow this type of activity. The American officer quickly responded that American law required American ships to survey any harbors they entered. He further stated that Americans were as bound to obey American laws as the Japanese were to obey theirs. Yezaiman was disgruntled but was made to understand that no further discussions were necessary until the Japanese government responded to Commodore Perry's demands.

Lieutenant Silas Bent of the steamer *Mississippi* was put in charge of the small boats and instructed not to venture beyond the range of the ship's guns. In the event of an attack, which could not be ruled out, reinforcement by additional armed boats would be in order. The survey by the men in the small boats was favorable; it revealed that deep water was found approximately 4 miles (6 kilometers) away, near the head of the bay, with readings of between 29 and 43 fathoms (174 and 258 feet) recorded. The current was running at between 2 and 3 knots.

While surveying the harbor, the small boats of the squadron also paid close attention to fortifications along the banks, which did not appear to be formidable. Their construction was primitive and showed little strength. The guns protruded through the embrasures and thus were ill-protected at best, making them easy targets for an assault. Japanese soldiers were present in good numbers and fully armed, but when the American boats came close to the shore, they disappeared into the enclosures. The survey boats were able to complete their soundings and return unmolested to their ships. The commodore's initial actions were fruitful and successful. Perry was satisfied that he had accomplished several objectives, which he listed as follows:

1. He had been able to survey the harbor successfully.
2. He had confined his visit to the harbor of Uraga.
3. He had refused to go to Nagasaki and was maintaining his position in the Bay of Yedo while awaiting an answer from the Japanese government.

During the wait for a reply from the governor, Commodore Perry wrote the following letter to the Emperor.

> United States Steam Frigate *Susquehanna*,
> Uraga, July 12, 1853
>
> The Commander-in-Chief of the United States Forces in these seas, being invested with full powers to negotiate treaties, is desirous of conferring with one of the highest officers of the Empire of Japan, in view of making arrangements for the presentation of the original of his letter of credence, as also the original of a letter with which he is charged, addressed to his Imperial Majesty by the President of the United States.
>
> It is hoped that an early day will be appointed for the proposed interview.
>
> To His Imperial Majesty the Emperor of Japan.

Also during their wait, the Americans intimidated the Japanese by challenging their large defensive forces, which included hundreds of guard boats, thousands of armed soldiers, and the many fortifications that protected the harbor. Com-

modore Perry ordered the *Susquehanna* to protect the survey
boats as they moved in a northerly direction up the Bay of
Yedo. Japanese soldiers appeared by the hundreds and were
funneled into boats along the bank. As each boat was filled,
it proceeded toward the American survey boats. The survey
boats alerted the *Susquehanna* to the danger of attack from
the Japanese boats. The American warship, belching heavy
black smoke from her stacks, increased her speed, to approach
and protect the survey boats. The Japanese guard boats abandoned their movement toward the American cutters.

After this incident, the East India Squadron remained at
anchor in a tranquil harbor. How the Japanese government
would respond to the demands of the commodore was the
question uppermost in the minds of the American sailors. The
ship's watch was on the alert for any sign of movement toward the American frigate *Susquehanna,* the commodore's
flagship. Finally, the appointed day was at hand—Tuesday,
July 12, 1853. At about nine-thirty in the morning, three
boats, larger than the guard boats, approached the *Susquehanna.* The lead boat had a black stripe across her sail,
indicating that she was carrying an official of distinction.
When the boat came near the American vessel, a man clad in
rich silk robes could be seen seated upon mats in the center
of the deck. The accompanying boats stood off from the *Susquehanna.* The governor, Kayama Yezaiman, accompanied
by two interpreters, Hori Tatsnoske and Fatcisko Tokushumo, was received on board with due formality. The party
were ushered before Captain Franklin Buchanan and Captain H. A. Adams, who welcomed them.

After some initial formalities, the governor said that there
had been many misunderstandings in the previous meeting.
This statement by the Japanese official prompted the commodore, who was in seclusion in his cabin, to reply that he had
already made his intentions quite clear. He advised his aides
to inform the governor that he himself would deliver a translation of the letter from the President, as well as the original.
He would also include a personal letter from himself addressed to the Emperor, when a higher-ranking officer was
available to accept the documents.

The governor responded that a building was being constructed in which the letters could be received, and that a

high-ranking personage, who had been duly appointed by the
Emperor himself, would receive the letters in the new building. The governor warned, however, that though the documents would be accepted in the Bay of Yedo, no answers
would be given there. The answers, he said, would be directed through the Dutch or Chinese interpreters, but only in
Nagasaki.

The governor's warning was reported at once to Commodore Perry, who wrote the following memorandum and directed it to be translated into Dutch and fully explained to the
governor.

> The Commander-in-Chief will not go to Nagasaki, and will
> receive no communication through either the Dutch or Chinese.
>   He has a letter from the President of the United States to
> deliver to the Emperor of Japan, or to his Secretary of Foreign
> Affairs, and he will deliver the original to none other—if this
> friendly letter of the President to the Emperor is not received
> and duly replied to, he will consider his country insulted, and
> will not hold himself accountable for the consequences. He
> expects a reply of some sort in a few days, and he will receive
> such reply nowhere but in this neighborhood [the Bay of
> Uraga].

Commodore Perry's response was relayed to the governor
by a translator, and he accepted it without comment or sign
of emotion. With the commodore's strong reply in hand, the
governor left the ship after less than three hours of initial
negotiations. However, the governor returned later that afternoon and asked to resume the discussion. Again the commodore remained in his cabin. The negotiations continued, cov-
ering points that would satisfy the commodore's demands.
Perry specified that the high-ranking official must prove that
he had been appointed by the Emperor to receive the documents. Discussion of original documents, as opposed to translations, consumed quite a bit of time. Finally, the commodore
agreed to submit both originals and translations of all documents at the same time. The governor explained that the
presentation would take place approximately a mile from the
shore, on the other side of a nearby hill. He asked whether the
commodore was prepared to wait for a reply. Perry's answer
was that he would not wait but would return in several

months to receive it. The governor promised that the ceremony would take place on Wednesday, July 13, 1853, at eight o'clock in the morning.

Once all the points of concern had been settled and the negotiations brought to a close, the Americans treated the governor and his interpreters to refreshments, including whiskey and brandy. The tone of the meeting became more social. The Japanese, who had been very reserved and solemn during the negotiations, became more relaxed. They smiled and nodded politely and often during their social conversation with the Americans. The Japanese were perceived by the Americans as being not only well-bred but highly educated as well. When the Orientals were shown a globe of the world, the interpreters studied it only briefly and then pointed out the United States. They placed their fingers on Washington and New York, stating with confidence that Washington was the capital city while New York was the center of commerce. They also identified England, France, Denmark, and other major countries. The Japanese were much better informed about world affairs than had been expected, perhaps (though the officers of the East India Squadron could not have known it) as a result of information obtained from Manjiro during the inquests at Kagoshima and Nagasaki.

One of the interpreters requested permission to view at close hand the ship's large steam engine and asked whether or not it was the same size as those used on American roadways. The Americans understood this question as a reference to American railroads.

The interpreters also inquired about the progress of the canal being cut through the land which, when finished, would unite the flow of currents of the Atlantic and Pacific oceans— an obvious reference to the Panama Canal, which was under construction at that time.

The American officers invited the Japanese to tour the entire ship. They accepted eagerly, leaving behind in their cabins the swords that indicated their rank and authority. The Americans took quick advantage of this carelessness to make a close examination of the style, quality, and workmanship of the swords, and found them to be of good-quality, highly polished steel, with mountings of pure gold.

While touring the warship, the Japanese closely examined its heavy, large gun, noticing that it was of immense size and capable of delivering a devastating blow. The American officers later said that the Japanese did not seem overly impressed or surprised, contrary to what they had expected. Rather, the members of the Japanese party merely nodded approvingly, leaving little doubt that the people of Japan were not as ill-informed about technology as the rest of the world had believed. Once again, though the Americans could not have known, it may be that the knowledge displayed by the Japanese had been derived from Manjiro.

The Japanese were obviously impressed by the manner in which the Americans on the *Susquehanna* had received them. As they departed, the governor promised to return on the following day with more news regarding the proposed meeting between a high-ranking official from the Emperor and Commodore Perry.

On the following day, Wednesday, July 13, the Americans waited patiently for the governor's return. Not until late in the afternoon did one of the ship's lookouts spot a craft making its way toward the *Susquehanna*, carrying Governor Kayama Yezaiman and his two interpreters. After boarding the American warship, the governor apologized for his tardiness and explained that it was due to the arrival in Yedo of Toda-Idzu-No-Kami, who had the title "First Counselor of the Empire." The governor was carrying a highly polished sandalwood box with the Emperor's seal on it. He said it was a sacred box containing a letter for the commodore, and he wouldn't allow anyone to touch it. He carefully removed the letter from the box and reverently handed it to Captain Buchanan, bowing politely several times. Captain Buchanan opened the letter and found that it was written in Dutch. Translated, it reads as follows:

> Emperor of Japan to his Highness, Toda, Prince of Idzu.
>
> I send you to Uraga to receive the letter of the President of the United States to me, which letter has recently been brought to Uraga by the Admiral, upon receiving which you will proceed to Yedo, and take the same to me.
>
> The Emperor's seal

The governor then presented his own affidavit verifying the authenticity of the Emperor's letter, which reads:

Six months in 1853

You can rest assured that the high officer who has been accredited by the Emperor of Japan himself, and who consequently comes here to Uraga from Yedo for the purpose of receiving the original and translated letters, is of very high rank, equal to that of Lord Admiral. I do assure that.

Signed: Kayama Yezaiman

Both of these letters were presented with the understanding that the person appointed to receive the President's letter from Commodore Perry was not to engage in any discussions or negotiations with the Americans. His only mission and authority was to accept the President's letter and to deliver it in person to the Emperor.

After presenting the letters from the Emperor and the governor, Governor Yezaiman informed the Americans that the formal meeting between Commodore Perry and Prince Toda was scheduled to take place early the next morning. He asked how many officers would accompany the commodore. Captain Buchanan replied that it was customary for the commodore, when delivering a communication from the President of the United States, to be accompanied by a full entourage of commissioned officers. He also said that it would be beneath the dignity of the commodore to travel a long distance in a small boat. Therefore, it was the commodore's intention to move his fleet to within viewing range of the house where the meeting was to take place.

The governor raised a question about whether or not the commodore intended to place the letters from the President directly into the hand of Toda-Idzu-No-Kami. He was told that that would not be necessary. In addition, the Japanese wanted to know whether the commodore was planning to leave Uraga after delivering the letters and, if so, when he would be returning for the answer. Dr. Williams, the Chinese interpreter for the Americans, relayed this inquiry directly to the commodore just as he had received it from his Japanese counterpart, Hori Tatsnoske. The commodore answered through Dr. Williams that he would return in the spring of the following year. This concluded the business at hand, and the Japanese party left the ship.

Following their departure, the commodore summoned all the squadron commanders to his flagship in order to formulate a protocol for the meeting between himself and the First Counselor. He told the commanders to draw up a list of all officers who would not be actually on duty at the time of the meeting, as well as all available marines. All the officers and marines on the list would accompany the commodore to the meeting.

At eight bells (eight o'clock) on the following morning, Thursday, July 14, 1853, the fleet was ordered to move farther up the Bay of Yedo, closer to the appointed meeting place. The officers and marines who were to accompany the commodore soon began to board the flagship. Just short of 100 fully uniformed naval officers and approximately 100 U. S. Marines were to be in the commodore's party, in addition to a group of musicians who would add the flair of martial music to this important occasion. The purpose of the entire protocol was to impress the Japanese officials. The commodore purposely delayed his emergence from his cabin in order to frustrate the Japanese, but eventually did appear, in full dress uniform. As he walked to the gangway, surrounded by his array of honor guards, the military band played spirited music. His waiting gig was manned by several smartly dressed enlisted men. As the gig approached land, a thirteen-gun salute acknowledged his rank. Trailing the commodore's gig were a number of barges containing the strong contingent of U.S. Marines. The commodore alit at the designated landing point amid much well-orchestrated ceremony.

Upon landing, the naval officers and marines quickly formed up, making an impressive appearance of authority, again for the benefit of the Japanese. Then the entire party marched to the meeting place. The commodore was flanked by two bodyguards, well-developed black sailors. Behind him marched two young sailors who each protectively carried the boxes containing the letters to be presented, which were carefully wrapped in scarlet cloth. A very impressive sight indeed!

Upon arriving at the meeting place, which measured approximately 40 feet (12 meters) square on the inside and had been especially designed for the ceremonious occasion, the commodore was ushered to a place of honor in the center of the room. Two Japanese officials, who were already seated and awaiting Commodore Perry's arrival, rose to their feet and bowed respectfully before him.

Silence prevailed in the impressive room for quite a while. Finally, one of the Japanese interpreters announced the names and titles of the two Japanese dignitaries. He first introduced Toda-Idzu-No-Kami, Prince of Idzu, and then Ido-Iwani-No-Kami, Ido, Prince of Iwani. Both were garbed in fine silk robes adorned with elaborately wrought figures of gold and silver.

Governor Yezaiman and his interpreters were in charge of the ceremonies. Turning to A. L. C. Portman and speaking Dutch, the Japanese interpreter asked whether the letters were ready to be delivered and said that Prince Toda was prepared to receive them. Portman, after conferring with the commodore, answered that the letters were ready. Perry beckoned to the two young sailors, who brought forward rosewood boxes adorned with gold mountings. As the sailors moved forward, the two black bodyguards walked beside them. A small table containing an open, red-velvet-lined box had been placed immediately in front of the Japanese officials. The guards carefully opened the rosewood boxes and placed the letter from the President, which was written on vellum and covered in blue silk, along with other documents, into the Japanese box. The other documents included the commodore's letter of credence and two communications from the commodore to the Emperor.

The President's letter and the other documents are printed below.

Millard Fillmore, President of the United States of America, to his Imperial Majesty, the Emperor of Japan.

GREAT AND GOOD FRIEND: I send you this public letter by Commodore Matthew C. Perry, an officer of the highest rank in the navy of the United States, and commander of the squadron now visiting your imperial majesty's dominions. I have directed Commodore Perry to assure your imperial majesty that I entertain the kindest feelings towards your majesty's person and government, and that I have no object in sending him to Japan but to propose to your imperial majesty that the United States and Japan should live in friendship and have commercial intercourse with each other.

The Constitution and laws of the United States forbid all interference with the religious or political concerns of other nations. I have particularly charged Commodore Perry to abstain from every act which could possibly disturb the tranquility of your imperial majesty's dominions.

The United States of America reach from ocean to ocean, and our Territory of Oregon and State of California lie directly opposite to the dominions of your imperial majesty. Our steamships can go from California to Japan in eighteen days.

Our great State of California produces about sixty millions of dollars in gold each year, besides silver, quick silver, precious stones, and many other valuable articles. Japan is also a rich and fertile country, and produces very valuable articles. Your imperial majesty's subjects are skilled in many of the arts. I am desirous that our two countries should trade with each other, for the benefit of both Japan and the United States.

We know that the ancient laws of your imperial majesty's government do not allow of foreign trade, except with the Chinese and the Dutch; but as the state of the world changes and new governments are formed, it seems wise, from time to time, to make new laws. There was a time when the ancient laws of your imperial majesty's government were first made.

About the same time America, which is sometime called the new world, was first discovered and settled by the Europeans. For a long time there were but a few people, and they were poor. They have now become quite numerous; their commerce is very extensive; and they think that if your imperial majesty were so far to change the ancient laws as to allow a free trade between the two countries it would be extremely beneficial to both.

If your imperial majesty is not satisfied that it would be safe altogether to abrogate the ancient laws which forbid foreign trade, they might be suspended for five or ten years, so as to try the experiment. If it does not prove as beneficial as was hoped, the ancient laws can be restored. The United States often limit their treaties with foreign States to a few years, and then renew them or not, as they please.

I have directed Commodore Perry to mention another thing to your imperial majesty. Many of our ships pass every year from California to China; and great numbers of our people pursue the whale fishery near the shores of Japan. It sometimes happens, in stormy weather, that one of our ships is wrecked on your imperial majesty's shores. In all such cases we ask, and expect, that our unfortunate people should be treated with kindness, and their property should be protected, til we can send a vessel and bring them away. We are very much in earnest in this.

Commodore Perry is also directed by me to represent to your imperial majesty that we understand that there is a great abundance of coal and provisions in the Empire of Japan. Our steamships, in crossing the great ocean, burn a great deal of coal, and it is not convenient to bring it all the way from America. We wish that our steamships and other vessels should be allowed to stop in Japan and supply themselves with coal, provisions, and water. They will pay for them in money, or anything else your imperial majesty's subjects may prefer; and we request your imperial majesty to appoint a convenient port, in the southern part of the Empire, where our vessels may stop for this purpose. We are very desirous of this.

These are the only objects for which I have sent Commodore Perry, with a powerful squadron, to pay a visit to your imperial majesty's renowned city of Yedo: friendship, commerce, a supply of coal and provisions, and protection for our shipwrecked people.

We have directed Commodore Perry to beg your imperial majesty's acceptance of a few presents. They are of no great value in themselves; but some of them may serve as specimens of articles manufactured in the United States, and they are intended as tokens of our sincere and respectful friendship.

May the Almighty have your imperial majesty in His great and holy keeping!

In witness whereof, I have caused the great seal of the United States to be hereunto affixed, and have subscribed the same with my name, at the city of Washington, in America, the seat of my government, on the thirteenth day of the month of November, in the year one thousand eight hundred and fifty-two.

[Seal attached]   Your good friend,

By the President: Millard Fillmore

                                   Edward Everett
                                   Secretary of State

Commodore Perry to the Emperor

United States Steam Frigate *Susquehanna*
off the coast of Japan, July 7, 1853

The undersigned, commander-in-chief of all the naval forces of the United States of America stationed in East India, China, and Japan seas, has been sent by his government to this country, on a friendly mission, with ample powers to negotiate with the government of Japan, touching certain matters which have been fully set forth in the letter of the President of the United States, copies of which, together with copies of the letter of credence of the undersigned, in the English, Dutch, and Chinese languages, are herewith transmitted.

The original of the President's letter, and of the letter of credence, prepared in a manner suited to the exalted station of your imperial majesty, will be presented by the undersigned in person, when it may please your majesty to appoint a day for his reception.

The undersigned has been commanded to state that the President entertains the most friendly feelings toward Japan, but has been surprised that and grieved to learn that when any of the people of the United States go, of their own accord, or are thrown by the perils of the sea, within the dominions of your imperial majesty, they are treated as if they were your worst enemies.

The undersigned refers to the cases of the American ships *Morrison*, *Lagoda*, and *Lawrence*. With the Americans, as indeed with all Christian people, it is considered a sacred duty to receive with kindness, and to succor and protect all, of whatever nation, who may be cast upon their shores, and such has been the course of the Americans with respect to all Japanese subjects who have fallen under their protection.

The government of the United States desires to obtain from that of Japan some positive assurance that persons who may hereafter be shipwrecked on the coast of Japan, or driven by stress of weather into her ports, shall be treated with humanity.

The undersigned is commanded to explain to the Japanese that the United States are connected with no government in Europe, and that their laws do not interfere with the religion of their own citizens, much less with that of other nations.

That they inhabit a great country which lies directly between Japan and Europe, and which was discovered by the nations of Europe about the same time that Japan herself was first visited by Europeans; that the portion of the American continent lying nearest to Europe was first settled by immigrants from that part of the world; that its population has rapidly spread through the country, until it has reached the shores of the Pacific ocean; that we have now large cities, from which, with the aid of steam vessels, we can reach Japan in eighteen or twenty days; that our commerce with all this region of the globe is rapidly increasing, and the Japan seas will soon be covered with our vessels.

Therefore, as the United States and Japan are becoming every day nearer and nearer to each other, the President desires to live in peace and friendship with your imperial majesty, but no friendship can long exist, unless Japan ceases to act toward Americans as if they were her enemies.

However wise this policy may originally have been, it is unwise and impracticable now that the intercourse between the two countries is so much more easy and rapid than it formally was.

The undersigned holds out all these arguments in the hope that the Japanese government will see the necessity of averting unfriendly collision between the two nations, by responding favorably to the positions of amity, which are now made in all sincerity.

Many of the large ships-of-war destined to visit Japan have not yet arrived in these seas, though they are hourly expected;

and the undersigned, as an evidence of his friendly intentions, has brought but four of the smaller ones, designing, should it become necessary, to return to Yedo in the ensuing spring with a much larger force.

But it is expected that the government of your imperial majesty will render such return unnecessary, by acceding at once to the very reasonable and pacific overtures contained in the President's letter, and which will be further explained by the undersigned on the first fitting occasion.

With the most profound respect for your imperial majesty, and entertaining a sincere hope that you may long live to enjoy health and happiness, the undersigned subscribes himself,

M. C. Perry

Commander-in-chief of the United States
Naval Forces in the East India,
China, and Japan seas.

To His Imperial Majesty, the Emperor of Japan

Commodore Perry to the Emperor.

United States Steam Frigate *Susquehanna*
Uraga, Yedo Bay, July 14, 1853.

It having been represented to the undersigned that the propositions submitted through him to the government of Japan are of so much importance, and involve so many momentous questions, that much time will be required to deliberate and decide upon their several bearings:

The undersigned, in consideration thereof, declares himself willing to await a reply to these propositions until his return to Yedo Bay in the ensuing spring, when he confidently hopes that all matters will be amicably arranged, and to the satisfaction of the two nations.

With profound respect,
M. C. Perry,
Commander-in-chief of the United States Naval Forces
in the East India, China, and Japan seas.

To His Imperial Majesty, the Emperor of Japan.

Letter of credence to Commodore Perry.

Millard Fillmore, President of the United States of America,
to His Imperial Majesty the Emperor of Japan.

Reposing special trust and confidence in the integrity, prudence and ability of Matthew C. Perry, a captain in the navy of the United States, I have invested him with full power, for and in

the name of the said United States, to meet and confer with any
person or persons furnished with like powers on the part of your
imperial majesty, and with him or them to negotiate, conclude,
and sign a convention or conventions, treaty or treaties, of and
concerning the friendship, commerce, and navigation of two
countries; and all matters and subjects connected therewith
which may be interesting to the two nations, submitting the
same to the President of the United States for his final ratification, by and with the advice and consent of the Senate of the
United States.

In testimony whereof, I have caused the seal of the United
States to be hereunto affixed.

Given under my hand, at the city of Washington, the thirteenth day of November, in the year one thousand eight hundred and fifty-two, and of the independence of the United
States of America the seventy-seventh.

By the President   Millard Fillmore

                                      Edward Everett
                                      Secretary of State

[U.S. seal attached]

Besides the English versions, translations of each letter into
both Dutch and Chinese were placed into the Imperial box by
Mr. Portman. As he put each translation into the box, he told
the Japanese interpreters which language it was written in.
Rising to his feet, Governor Kayama Yezaiman approached
the Prince of Idzu, lowered himself to a prostrate position,
and accepted a scroll of papers. Next he prostrated himself
before Commodore Perry and presented the scroll to him. Mr.
Portman asked what the papers were, and the answer was
that they were the Imperial receipt. The receipt had been
translated into Dutch by the Japanese interpreter, and a lit-
eral English translation reads as follows:

The letter of the President of the United States of North
America, and copy, are hereby received and delivered to the
Emperor. Many times it has been communicated that business
relating to foreign countries cannot be transacted here in Uraga,
but in Nagasaki. Now it has been observed that the Admiral, in
his quality of ambassador of the President, would be insulted by
it; the justice of this has been acknowledged; consequently, the
above mentioned letter is hereby received, in opposition to the
Japanese law.

Because the place is not designed to treat of anything from

foreigners, so neither can conference nor entertainment take place. The letter being received you will leave here.

[Here follow facsimiles of signatures in Japanese.]

The ninth of the sixth month.

The Japanese interpreter, however, lacked skill, and his translation does not represent an exact interpretation of the original Japanese letter. The translation below has been suggested as more appropriate.

> The letter of the President of the United States of North America, and copy, are hereby received, and will be delivered to the Emperor.
>
> It has been many times intimated that business relating to foreign countries cannot be transacted here in Uraga, but at Nagasaki; nevertheless, as it has been observed that the Admiral, in his quality of ambassador of the President, would feel himself insulted by a refusal to receive the letter at this place, the justice of which has been acknowledged, the above mentioned letter is hereby received, in opposition to Japanese law.
>
> As this is not a place where in to negotiate with foreigners, so neither can conferences nor entertainment be held. Therefore, as the letter has been received you can depart.

After the contents of the receipt were translated to the commodore, he thought for a moment and then directed his interpreter to inform the Japanese that it was his intention to leave within a few days with his entire squadron. They would return to the Loo Choos before setting a heading for Canton, China. He further instructed Mr. Portman to say that he would be returning in the spring, probably in April or May. Thus the conference was concluded. Commodore Perry returned to his gig, again accompanied by his entourage and the sound of martial music.

11

Ratification of the Kanagawa Treaty

Even after Commodore Matthew C. Perry and his Black Ships left Yedo Bay in July 1853, officials of the Japanese government at Yedo remained concerned about Perry's boldness and arrogance. The American commodore had issued an ultimatum, and the shogun was worried by his promise to return in six or seven months to obtain an answer to President Millard Fillmore's request that Japan change its policy of isolation. The shogun had no naval ships or forces capable of repelling an armed aggression. It was therefore necessary to formulate a meaningful diplomatic response to the American proposal.

After much discussion with government officials, the shogun decided to send for Manjiro, hoping that he might help to bolster the Tokugawa's position in this delicate matter.

In late September 1853 a messenger-runner arrived at the castle of Lord Yamanouchi in Kochi, carrying a box adorned with the seal of the Tokugawa. Inside the box was a message from the shogun to Lord Yamanouchi, ordering that Manjiro be delivered to him in Yedo at once.

Lord Yamanouchi, in response to the shogun's urgent request, summoned "Honorable Teacher" Manjiro and ordered him, with no explanation, to prepare for a journey to the capital city. Manjiro was shaken by the demand that he return to the Tokugawa Bakufu, but, as he had no right to refuse an official summons, he immediately gathered his belongings. He was led to a junk for the journey to the port city of Osaka on the main island of Honshu, nearly 150 miles (241 kilometers) northeast of Kochi. Arriving in Osaka, Manjiro was taken overland along the main highway, which was called "Tokaido," to Yedo and the Bakufu.

Some of the officials, in discussing Manjiro, had argued that he could be very helpful to the Japanese government in deter-

mining the true intentions of the American government because of his experience of living among the Americans. Others, however, had argued against using him, pointing out that
he might have already deceived his countrymen and might be
acting in the interest of the foreigners rather than of his own
country. After all, he was indebted to Americans for his rescue from the small Pacific atoll, and he had been taken alone
to America, where he was isolated from any Japanese influence. The question, these Japanese officials insisted, was
whether the education he professed to have acquired in
America included training to act as a spy against his own
country. Though the officials debated these matters at length,
they finally decided that only time would reveal Manjiro's
true allegiance.

Despite the insistence of the shogun's retainer, Lord Egawa
Tarozaemon, it was decided not to use Manjiro as an interpreter when Commodore Perry returned. Instead, Manjiro
was told that he would again be questioned by government
officials, in an effort to elicit information that would help them
in a major decision which could affect the fate and future of
his country. He was ordered to deliberate carefully about
each question before offering an answer.

The place chosen for the interrogations was near the Imperial Palace, and Prime Minister Abe Hasahiro questioned
Manjiro personally. Kawaji Toshiakira, a retainer from the
shogunate who was minister of finance, also participated in
the questioning. Another person in attendance was High
Commissioner Hayashi Daigaku-No-Kami, who was one of
the Emperor's chosen negotiators. The High Commissioner
spoke, read, and wrote Chinese fluently. Also present was
Egawa Tarozaemon, who was fluent in both spoken and written Dutch. Tarozaemon was especially interested in the
young man from Nakanohama. He had listened to and
watched Manjiro very closely during the interrogation in
Nagasaki more than a year before. Manjiro's stories about the
large oceangoing ships of the Americans had piqued his interest, for he envisioned increasing the size of Japanese ships.

Many of the questions posed by the Bakufu hinted at the
contents of the letters presented by Commodore Perry. Manjiro answered all the questions as simply and directly as possible, holding back nothing about his understanding and knowledge of the foreigners.

Through months of sporadic questioning, Manjiro was able to ward off all implications of wrongdoing or complicity with the Americans, though some members of the Bakufu still refused to believe him. Nevertheless, the Bakufu rewarded Manjiro for the valuable information he had provided to the Tokugawa officials about places outside Japan, especially America. His reward was elevation to a higher rank, that of samurai, along with the respect and authority of the rank. As a mark of his new rank, he was allowed to wear two swords and to assume a family name, which had not been allowed previously because of his inferior status. Manjiro selected "Nakahama" as his family name, after the village of Nakanohama where he had been born. He was thereafter called "Nakahama Manjiro the Samurai."

While questioning Manjiro, the Tokugawa had been formulating policy about how to respond to the crisis brought about by Commodore Perry. Mito Nariaki, Lord of Mito, held a deep-seated opposition to the opening of Japanese ports to foreigners. A letter from Mito to Lord Tarozaemon reads as follows:

Lord of Ise to Egawa Tarozaemon, January 23

First Year of Ansei (lunar calendar)

In the course of our conversation during your visit a little while ago, you related in detail regards Manjiro and explained that, since you are to go aboard the ship to persuade the squadron to turn back, you would be immensely inconvenienced without a person to act as interpreter. As for Manjiro, it was your assurance that, being in a position to fathom his inmost heart, you would take it upon yourself to guarantee that he would never act to the prejudice of the Shogunate. Such being the case, and taking into consideration such a circumstance as might arise at any moment to call you urgently to depart, my hasty conclusion then was to agree to what you had suggested. Afterward, however, I turned the whole matter over in my mind very carefully. There is no reason whatsoever to be apprehensive about your guarantee for things. It is very apparent that Manjiro himself never cherishes a treacherous desire. But foreign motives are difficult to speculate upon. That an unforeseen situation might arise on board the ship in which Manjiro might be taken away with the foreigners is beyond anybody's guarantee. Furthermore, there are persons, among them Grand Lord of Mito, who entertain serious apprehensions. Under the circumstances, in the event that you might be called upon to visit the ship within this night, it is advisable that you refrain from taking Manjiro with you. It is my intention to take up the matter at the Castle when I attend there tomorrow, and let you hear the consequences as quickly as possible. Everything we do is in the cause of the Shogun. You are advised to have patience.

Eleven days later, Lord Mito sent a second letter to Lord Tarozaemon, again insisting that Manjiro must have no contact with the Americans. The letter reads as follows:

The Lord of Mito to Egawa Tarozaemon

February 2

Egawa Esq:

Pleased to know that Egawa is progressing so well in this cold weather. It is a thousand pities that the Americans came before even the half-way was accomplished in the manufacture of guns. Mito wholeheartedly concurs in the wish that, even one by one, the guns will be finished with speed and the ones that are ready fully equipped with carriages immediately. As regards Manjiro, Egawa has seen through his heart and found it clear of all suspicion. Manjiro is to be praised for yearning so much for home, and eventually coming back. But consider that the Americans took advantage of Manjiro's youth to separate him from others and did a favor by teaching writing and arithmetic. In so doing who can tell that there was not a doubtful scheme in mind? Manjiro was saved from death and put under obligation of gratitude for upbringing from early boyhood to twenty years of age. That it will not be to Manjiro's liking to do anything to the disadvantage of the Americans is natural. Therefore even if Egawa sees well, it would be advisable that all chances be eliminated of meeting anyone of the Americans when they come ashore, and that Manjiro be kept in ignorance of secret conferences, not to mention restrained from going on board the ships. Depending on how Egawa makes use of the man, it will help toward enlightenment on the state of affairs in America, and it is left to Egawa's good sense and discretion to turn Manjiro into an instrument to be employed in defense. Though fully relying on Egawa's tactfulness, still apprehension has caused these few lines. Pray excuse this scribble in haste before attending the Castle.

[Signed] The Hermit of Mito

P.S. It will be imprudent, in view of the times, to leave that man loose at pasture, but to make too confined and ill at ease would reduce usefulness. Treat generously, while guarding carefully. There was once a dragon tamed and domesticated that one day drove through wind and cloud in the midst of a hurricane and took flight. Once that man changed his mind and was taken away on an American ship it would be to repent too late. With regard to dealings with Americans Mito agrees that lacking preparation for defense the Americans should be tactfully persuaded to leave in peace. Once successful, demands will know no bounds. Just like Kappa (a legendary river monster), and Raiju (a creature connected with the God of Thunder), the Americans are rampant only because of being on water and the strength of fire-arms. Tumbling about in a field, a Kappa or a Raiju is a mere nothing. Until the time when well prepared with ships and guns, it is hoped that, dealing with those Americans, Nippon will have the high spirit of fighting a hand to hand combat with lightening speed. Mito hopes and believes that Egawa's pluck and courage will not fail to make the invaders' blood run cold. Here Mito takes the opportunity to manifest notorious obstinacy.

While Manjiro was in Yedo assisting the Japanese government, the East India Squadron returned to the Loo Choo Islands for diplomatic purposes, and to establish a coal and supply depot. At eight o'clock in the morning on August 1, 1853, Commodore Matthew C. Perry and his squadron set out for the port of Hong Kong, China. Prior to the departure, the commodore had ordered Commander John Kelly of the *Plymouth* to proceed to the Bonin Islands and to visit the settlements of Port Lloyd. In addition, he was to station the American warship in the vicinity of the Loo Choos, to begin surveying the Bonin Islands, and to inquire into the well-being of Nathaniel Savory and John Smith. Originally from Massachusetts, Savory and Smith had previously sailed on the *Susquehanna* and had established a colony, called "Colony of Peel Island," in the Bonin Islands. Upon his arrival at the Bonin Islands, Commander Kelly soon learned that the settlers on Peel Island, the principal island of the group, had organized a municipal government under the title "The Colony of Peel Island." Thirteen articles to govern this colony had been drafted, and Nathaniel Savory had been elected to serve as chief magistrate.

When the East India Squadron arrived in Hong Kong on August 7, the typhoon season was approaching. Many of Perry's ships were in need of repair, and their crews required relaxation. Perry therefore decided to remain on the China coast until it was time to resume negotiations with Japan.

After a stay of six months, the squadron returned to the Loo Choo Islands, to the port of Naha. From there, the ships went to the Bay of Yedo, reaching the outer bay on February 11, 1854. The squadron came to anchor about 12 miles (19 kilometers) beyond the town of Uraga, and approximately 20 miles (32 kilometers) from Yedo.

Two Japanese government boats immediately came alongside the *Susquehanna*. Commander H. A. Adams (who was designated as captain of the fleet), instructed them to go to the *Powhatan*. Captain Adams, A. L. C. Portman (the Dutch interpreter), and Dr. Wells Williams (the Chinese interpreter) went by barge to the *Powhatan*, followed closely by the Japanese government boats. The official Japanese party included a high-ranking dignitary named Kura-Kawa-Kahie and the same two interpreters, Hori Tatsnoske and Fatcisko Tokushumo, who had served the Japanese during the commodore's first visit to Uraga six months earlier. Also in the party were three cross-eyed men wearing gray robes, who were spies for the Japanese government.

Kura-Kawa-Kahie told Perry, through Captain Adams, that he should return to Uraga, where the first meeting had taken place and where two high-ranking officials were waiting for him. Captain Adams stated that the commodore had no intention of returning to Uraga. The Japanese replied that the Emperor himself had chosen the place for negotiations. Captain Adams said that the commodore would agree to go ashore only where they now were, to meet with representatives of the government. Otherwise, he would move his ships farther up Yedo Bay, perhaps even as far as Yedo itself.

The negotiations between the American and the Japanese representatives continued. Each side rejected every meeting place the other suggested. Speaking through Tatsnoske, the Japanese official finally said that he would seek further counsel. He also requested that the Americans avoid any further surveying of the harbor, warning that such surveying would be against Japanese law. The Japanese party then left the *Powhatan*, stating that it would be several days before they could return.

On February 15, the Japanese party returned amid the usual ceremonial protocol afforded foreign dignitaries. Some rumors about the death of the Emperor had reached the squadron. Captain Adams asked whether the rumors were true. The answer was, "Yes, a very high man died lately." Captain Adams asked to know the rank of the man who had died, and the Japanese official said only, "He was a prince." The meetings continued for several days. On February 19, Commodore Perry transferred his flag to the *Powhatan*, but not until February 23 did Governor Kayama Yezaiman of Uraga, who had been an active participant during Perry's first visit, come to the ship with the Japanese negotiators. He explained that his absence had been due to illness and said that he had come to the ship to encourage Commodore Perry to reconsider Uraga as the meeting site. He also said that a very high official would visit the *Powhatan* the next day.

On February 24, not waiting for the high official to arrive, Commodore Perry moved his entire squadron to within view of Yedo. The squadron came to anchor near the town of Kanagawa. Soon afterward, Captain Adams brought to the flagship a letter from the high official, Hayashi-Daigaku-No-Kami, who had been sent by the Emperor. The letter requested that the commodore meet with a Japanese official in Uraga. Shortly thereafter, Governor Yezaiman arrived to request an answer to Hayashi-Daigaku-No-Kami's letter. Convinced now that the commodore could not be convinced to go to Uraga, the governor suggested that the talks be held at Yoku-hama, almost directly abreast of the squadron's present anchorage.

Commodore Perry waited until March 1 to respond to Yezaiman's suggestion that he meet with government officials in Yoku-hama. He answered with the following letter:

His Highness Hayashi-Daigaku-No-Kami:

United States Flag-ship Powhatan, At anchor off the town of Yoku-hama, Yedo Bay, March 1, 1854.

YOUR EXCELLENCY: The letter of your excellency from Uraga was duly delivered by Captain Adams; and shortly after, when it was ascertained that I could not agree to return to Uraga, Kayama Yezaiman suggested that the negotiations might be conducted at a village opposite the present anchorage of the squadron.

Being exceedingly desirous of meeting the wishes of your excellency, in every way consistent with the honor and interest of my country, and learning that the place pointed out was in all respects convenient for the purpose, I at once consented to defer my visit to Yedo until after the completion of the negotiations.

I the more readily entered into this arrangement, as, on examination of the port by the surveying boats, it has been found that the ships can approach near to the city, where I propose at some future time to anchor them, as well as do honor to his Imperial Majesty by salutes, &c., as to be in full view of the palace, and convenient to be visited by such of the court as may desire to examine the steamers and their machinery, and I hardly need say that they will be kindly and politely received.

With the most profound respect,

M. C. Perry,

Commander in-chief United States Naval Forces East India, China, and Japan Seas, and Special Ambassador to Japan.

His Highness Hayashi-Daigaku-No-Kami, &c., &c., &c.

Now that the site for the negotiations had been agreed upon, the Japanese began reconstructing, near the shore, the same building that had been previously used in Uraga for the first exchange of letters between Commodore Perry and representatives of the Tokugawa in 1853. The building had been dismantled and moved to Kanagawa for the purpose of the treaty negotiations. The commodore moved his fleet to within gun range of the meeting place, arranging the ships so that their guns would cover a range of about 5 miles (8 kilometers) on either side of the selected meeting site.

Through the Dutch interpreter, Mr. Portman, the commodore requested that Governor Yezaiman provide him with the names and credentials of the High Commissioner. The following notice was promptly forwarded to the *Powhatan*.

Hayashi Daigaku-No-Kami, Ido-Tsus-Sima-No-Kami, Izawa Mema-Saki-No-Kami, U Dono Mimbusco:

You are hereby empowered to hold interviews with his excellency the American Ambassador on his arrival, and to negotiate concerning the business which has been communicated to you.

Ka-Ei-Silsi-Neu

Siogoots

[Seal of the Emperor]

When asked if the High Commissioner with whom Commodore Perry was to meet was of rank equal to that of the commodore, Governor Yezaiman answered that he was. It was agreed that the meeting would be held on March 8, 1854, in the building that was being reconstructed especially for that purpose.

Early on the morning of the meeting, the Americans saw a large barge moving down the river toward the meeting site. When the barge, which was handsomely decorated and displayed banners of various designs, reached the landing site, a number of Japanese commissioners, all dressed in fine silk, debarked into smaller craft to effect the landing.

The Americans meantime were assembling—a turnout of approximately 500 men, all in parade dress including badges, caps, swords, and pistols. The fixed bayonets of the marines gleamed in the sunlight. Once the entire escort was assembled, Commodore Perry appeared on the quarterdeck of the *Powhatan*, as the U.S. naval band struck up an impressive musical selection. When he stepped into his barge, batteries thundered a seventeen-gun salute. Once on land, Commodore Perry and his entourage marched to the meeting place in military order, accompanied by a military cadence played by the naval band.

Perry was greeted by an honor guard of Japanese soldiers and officials. As the commodore and his party entered the building that the Americans were later to call the "treaty house," howitzers bellowed a twenty-one-gun salute in honor of the Emperor, followed by a seventeen-gun salute in honor of High Commissioner Hayashi Daigaku-No-Kami. The *Powhatan* smartly raised the Japanese colors at the foremast, acknowledging the sovereignty of Japan.

Once Commodore Perry and his staff were properly seated, five Japanese commissioners made their ceremonial entrance. Besides Hayashi Daigaku-No-Kami, they included Ido, Prince of Tsus-Sima; Prince of Mimasaki, who was the youngest member of the Japanese party; Udono, who was not a Prince but was a high rank and was known as "Mimbu-Shiyoyu"; and Matsusaki Michitaro.

The principal interpreter for the Japanese for this occasion was Moryama Yenoske, who assumed a position on his knees immediately before the High Commissioner. After all the principals were seated, the room became noticeably still. A prolonged silence was interrupted by Yenoske, who asked about the well-being of the commodore. This inquiry was followed by the usual cordial exchange of mostly meaningless messages.

The High Commissioner then gave Commodore Perry a long roll of paper, and the Japanese interpreter told him it contained the Emperor's answer to the letter from the President which the commodore had delivered the previous July. A translation of the Emperor's answer follows.

The return of your excellency, as ambassador of the United States to this Empire, has been expected according to the letter of his Majesty the President, which letter your excellency delivered last year to his Majesty the Emperor of this Empire.

It is quite impossible to give satisfactory answers at once to all the proposals of your government, as it is most positively forbidden by the laws of our Imperial ancestors; but for us to continue attached to the ancient laws, seems to misunderstand the spirit of the age; however, we are governed now by imperative necessity.

At the visit of your excellency last year to this Empire, his Majesty the former Emperor was sick, and is now dead. Subsequently, his Majesty the present Emperor ascended the throne; the many occupations in consequence thereof are not yet finished, and there is no time to settle other business thoroughly. Moreover, his Majesty the new Emperor, at the succession to the throne, promised to the princes and high officers of the Empire to observe the laws. It is therefore evident that he cannot now bring about any alteration in the ancient laws.

Last autumn, at the departure of the Dutch ship, the superintendent of the Dutch trade in Japan was requested to inform your government of this event, and a reply in writing has been received.

At Nangasaki [sic] arrived recently the Russian ambassador to communicate a wish of his government. He has since left the said place, because no answer would be given to any nation that might communicate similar wishes. However, we admit the urgency of, and shall entirely comply with, the proposals of your government concerning coal, wood, water, provisions, and the saving of ships and their crews in distress. After being informed which harbor your excellency selects, that harbor shall be prepared, which preparation it is estimated will take about five years. Meanwhile a commencement can be made with the coal at Nangasaki [sic] by the next Japanese first month (Siogoots) (16th of February, 1855).

Having no precedent with respect to coal, we request your excellency to furnish us with an estimate, and upon due consideration this will be complied with, if not in opposition to our laws. What do you understand by provisions, and how much coal?

Finally, anything ships may be in want of that can be furnished from the production of this Empire shall be supplied. The prices of merchandise and articles of barter to be fixed by Kurakawa Kahei and Moryama Yenoske. After settling the points before mentioned, the treaty can be concluded and signed at the next interview.

Seals attached by order of the high gentlemen.

Moryama Yenoske.

Below are some notes that were handed to First Commissioner on Wednesday, March 8.

The American ambassador learns with pleasure that the Japanese government is disposed to enter into some friendly arrangement with the United States. As such is happily the case, it would be much more advantageous to both nations, and especially to Japan, if a treaty is agreed upon, even if it be of short duration; for reason that the citizens and subjects of both the contracting powers would be mutually bound by law to conform to all its stipulations, and thus prevent mistakes and consequent disputes.

This is the practice with all other nations; and such is the present condition of the world, that these treaties have become necessary to avert contention and war. The obligations to conform to them are enjoined as well by considerations of honor, as the preservation of the peace and prosperity of the respective countries; and it would be impossible for the western nations to preserve friendly intercourse if it were not for similar treaties.

Although we have abundance of prepared provisions in the squadron, it would be desirable to obtain daily supplies of fresh meat, vegetables, &c., for which we would pay the prices demanded. Wood and water will, of course, be wanted, and for a supply of which we shall be thankful.

The health of the officers and men require that they should have exercise on shore; and though I have hitherto, out of respect to the Japanese laws, forbidden any one to land except for purposes of duty, I feel assured that some arrangement will be made to admit of some reasonable intercourse with the neighborhood.

Copies of the surveys which the officers are employed in making will be presented to the Imperial government; and, to make them more perfect, it will be necessary to place signal-poles at some points on shore by which to measure the

angles; therefore it is requested that the officers landing for such
purposes may not be molested.

It is thought that the business of the negotiation would be
facilitated by submitting the several questions and replies that
may arise in writing.

M. C. Perry

United States Flag-ship, *Powhatan*,
Yedo Bay, off the town of
Yoku-hama, March 1, 1854.

YOUR EXCELLENCY: In presenting for the consideration of
your highness the accompanying draught of a treaty, which, in
all its essential features, is identical with that at present
subsisting between the United States and China, I again venture
to urge upon the Imperial government of Japan the importance
of establishing a friendly understanding with the nation which
I have the honor on this occasion to represent.

It would be needless in me to reiterate the arguments already
advanced in support of a measure so fraught with the best
interests of the two nations, and so necessary to the peace and
prosperity of Japan.

I have in a former communication remarked that the
President of the United States entertains the strongest desire,
and cherishes a most fervent hope, that the mission which he
has intrusted to my charge may result in the accomplishment of
a treaty mutually beneficial, and tending to avert, by timely
negotiation, the consequences that would otherwise grow out of
collisions certain to arise, should the present undefined relations
between the two countries much longer continue.

In the increasing number of American ships almost daily
passing and repassing the territories of Japan, the President
is apprehensive of the occurrence of some further act of hostility towards the unoffending citizens of the United States who
may be thrown by misfortune upon your shores, and hence
his wish to establish a treaty of friendship, which shall give assurance of the discontinuance of a course of policy, on the
part of the Japanese, altogether at variance with the usages
of other nations, and no longer to be tolerated by the United
States.

As an evidence of the friendly intentions of the President, and
to pay the highest honor to his Imperial Majesty, he has sent me
in command of a number of ships—to be increased by others
which are to follow—not only to bear to his Majesty the letter
which I have already presented, but to evince, by every suitable
act of kindness, the cordial feelings entertained by him towards
Japan.

That there might be sufficient time allowed for a full consideration of the just and reasonable demands of the President, I took upon myself to withdraw the ships in July last from the coast, and have now, after an absence of seven months, returned, in the full expectation of a most satisfactory arrangement.

Another proof of the friendly disposition of the President has been given in his sending for exhibition to the Imperial court three of the magnificent steamers of the United States, of which there are many thousands, large and small, in America; and he has also sent, for presentation to the Emperor, many specimens of the most useful inventions of our country.

Therefore, after all these demonstrations of good will, it would be strange if the Japanese government did not seize upon this very favorable occasion to secure a friendly intercourse with a people anxious to prevent, by wise and prudent foresight, all causes of future misunderstanding and strife.

It will be observed that there is no western nation so intimately connected with the peace and welfare of Japan as the United States, a part of whose territory lies opposite the Imperial coast, and whose commerce covers the Pacific ocean and Japan seas; not less than five hundred large ships being engaged exclusively in those regions in pursuit of whales, the crews of many of which suffer for want of water and other refreshments; and it would seem nothing more than common humanity to receive those who may seek shelter in the ports of Japan with kindness and hospitality.

The government of China has derived much benefit from its treaty with the United States. The purchase of teas by the Americans during the present year will amount to three million six hundred thousand (3,600,000) taels, and of raw and manufactured silks to nearly three millions (3,000,000) of taels.

Nearly thirty thousand subjects of the Emperor of China have visited America, where they have been kindly received, and permitted by the American laws to engage in whatever occupation best suited them. They have also been allowed to erect temples, and to enjoy in all freedom their religious rites. All have accumulated money, and some have returned to China, after a short absence, with sums varying from 300 to 10,000 taels.

I have adverted to these facts merely to show the advantages that would grow out of such a treaty as I now propose, and to remark again that some amicable arrangement between the two nations has become positively necessary, and for reasons already explained.

Indeed, I shall not dare to return to the United States without carrying with me satisfactory responses to all the proposals of the President, and I must remain until such are placed in my possession.

With the most profound respect,

M. C. Perry

Commander-in-chief U.S. Naval Forces East India, China, and Japan seas, and Special Ambassador to Japan.

His Highness Hayashi-Daigaku-No-Kami, &c., &c.

On Thursday, March 9, Kura-Kawa-Kahie, the prefect, representing the Emperor, and the chief interpreter Yenoske, came on board the *Powhatan* with a copy of the Emperor's reply to the President's letter, duly certified and signed by the four commissioners.

Captain Adams asked Yenoske what parts of Japan would be open to trade and also stated that five years was too long to wait. He said that the commodore would never submit to having a place like Dezima (Nagasaki) set aside for American use.

The following is the treaty as agreed upon:

The United States of America and the Empire of Japan, desiring to establish firm, lasting, and sincere friendship between the two nations, have resolved to fix, in a manner clear and positive, by means of a treaty or general convention of peace and amity, the rules which shall in future be mutually observed in the intercourse of their respective countries; for which most desirable object the President of the United States has conferred full powers on his commissioner, Matthew Calbraith Perry, special ambassador of the United States to Japan; and the august sovereign of Japan has given similar full powers to his commissioners, Hayashi-Daigaku-No-Kami, Ido, Prince of Tsus-Sima, Izawa, Prince of Mimasaki, and Udono, member of the Board of Revenue.

And the said commissioners, after having exchanged their said full powers, and duly considered the premises, have agreed to the following articles:

Article I.

There shall be a perfect, permanent, and universal peace, and a sincere and cordial amity, between the United States of America, on the one part, and the Empire of Japan on the other, and between their people, respectively, without exception of persons or places.

Article II.

The port of Simoda, in the principality of Idzu, and the port of Hakodadi, in the principality of Matsmai, are granted by the Japanese as ports for the reception of American ships, where they can be supplied with wood, water, provisions, and coal, and other articles their necessities may require, as far as the Japanese have them. The time for opening the first named port is immediately on signing this treaty; the last named port is to be opened immediately after the same day in the ensuing Japanese year.

Note:—A tariff of prices shall be given by the Japanese officers of the things which they can furnish, payment for which shall be made in gold and silver coin.

Article III.

Whenever ships of the United States are thrown or wrecked on the coast of Japan, the Japanese vessels will assist them, and carry their crews to Simoda or Hakodadi, and hand them over to their countrymen appointed to receive them. Whatever articles the shipwrecked men may have preserved shall likewise be restored, and the expenses incurred in the rescue and support of Americans and Japanese who may thus be thrown upon the shores of either nation are not to be refunded.

Article IV.

Those shipwrecked persons and other citizens of the United States shall be free as in other countries, and not subjected to confinement, but shall be amenable to just laws.

Article V.

Shipwrecked men, and other citizens of the United States, temporarily living at Simoda and Hakodadi, shall not be subject to such restrictions and confinement as the Dutch and Chinese are at Nagasaki; but shall be free at Simoda to go where they please within the limits of seven Japanese miles (or ri) from a small island in the harbor of Simoda, marked on the accompanying chart, hereto appended; and shall in like manner be free to go where they please at Hakodadi, within limits to be defined after the visit of the United States squadron to that place.

Article VI.

If there be any other sort of goods wanted, or any business which shall require to be arranged, there shall be careful deliberation between the parties in order to settle such matters.

Article VII.

It is agreed that ships of the United States resorting to the ports open to them shall be permitted to exchange gold and silver coin and articles of goods for other articles of goods, under such regulations as shall be temporarily established by the Japanese government for that purpose. It is stipulated, however, that the ships of the United States shall be permitted to carry away whatever articles they are unwilling to exchange.

Article VIII.

Wood, water, provisions, coal, and goods required, shall only be procured through the agency of Japanese officers appointed for that purpose, and in no other manner.

Article IX.

It is agreed, that if, at any future day, the government of Japan shall grant to any other nation or nations privileges and advantages which are not herein granted to the United States and the citizens thereof, that these same privileges and advantages shall be granted likewise to the United States and to the citizens thereof without any consultation or delay.

Article X.

Ships of the United States shall be permitted to resort to no other ports in Japan but Simoda and Hakodadi, unless in distress or forced by stress of weather.

Article XI.

There shall be appointed by the government of the United States consuls or agents to reside in Simoda at any time after the expiration of eighteen months from the date of the signing of this treaty; provided that either of the two governments deem such arrangement necessary.

Article XII.

The present convention, having been concluded and duly signed, shall be obligatory, and faithfully observed by the United States of America and Japan, and by the citizens and subjects of each respective power; and it is to be ratified and approved by the President of the United States, by and with the advice and consent of the Senate thereof, and by the august Sovereign of Japan, and the ratification shall be exchanged within eighteen months from the date of the signature thereof, or sooner if practicable.

In faith whereof, we, the respective plenipotentiaries of the United States of America and the Empire of Japan, aforesaid, have signed and sealed these presents.

Done at Kanagawa, this thirty-first day of March, in the year of our Lord Jesus Christ one thousand eight hundred and fifty-four, and of Kayei the seventh year, third month, and third day.

It was Captain H. A. Adams who was dispatched on the *Saratoga* on April 4, 1854, to carry the proposed treaty to the United States. He arrived in Washington on July 12, after a journey of three months and eight days. The treaty was soon approved by the President and ratified by the Senate, and Captain Adams was again dispatched to Japan, leaving from New York on September 30, 1854, and proceeding directly to Japan. He arrived at Shimoda on January 26, 1855, carrying with him the ratified copy of the treaty, which both sides were in agreement with. The exchanges of the treaty were formally made on February 21, 1855, following the official signing of the agreement by the Emperor and the Supreme Council. As soon as the formalities were concluded, the *Powhatan* displayed the Japanese flag at her foremast, and fired a seventeen-gun salute.

On April 23, 1855, Commodore Perry arrived at the Brooklyn Navy Yard on board the *Mississippi*. The next day the commodore ordered that his flag be hauled down, thus formally concluding the East India Squadron's expedition to Japan.

This detailed account of Commodore Perry's negotiations with Japan, including his initial landing at Loo Choo and his arrival at Yedo Bay, has been given as a preliminary to pointing out some important facts concerning the story of Manjiro. Many historians have cited Manjiro as an interpreter during the negotiations between the Americans and the Japanese in 1854. However, a close examination of the facts of the East India Squadron's expedition to Japan, as compared to the facts of Manjiro's life, brings this theory into question.

First, Manjiro was but fourteen years of age when he was shipwrecked, and had received no schooling of any kind. Thus it is reasonable to assume that in 1854 he could neither read nor write the Japanese language.

Second, Captain Whitfield took Manjiro to America and afforded him a basic American education—meaning that he learned to read and write only in English.

Third, Commodore Perry had in his employ Chinese and

Dutch interpreters, Dr. Wells Williams and A. L. C. Portman, while the Japanese had in their service Moryama Yenoske and Hori Tatsnoske, who were able to read and write in Chinese and Dutch, respectively. All communications between Commodore Perry and the Japanese government were written in either Chinese or Dutch, or in both. Therefore, it can be reasonably surmised that Manjiro was not needed as an interpreter.

It may be, however, that he was shown some of the documents exchanged between the Japanese and the Americans, though he would have been unable to read them. He may also have been questioned further on some points, with the thought of trapping him into admission of complicity with the Americans. Manjiro himself later said that he had been in Yedo at the time of Perry's visit but offered no evidence that he had had any knowledge of the mission of the Americans.

The obvious conclusion, therefore, is that Manjiro was not, in fact, an interpreter but may have been used by the Tokugawa Bakufu as a resource in attempts to clarify some points of confusion.

12

The Episode of
the Kanrin-Maru

Throughout the negotiations between Commodore Perry and the representatives of the Tokugawa, Manjiro remained in Yedo at the residence of Lord Egawa Tarozaemon. He had little time to himself, as the questioning was almost continuous. No matter how hard he was pressed, Manjiro was always interesting and informative on a range of subjects. He was always willing to offer his own views and theories on matters regarding the Americans. The lord was quite impressed with Manjiro's conduct and attitude under the stress of questioning, and became his close supporter and protector.

Lord Tarozaemon soon came to feel that this important young man should not be denied the companionship of a woman. He arranged for his ward to meet a seventeen-year-old woman named Tetsu, the young daughter of a samurai fencing-school master. Although he found Tetsu quite pretty, Manjiro felt that an American-style marriage might suit him better. He thought he would prefer to choose his own wife. At that time, the accepted practice in Japan was for a young man's wife to be selected for him by a third party, and the high and influential Egawa therefore felt free to disregard Manjiro's preference. Tetsu was brought to the great Egawa mansion several times so that she and Manjiro could become acquainted. Finally, after much encouragement, a wedding ceremony was arranged. After the ceremony in 1854 (exact date unknown), the couple resided in the great mansion of Lord Tarozaemon.

Despite the circumstances of the marriage, Manjiro became quite contented and happy after marrying Tetsu. Their first child, a girl whom they named "Suzu," was born within the first year of their marriage. During a visit with his mother in Nakanohama, Manjiro attempted to persuade her to come

Manjiro's first wife, Tetsu. Circa 1860. (Courtesy Millicent Library, Fairhaven, Massachusetts)

and live with them, but Shio could not agree to leave her home to live in the great city, being unaccustomed to city life. The better times that Manjiro was enjoying, however, were soon interrupted by grief. Lord Egawa Tarozaemon died in 1855, leaving Manjiro again at the mercy of the Bakufu. Though mindful that many of those in high places were not as tolerant and understanding as was his friend Tarozaemon, and though distrustful eyes watched his every move, he persevered. As previously mentioned, Lord Tarozaemon had been Manjiro's lord protector. Following his death, Manjiro was doubly careful about whom he spoke with, whom he associated with, and what he said. Mistrust of Manjiro by many samurai was an ongoing factor in his life for many years.

On July 7, 1857, Tetsu gave birth to a second child, a boy whom she and Manjiro named "Toichiro." In 1858 Tetsu presented Manjiro with their third child, a daughter whom they named "Kyo."

Though under suspicion, Manjiro reaped acclaim and made progress, continuing to broaden the scope of his importance within the Bakufu regime. As before, he was usually able to convince those who at first were distant from him that the seemingly unbelievable stories he told were really true.

One of the official duties assigned to him by Lord Tarozaemon in 1855 was to make surveys and plot courses along the coastal regions of Japan, as part of the process of preparing the country to receive deep-drafted foreign vessels. This step, forced upon the country by Commodore Perry, was followed by the lifting of the Tokugawa's ancient restrictions upon the size of Japanese vessels. Manjiro's revelations concerning the huge vessels of the West and their ability to sail for weeks and even months without the guidance of landfall were an influence in this regard.

Manjiro's American whaleboat, the *Adventurer,* was returned to him by the Bakufu in 1859, along with some of the other articles that had been confiscated earlier. He enjoyed telling others about how whaleboats were used in chasing whales. With the help of boatbuilders, and using the *Adventurer* as a model, he produced a good number of "banana boats," as they were commonly referred to by the Japanese, who found them strange-looking but intriguing.

In the months that followed the building of the whaleboats,

Manjiro was given additional projects and responsibilities. The Bakufu decided to construct a large, two-masted sailing ship, and placed Manjiro in the important position of overseeing its construction. However, the Tokugawa officials knew that the skills involved in sailing such a large vessel were complex and unknown to Japanese seamen. By this time, they were well aware of Manjiro's sailing skills. They decided to have him translate into Japanese the classic American sailing book, Nathaniel Bowditch's *The New American Practical Navigator*, which Manjiro had told them contained the secrets to sailing. Since the time of his release by the Tokugawa officials in 1853, Manjiro, in his thirst for knowledge, had studied hard, working to master both the reading and the writing of Japanese. Even so, while translating *The New American Practical Navigator* he required the assistance of scribes possessing greater expertise in the field of writing, as well as a number of calligraphers.

This unprecedented undertaking, which proved to be Manjiro's most noted accomplishment, was to consume approximately two years of painstaking work. He later noted that the laborious task had caused him to age by several years. He knew, however, that Japan's future success in dealing with other nations of the world would depend in part upon her ability to tap the vast reaches of the oceans.

Once the translation was done, the Bakufu organized a naval school, to train the many young, aspiring mariners of Japan. Now, thanks to Manjiro's knowledge and the vision of such leaders as Lord Egawa Tarozaemon, the young men of Japan had access to formal maritime training. So great was the need for navigational schooling that the Bakufu constructed several more schools in order to satisfy the demand.

The officials of the Bakufu were initially ecstatic. Manjiro himself had made two copies of the Bowditch work, and other copies had been made by his assistants. The Tokugawa government was certain that Japan would be capable of dealing with even the most knowledgeable of oceangoing nations.

As the thirst to acquire knowledge of the technology of navigation spread quickly through the nation, however, Japan's boatbuilding facilities and specialized maritime schools became unable to keep up with the demand. The shortage of teaching facilities was somewhat alleviated by the construction in Yedo (now Tokyo) of a modern school dedicated to the sole purpose of offering advanced naval training to the young men of the Empire. However, because an unexpectedly large number of enthusiastic young men had aspirations to be included in Japan's naval plans, there were not enough qualified instructors available to staff the school. Once again the Bakufu called upon Manjiro, this time for help in the training of navigators. He was appointed one of the chief instructors at the Gunkankyojujo Naval School at Tsukiji, near Tokyo Bay.

As Japan's world trade slowly expanded, and with the opening of her sealed harbors to foreigners, the formerly contented though downtrodden masses of Japanese people developed a new and challenging relationship with their government. No longer were they contented to conform obediently to the wishes of the Tokugawa. Instead, feelings of discontent and unrest spread across the empire. Resentment of the shogun and his bureaucratic Bakufu regime was evident everywhere. Reports were received of clashes between rival clans. Uprisings and riots were on the increase throughout the provinces. The shogun and his armies of samurai were unable to stem the rising tide of discontent. The once-stalwart grip of the Bakufu was weakening. The political climate of Japan was under siege by the Japanese people themselves.

Even during this unprecedented political and social unrest, Manjiro was yearning once again to see his mother's kind and loving face. The now-famous naval instructor from Shikoku Island respectfully requested to be temporarily relieved from his duties so that he could return to Nakanohama and visit his aging mother. In addition, he needed a rest, for he had been overworked by the Bakufu, and his health had suffered. He waited patiently for an answer. In the autumn of 1857, after much delay, word came that his request was granted. However, the time allowed was much less than he had hoped.

Manjiro traveled to his mother's home in Nakanohama with anticipation, and his journey was pleasant. As he traveled from village to village, he enjoyed the recognition he received from the peasants, especially the children. Throughout the journey, he was given the courtesies and acknowledgments due to a high-ranking lord or a respected samurai.

Manjiro and Shio were happy to be together again. He

proudly told her about his many accomplishments on behalf of the Bakufu in Yedo. He also reminisced about his involvement with the opening of Japanese ports to other nations. He talked about his role at the naval school and his rise to a degree of acclaim that was almost unbelievable for a man from such a low-class background. His mother was delighted to hear his tales and was proud of her successful son.

Manjiro thoroughly enjoyed his much-needed rest from the demands of his position. When it was time to return to his duties and responsibilities in Yedo, he said a warm goodbye to his mother, fearful that he might never again have the opportunity to look upon her face.

Arriving back in the capital city, he was astounded to learn of the death of yet another supporter and good friend, Lord Abe Ise-No-Kami, the Premier. It was Egawa Tarozaemon and Lord Abe together who had been chiefly responsible for Manjiro's rise to an important position in the government. Though he was despondent, he resumed his duties at the naval school. Soon he was again overwhelmed by his burdensome workload.

In 1858, Manjiro was ordered by the Bakufu to report without delay to the port city of Hakodate, to assume new duties as instructor of whaling in the government school. He arrived in Hakodate sometime in November of that year. This assignment pleased Manjiro more than any other he had received, because it allowed him to return to whaling, the occupation he had chosen in his youth. Stories of his vast knowledge of whaling had preceded him to Hakodate, and he was welcomed with great enthusiasm. It was widely known that no man in Japan was more knowledgeable about deep-draft whaling than was Manjiro from Nakanohama.

His first goal was to encourage the development of a greater interest in whaling among higher government officials. Soon his tireless efforts began to show results. In 1859, the Bakufu informed the government office in Hakodate that it had decided to entertain Manjiro's suggestions and would pursue whaling on a commercial basis. The Tokugawa shogunate had recently received a large schooner named the *Kimigata I* as a gift from the Russian government, to commemorate the friendship between the two governments. The Bakufu ordered Manjiro to make whatever adjustments were necessary to prepare this vessel for the pursuit of whales.

Feeling that his dreams had come true, Manjiro immediately began to refurbish the *Kimigata I* in the style of an American whaler, painting the hull black and adding the necessary equipment, with the exception of a tryworks, or rendering plant. The Japanese took whales for eating (whereas the Americans took whales for their oil) and therefore had no need to build a tryworks. After the refurbishment was finished, the schooner could easily have been taken for an American ship, when observed from a distance.

Manjiro's big moment came late in 1859, when he sailed as the ship's master in the newly refurbished whaleship. He was anxious to try out the results of his efforts. Many Japanese officials were at dockside when the large vessel quietly slipped out of her berth and set a course for the deep, open sea, where whales were active. Before long, however, there were unexpected setbacks. The worst of these was a strong tempest, which arose suddenly. Howling gale-force winds attacked the Japanese whaler and drove it off course.

Responding to Manjiro's every command, the crew worked desperately to save their ship. When they were unable to bring the vessel under control, Nakahama ordered the masts to be cut down. This decision proved to be a sound one, as it enabled him to bring the ship under control and prevent it from being torn apart. Though ravaged, the ship was able to limp back to the port of Shimoda. Manjiro once again had shown his determination and courage.

While the ship was undergoing repairs, Manjiro received word that the Bakufu required his immediate return to Yedo for a more pressing assignment. Though dejected by this news, Manjiro had no say in the matter; he reluctantly reported to the government office in the capital city. He was informed that a meeting had taken place between the shogunate and the first American Consul General to Japan, Townsend Harris (1804–1878), who had arrived in Japan some months before. The Treaty of Amity and Commerce between Japan and the United States had been agreed upon, and an official delegation was being chosen by the Tokugawa government to visit Washington, D.C., for the actual signing of the covenant. Because of Manjiro's experience with and knowledge of the Americans and their ways, he had been selected as a member of the Tokugawa delegation. Among the duties of the Honorable Navigator-Teacher would be assisting the officials of the delegation in the capacity of interpreter and clarifying points related to American customs and courtesies and to his experience in global navigation.

The U.S. government, as a gesture of goodwill, offered the steam-powered frigate *Powhatan*, which had been the flagship of Commodore Matthew C. Perry when he visited Uraga in 1854, to transport the Japanese envoys to the United States. When this impressive-looking, steam-powered vessel arrived in Yedo, commanded by flag officer Commodore Josiah Tatnall and Captain George F. Pearson, it received an exhilarating welcome from the Japanese.

The Tokugawa, in a countermove intended to impress the American leadership, had assigned an escort vessel to accompany the *Powhatan*. The ship chosen for this duty was the 300-ton sailing ship *Kanrin-Maru* (also referred to as the *Candin Murro*). The 219-foot (718.5-meter) clipper ship, which had been built for the Japanese in the Netherlands, had recently been acquired from the Dutch. The ship was equipped with a small steam engine designed to be used solely for maneuvering the large vessel in close quarters. The Japanese appointed Katsu Rintaru (also known as "Katsu-Awa"), who had recently completed extensive navigation courses at the Bakufu naval school, as the captain of their prized ship.

The highest-ranking government officer who was to travel on the *Kanrin-Maru* was Admiral Kimura, Lord of Settsu-No-Kami. The Bakufu, to show evidence of Japan's sincerity with respect to the Treaty of Amity, volunteered to transport an American naval officer, Captain John Mercer Brooke of the U.S. schooner *Fenimore Cooper*, which had been shipwrecked in Japanese territorial waters of Yedo Bay earlier in 1859 while surveying. Brooke, who held the rank of lieutenant, and eleven other members of the *Fenimore Cooper*'s crew were to return to the United States aboard the *Kanrin-Maru*.

The plan was that the American officers were to assist the Japanese captain if needed. Brooke possessed much expertise and had had vast experience in sailing. Captain Katsu was not pleased by this plan but accepted his orders without comment. He felt that it was not necessary to have an American officer on board, seemingly waiting for the Japanese captain and crew to falter. Katsu was confident that the Japanese were as well qualified to navigate the oceans as anyone.

According to John Brooke's personal journal, the Americans on board the Japanese ship instructed their counterparts in the proper use of small arms before the departure of the *Kanrin-Maru,* as it lay at anchor in the Harbor of Uraga. Brooke later noted that Manjiro read to the ship's captain and the Japanese Admiral Kimura an account of the battles of the Mexican War (1846–1848). Tales of the war, including the brilliant march of General Zachary Taylor (1785–1850), were very interesting to the high-ranking Japanese officer. The admiral asked Lieutenant Brooke whether he would be able to purchase a vessel while in San Francisco. Brooke advised against that idea and suggested that the admiral consult with the Secretary of the Navy in Washington about having a ship built in New York for the Japanese. Lieutenant Brooke also noted in his journal that he was astonished by the intelligence of the Japanese officers.

On the morning of February 9, 1860, the winds over Uraga freshened from the north, accompanied by a low cloud cover. The *Kanrin-Maru* was scheduled to sail on the following day, in conjunction with the *Powhatan*'s departure from Yokohama. Lieutenant Brooke wrote in his journal that the decks of the *Kanrin-Maru* were leaking badly and that caulking crews were busily repairing them. He noted that the Japanese officers did not wear any particular uniform, and went on to write:

> Manjiro is certainly one of the most remarkable men I ever saw. He has translated Bowditch into the Japanese language. Manjiro is an adventurous character. I shall get the principal incidents of his life from him. He is very communicative and I am satisfied that he has had more to do with the opening of Japan than any other man living. This morning he requested me to explain the object of making observations of wet and dry bulb thermometers which I did to his satisfaction. I anticipate much pleasure in teaching him when we have leisure. Manjiro offered to accompany Mr. Kern and myself on shore if we wished to go. The original galley of the ship has been removed and another adapted to Japanese cooking of rice substituted. We employ braziers for our cooking purposes. The captain is better today. He spells his name "Cats lin-taro."
>
> EVENING.   The captain went on shore this afternoon to expedite the watering party. He seemed to apprehend that we would not get off tomorrow. But this evening Manjiro says we may start between 8 and 10 o'clock tomorrow.

On the morning of February 10, 1860, the *Powhatan* left her berth in Yokohama Harbor, carrying the Japanese embassy, which included the first ambassador, Shimmi Buzen-No-Kami Masaaki. The second deputy ambassador was Muragaki Awaji-No-Kami Norimasa, and the third was Censor Oguri Bungo-No-Kami Tadayori. She was soon joined by the *Kanrin-Maru,* which, besides serving as escort ship and transporting the American sailors, carried some of the baggage of the official party (including that of the aides).

When they reached the open sea, the two ships began to encounter heavy weather. The damaging winds (probably a typhoon) and violent surf soon began to take a toll on the *Powhatan.* Captain Pearson decided to make for the port of Honolulu instead of sailing directly to San Francisco as planned, so as to make the necessary repairs. The *Powhatan* reached Honolulu on March 5, 1860.

Meanwhile, the *Kanrin-Maru* was battling to maintain her projected heading. Commander Katsu had been reported ill prior to their departure from Japan, and had been unable to overcome his illness. He was no longer capable of conducting his duties properly, and rather than risking taking any action which might be misinterpreted as a sign of incompetence, especially in view of the extreme weather, he summoned Lieutenant Brooke and Manjiro to his quarters and entrusted them with the responsibility for sailing the ship, under the command of an acting captain named Suzufuji Yujiro. Lieutenant Brooke was put in charge of sailing, while Manjiro was chosen to assist as navigator.

Nakahama accepted his appointment as navigator and reported at once to the quarterdeck. Lieutenant Brooke and Manjiro worked together to assess what action should be taken to save the ship. As they deliberated, the violent winds continued.

The crewman were ordered aloft to secure the topsails. At first they were unsuccessful, but after several attempts, they were able to make fast the sails to the mastheads. This allowed Lieutenant Brooke to bring the ship under control, despite heavy damage that the ship's rigging had sustained. Utilizing all their nautical skills, Lieutenant Brooke and Manjiro were finally able to bring the ship back on course. Their decisive and timely actions were later hailed as acts which could only have been achieved by persons thoroughly knowledgeable in navigation techniques and with a full understanding of the behavior of the seas. During the entire storm, Captain Katsu was confined to his cabin.

The *Kanrin-Maru* reached San Francisco after a voyage of thirty-seven days, somewhat disarranged by her harrowing experience. By this time, Captain Katsu was well enough to resume command of his vessel. Manjiro had become the first Japanese to successfully navigate a ship across the vast Pacific Ocean. He guided the damaged vessel to the anchorage, where she was greeted with much fanfare. The *Kanrin-Maru* was docked at nearby Mare Island, where her damage could be assessed and needed repairs made, prior to her return to Japan.

Manjiro waited anxiously for the arrival of the official delegation. The *Powhatan* entered port several days after the *Kanrin-Maru*. She had left Honolulu on March 18, 1860, after having been repaired. On March 30, 1860, the following article appeared in the *Daily Alta*, a newspaper published in San Francisco.

Daily Alta, California

San Francisco, Friday March 30, 1860

Arrival of the Japanese Embassy, the U.S. Steamer *Powhatan*, flag officer Tarnall, arrived at this port yesterday morning from Kanaghawa via Honolulu, having on board the Japanese Embassy, consisting of seventy—viz: four ambassadors, eighteen attached of the Embassy, and fifty servants and attendants. The names of the principals and full details in relation to them, will be found in our last evening's edition (first page) where the interesting letter of our Honolulu correspondent is mainly devoted to them. The *Powhatan* is 4½ days from Kanaghawa via Honolulu. Her destination will be found under the usual head. She was ten days at Honolulu where the commander put in at the wish of the Japanese, who were exceedingly desirous of seeing the place. There they were received with general courtesies, and of course presented to their Majesties the Hawaiian King and Queen.

Visit to the *Powhatan*

We are indebted to Captain Pease, of the U.S. Revenue Cutter *William L. Marcy*, for his kindness in furnishing his boat in which we visited the *Powhatan* shortly after she anchored off

Vallejo Street Wharf. The ship looks well and though just from
sea, was as neat and trim as though she had been in port a week.
We were courteously shown over her by Lieutenant Treachard.
The Japanese occupy a large space on board—two rows of
houses having been constructed on either side of the quarterdeck for them. Their habits are represented to have been orderly, and their conduct on the passage that of guests. The
officers of the ship said that they could not have had less trouble
with the same number of any other nation. They have been
carefully observant of everything on board from the day of their
starting. Their draughtsmen have taken copies of the machinery, and notes have been made of everything that has transpired
on board by a censor, or secretary, who has also had a copy
made, which with what has transpired up to their departure
hence, will be forwarded to the Emperor by the next vessel
leaving for Japan. A journal was also left at Honolulu for the
same destination. A number of them have made considerable
progress in English. There are two or three interpreters with the
Embassy, but we hear that none of them can compare with
Captain Manjiro of the *Kandinmarro*, who may perhaps accompany the ambassadors to Washington. The appearance of these
visitors differ in few if any, particulars, from that of the admiral
and his crew. The dress of the ambassadors may be a little
richer, but in other respects they are identical. Those who have
seen these people of the *Kandinmarro* have a perfect idea of the
newer comers. Their food on board has been mostly rice, for the
cooking of which they have had place of their own and the
culinary operations have been performed by native cooks. They
stood the passage very well, few of them having suffered much
with sea sickness. Lieutenant Treachard represents the weather
as having been unusually rough and affording not only an opportunity of teaching the Japanese, but of the ship herself. The
three principal dignitaries on board are hereditary princes, or
rulers of provinces in their native land.

The Japanese embassy received guided tours around San
Francisco, wearing their strange-looking silk finery. Manjiro,
with his experience and knowledge of American manners,
proved to be of great service.

The Japanese delegation were escorted to the main ballroom of a large, magnificent international hotel which had
been chosen for two official parties. At the first of these parties, which was held on the evening of April 2, 1860, Manjiro
proudly introduced members of the Japanese embassy to the
Americans, taking special care to pronounce each name correctly.

The Japanese dignitaries watched with great interest the exercise of courtesies and protocol when George Wallace, the secretary and representative of Downey, Governor of California, was introduced. The Japanese were appalled to see that Wallace entered the ballroom unattended, for the Japanese custom was that high officials never appeared in public without armed samurai as escorts. The Americans were impressed by the way the Oriental party conducted themselves throughout this first ceremonious occasion.

The next day (April 3), the representatives from Japan were given an overview of the city, including many places their hosts thought would be of interest to them. This event was written up in the *San Francisco Herald* on April 4, 1860, as follows:

The Japanese in Town

A number of our Japanese visitors yesterday amused themselves by promenading around town, the weather being beautifully bright and the streets dry enough to permit of pleasant locomotion. Quite a number of fine stores were inspected by the strangers, who openly expressed admiration of many things they beheld. One of them astonished a stationer not a little by asking, in excellent English, for a copy of *Webster's Dictionary*, with the value of which he appeared quite familiar. It is said that the interpreter of the Admiral commanding the *Candinmurro*, had quite a large school for his young countrymen in Kanagawa, to whom he was teaching the English language when called away upon his present mission. The Japanese are of lighter mould than our people, being neither so tall nor so thickly set; but their features are rather fine, the forehead high, for the most part, with sufficient breadth to denote decision, the eyes black and observing, the face rather delicate and nose thin, spirited and aquiline. The chin is sharp pointed but by no means feminine. Their average height is about five feet seven or eight inches, none of those whom we have seen exceeding five feet ten inches. It is nevertheless true, that in Japan they breed or cultivate a race of athletes, or gladiators who are of monstroua [sic] proportions, and who are reported to be remarkably powerful, but altogether animal. The better class of Japanese regard those creatures with about the same degree of respect we pay to a ferocious bull dog. The report of Commodore Perry's Expedition gives pretty full details of Japanese public displays, in which these athletes play prominent parts. The distinction between the Japanese and Chinese is very marked, the former being a superior race, intellectually. It would be difficult to set any limit to the exceeding benefit that must result to California should the amicable disposition now manifested toward us by the Japanese be carried to fruition. We must, however, remember that they are suspicious of foreign nations, and not without reason, and should endeavor to conciliate their kindest feelings.

City Intelligence

GOV. DOWNEY AND THE JAPANESE—Governor Downey was in the city Monday, and during the morning sent his private Secretary, Mr. George Wallace, with a courteous invitation to the Japanese Ambassadors to visit the Capital of the State, where he (Gov. Downey) would be happy to entertain them at the Executive mansion. The Ambassadors replied that their engagements and the necessity of taking an early departure from California en route for Washington forced them, much to their regret, to decline the invitation. The absence of the Governor at the public reception given on Monday was in compliance with the rules of etiquette and the necessity of maintaining the respect due the Chief Magistrate of the State. The municipal authorities of the city were the parties who entertained and welcomed the Ambassadors, and of course the Governor, as the representative of the State, could not be present on such an occasion.

During the next several days, the Japanese envoys were taken on an extended and gracious tour in and around the city of San Francisco. One place in particular which was of great interest to the Embassy officials was noted in the April 4, 1860, edition of a San Francisco newspaper, as follows:

Daily Evening Bulletin,

Local Matters

THE JAPANESE—A deputation of the Japanese, in company with some of the officers of the *Powhatan* visited the Mint this morning.

Yesterday the Captain of the *Candinmarro* was in town, looking up its lions. On Montgomery street he and his men had a tail full 40 yards in length of curious Americans, many of whom looked very intelligent, and wore dresses of great varieties and pattern, but mostly of dark or dingy colors.

The *Candinmarro* expects to return to Japan in 2 or 3 weeks at the farthest.

The *Powhatan* will be here tomorrow, and probably will sail for Panama in a day or two thereafter.

After nearly a week of tiring receptions and official functions, the delegation from Japan were escorted aboard the

Powhatan, to begin the second leg of their long journey to Washington. The *Powhatan* sailed from San Francisco to Panama, where the Japanese were transferred to a steam train that carried them across Panama to the coast of the Atlantic. There, they were taken aboard another American warship, the *Roanoke.* As the *Roanoke* sailed north along the East Coast, the visiting dignitaries were afforded every courtesy.

Before the Japanese party left San Francisco, the chief of the Japanese delegation had ordered Manjiro to remain aboard the *Kanrin-Maru* while it was being repaired, explaining that because Manjiro was familiar with such matters, he should be responsible for overseeing the necessary repairs. In truth, however, a secret letter had been circulating among the samurai which, in essence, warned that Manjiro was an American spy and should not be trusted. It was for this reason that he was not allowed to accompany the delegation to Washington. Manjiro was not at that time made aware of the letter that was being passed from samurai to samurai. (However, a copy of the letter was found among his personal papers following his death in 1898.)

While overseeing the repairs to the *Kanrin-Maru,* Manjiro was also able to take some time for himself in San Francisco. He found the city almost unrecognizable, it had changed so much. Gone were the dust-strewn roadways, which had been replaced by stone paving blocks. The crowds of shanties and huts had also vanished, giving way to more formidable structures made of stone and brick. He purchased a number of articles to take back to Japan, including a daguerreotype camera. His plan was to take a picture of his mother so that he could always have with him her likeness, to help him remember her. He also purchased an early-model sewing machine, planning to introduce Japan to the concept of sewing apparel by machine rather than by hand.

When the Japanese embassy arrived in the U.S. capital, wearing their Oriental silks and carrying their traditional swords, they were greeted with a stupendous welcoming celebration. Their clothing drew much attention, and they thoroughly enjoyed the warm reception they received.

The climax of the visit occurred at the signing of the Treaty of Amity and Commerce. President James Buchanan (1857–1861) extended greetings on behalf of the American people. He expressed his profound gratitude to the leaders of Japan

for their foresight and wisdom in reaching this notable agreement with the people of the United States of America.

After the treaty was signed, the delegation proceeded to
New York, where they were entertained in grand fashion.
Then it was time to return to Japan. Boarding the *Roanoke*,
the delegates began their voyage back to San Francisco,
where the *Kanrin-Maru* and Manjiro were waiting for them.
When the high-ranking envoys arrived, Manjiro told them
that three of the Japanese crewmen of the *Kanrin-Maru* had
died and were buried in Laurel Hill Cemetery. (Some years
later, they were reinterred in the Japanese cemetery in San
Mateo, California.)

Their mission completed, the Japanese embassy sailed from
San Francisco aboard the *Kanrin-Maru*. A stopover at
Honolulu for supplies allowed Manjiro to go ashore to visit old
friends and acquaintances. It also revived memories of his
first arrival in Honolulu and of the Japanese friends he had
left behind when he went to America for the first time. He
thought too of the time he had spent in Hawaii while serving
on the *Franklin*, and of the help he and his shipwrecked
companions had received from the Reverend Samuel C.
Damon prior to their departure on the *Sarah Boyd*.

Reverend Damon was no longer living in the same place,
but after some searching, Manjiro found his new home.
Damon stared in astonishment at his young friend, who was
now recognized as Captain Manjiro of the Imperial Navy (an
unofficial rank he acquired because of his heroic actions while
on board the *Kanrin-Maru*). The two had a warm reunion,
and Manjiro invited the Reverend Damon to visit him on the
Kanrin-Maru. The Reverend Damon later published in his
newspaper an account of his conversations with Manjiro, as
follows:

The Friend

June 1, 1860

[Manjiro was quoted as having said,] "At the end of two and a
half years, we were allowed to proceed to our homes, and, so far
as I know, all my companions safely reached their homes, and
were welcomed by their friends. I went to Xicoco; after thirteen
years' absence, I was joyfully welcomed by my mother. My
father died before I left home. My mother had mourned for me

as dead; under that impression, she had built for me a tomb. I remained at home three days and three nights. I was then removed, with my good boat *Adventurer* to Yeddo, where I was promoted to the rank of an Imperial officer, wearing two swords! For several years I was employed in Yeddo. I was for a long time occupied in translating 'Bowditch's Navigator;' it was a long and laborious work. I have built many boats after the model of the American whaleboat *Adventurer*.—My old whale-boat is now in a government store-house at the city of Yeddo. I have been very often consulted respecting questions relating to Americans and foreigners. I have had charge of some of the presents which were brought by Commodore Perry. I was in Yeddo at the period of Commodore Perry's visit, but was not introduced to any of the officers of the expedition. I am thirty-six years old. I am married, and have three children. I am captain in the navy, and at home, have charge of a vessel."

By no means were these all the interesting statements which he made, in answer to our many inquiries about Japan, its government, its religion, its institutions, its people, &c.

Since writing the above, we have returned the call, and been very kindly welcomed on board the *Candinmarrah,* and were introduced to the Admiral and Capt. Katslintarro. Our surprise and astonishment were great when Captain Mungero presented us a translation of Bowditch's great American work upon Navigation. The translation, with the logarithmic tables, had been made by Captain Mungero. He said it tried his patience, and made him grow old by about three years faster than he should! He remarked that about twenty copies had been made into Japanese, one of which was deposited in the Royal Palace. It had not yet been printed in Japanese style. The copy before us is most beautifully executed. It is surely a most creditable per-formance, and evidently shows that Captain Mungero is a man of decided ability. He is the first native of the Japanese Empire who navigated a vessel, out of sight of land, according to scien-tific principles. We hope, when our friend, Capt. Whitfield, of Fairhaven, reads this statement, he may feel rewarded for his trouble and expense in educating this Japanese sailor-boy. He speaks in the most grateful manner of those who befriended him, when a stranger in a strange land, and has left with us a letter and present, to be forwarded to his friend and benefactor, Capt. Whitfield. We could add much more, gathered during our pleasant interviews.

Captain Mungero returns to Japan, taking with him many curiosities and works of art, procured in San Francisco; among them a daguerreotype apparatus, for the purpose of taking the likeness of his mother, "and when that is done," he said, "it will be useless!"—a most beautiful instance of filial affection.

It is most gratifying to learn that the views we entertain and published nine years ago respecting Capt. Mungero, have been fully realized. He did return to his native land, and there acted no unimportant part in preparing the way for the opening of Japan to intercourse with foreign nations. The end is not yet. If we live a few years, other events equally worthy of record will have occurred. We shall anxiously await the development of the future.

Nine years ago, we wrote, "Success to Captain Mung, commanding the whaleboat *Adventurer*," but we now add, Success to Captain Mungero, of the Imperial Navy of Japan. Acting Interpreter of the *Candinmarrah*, and Translator of 'Bowditch's Navigator.' Long may he be spared to benefit his native land, to the interests, prosperity, civilization, and progress of which, he is most ardently devoted. His love for Japan is great.

"Cast thy bread upon the waters, for thou shalt find it after many days."

The letter to which Reverend Damon referred, from Manjiro to Captain Whitfield, is reproduced below.

Sandwich Islands, 1860

Captain William H. Whitfield.

My Honored friend—I am very happy to say that i had an opportunity to say to you a few lines. I am still living and hope you were the same blessing. i wish to meet you in this world once more. How happy we would be. Give my best respect to Mrs. and Miss Amelia Whitfield, i long to see them. Capt. you must not send your boys to the whaling business; you must send them to Japan, i will take care of him or them if you will. Let me know before send and I will make the arrangement for it.

Now I will let you know how am i arrived to my Native Country. You know that i have been to the Gold Mine; here stayed 4 month, average eight Dolls per day, beside expenses, from here i made my mind to get back and to see Dear Mother and also Shipped in one of the American Merchant men. In this vessel i arrived to Sandwich Island. I found our friend Mr. Damon and through his kindness bought a whale boat and put her into a Merchantman. this vessel was going to Shanghai in China.

It was January very cold that part of country; Time i went on shore south off Great Loo Choo it was gail with snow. The Capt. of vessel he wish me to stay with him and to go to China, but i refused it, because i wanted to see Mother. The boat is ready for me to get in, myself, Dennovo & Goyesman jump into the boat, parted with ship at 4 P.M. After ten hours hard pull we arrived lee of Island and anchored until morning. i went on shore amongst the Loo Choose, but i cannot understand their language, i have forgot all Japanese words. I stay here six months,

under care of the King of Loo Choo, waiting for Japanese junk
to come.

In the month of July get on board junk and went into the
Harbour of Nagashirki Island, off Kie-u-see-u, waiting to get
permition for 30 month before we get to our residence. After all
the things is properly regulated we were send to our residence.
It was great joy to Mother and all the relation. i have stay with
my mother only 3 day and night the Emperor called me to Jedo.
Now i became one emperian officer. At this time i am attached
this vessel.

This war steamer were send by Emperor of Japan to the
Compliment of the President of America. We went to San Francisco, California, and now homeward bound, at Sandwich to
touch Island to secure some coal and provition. I wish to send
the letter from San Francisco but so many Japanese eyes i can't.
i wrote this between passage from San Francisco to Island.
Excuse me many mistakes. i can write better after our arrived
Japan Jedo.

I wish for you to come to Japan. I will now lead my Dear
Friend to my house, now the port open to all nations. I found our
friend Samuel C. Damon. We was so happy each other I cannot
write it all. When I get home I will write better acct. I will send
to you sut of my clothe. It is not new, but only for remember me.

I remain your friend,

John Mungero

The Reverend Damon also wrote to Captain Whitfield,
after the departure of the *Kanrin-Maru*. His letter reads as
follows:

June 1860

Captain W. H. Whitfield

Dear Sir,

Accompanying this letter I forward to you a communication
from your protege, John Mung, the Japanese. You will be doubt-
less as much surprised to hear from him as I was to see him. I
have written out an account of his visit to Honolulu for the next
No. of "The Friend". This I shall send to you, and it will furnish
you the information which I am confident will be most interesting to you. He speaks of you with the most greatful feelings and
also of your family. He wished to learn all about your children.
I have taken the liberty to read the letter, which he left with me
for you, and also to retain a copy of the same. It is a very great
source of satisfaction to me to have seen him again. For years I
have striven to learn something about him, but I could not

obtain the least information. Judge then of my great surprise to have him come to my study, dressed like a Japanese official, with "his two swords".

He was very free and communicative, often called, and brought the captain of the steamer, who was a man of much intelligence. John has really become a man of importance in Japan. I could not state in print all he told me about his position, but let me say that it is my decided opinion that John Mung acted a most important part in opening Japan. The information which he furnished the Japanese Government was of immense importance. His translation of Bowditch's Navigation is most remarkable.

He left with me to be forwarded to you a suit of his Japanese costume! Unless I can send it by some gentleman going overland, I will forward the same by some New Bedford whaleship.

I have become so much interested in John that I want you to write me and tell me when and where you first found him for I am quite astonished at the ability which he displays.

I think when you write him you had better send your letter to my care, for we have frequent opportunities of sending letters to Japan. A vessel, the *Leo*, arrived from Japan today. Do you feel like paying a visit? He is placed in a position where he is constantly watched, in other words, there are "many eyes in Japan", so he says. The reason why he had not written us is that he could not get his letters out of the country. He told me that at the end of two years, or when Yedo was open to foreigners that he hoped I would visit Japan. He offered me the hospitality of his house.

Your honorable friends, the Diamonds, the Smiths, the Damons, the Harris, are all well.

Now I shall expect a letter from you and if you send one for John Mung, alias Captain Mungero, etc., I will send it to him by the very earliest opportunity.

Yours,

Sam C. Damon

P.S. Remember me to your fellow townsman, Captain S. Cox and family

Manjiro's letter and package and Damon's letter reached Fairhaven some months later, thanks to the kindness of a homeward-bound New Bedford whaleship.

When the Japanese vessel was ready to leave Honolulu, having been reprovisioned with fuel and supplies, Manjiro went to Damon's home to say goodbye. As usual at partings, the Imperial naval officer had to search for words to express

Manjiro's samurai sword, which he presented to the Reverend Damon in 1860. Circa 1870. (Courtesy Millicent Library, Fairhaven, Massachusetts)

his thankful feelings. He presented his own personal samurai sword to his friend Damon as a token of everlasting friendship. Even today, the sword is still a treasured artifact of the Damon family heirs. (It is in the possession of Dwight Damon of Honolulu, the great-great-grandson of Samuel C. Damon.)

The *Kanrin-Maru* arrived in Yedo, Japan, on June 24, 1860. An armed escort from the shogun greeted the embassy party, including Manjiro, and immediately escorted them to his palace for a report on their successful mission.

News of the return and success of the *Kanrin-Maru* soon swept throughout the capital city. The name "Nakahama Manjiro" was continuing its rise to importance. The poor, lowly son of a fisherman had successfully changed his destiny by becoming a powerful member of the Tokugawa.

13

Manjiro's Role in the Reconstruction of Japan

When the Japanese delegation to the United States returned to Japan on the *Kanrin-Maru* in June 1860, they learned that the unrest among their people had deepened and feelings against the Tokugawa Bakufu were running high. They also learned that some high authorities were having second thoughts about Japan's recently signed treaty with the United States. Despite general feeling of satisfaction with the opening of Japanese ports to foreigners, times were dangerous for those of high rank. An alarming number of officials of the Tokugawa had been accosted and harassed by roving gangs who advocated restoration of governmental power to Emperor Meiji.

It was Lord Chikamies, an ambassador with the Japanese mission, who reported on the success of the mission to the United States. The shogun expressed profound satisfaction with the report. He also warned the envoy to be alert for enemies of the government who might be working within the Bakufu, and talked about several uprisings. He cautioned against further relaxation of restrictions and said that opposition to the Tokugawa was spreading like a cancer from clan to clan.

Manjiro, though he was now acclaimed and held the title "Imperial Navigator," did not escape the "watching eyes" of the Bakufu. Shortly after his return on the *Kanrin-Maru,* he was invited aboard an American ship which had recently arrived in Yokohama. Because of this innocent visit, he was accused of secretly disclosing information to the Americans. Despite his plea of innocence, Manjiro was relieved of his duties as instructor at the naval school—an act that seemed to destroy all he had accomplished and that did dispel much of the goodwill that he had acquired through his work for the government.

Dejected, bewildered, and dismayed, he returned to his home after being informed of his discharge. Before long, however, his spirits were lifted by the arrival of a messenger who bore several gift packages from the Bakufu. Manjiro accepted the packages without questioning the meaning of the gesture. The gifts included several pieces of gold, two suits of clothing, and the most valuable prize of all, the honor of wearing the respected "crested dress." This mode of attire was symbolic of a ranking officer of the feudal system. Commoners prostrated themselves before officials dressed in the crested clothing. The gifts, as it turned out, were only tokens of recognition for his meritorious service with the recently returned mission.

In 1861, the samurai from Tosa province was recalled by the Bakufu, to serve as interpreter and adviser to a newly formed commission that was to take control of the Agasawara Islands (also known as the "Bonin Islands"). Commodore Matthew C. Perry, during his mission to Japan in 1853–1854, had proposed that the Bonin Islands become an open port where American ships, especially whaleships operating in that quarter of the world, could be reprovisioned and serviced.

The *Kanrin-Maru*, with Manjiro on board as interpreter, led the three smaller ships of the squadron. Their aim was to seize control of the disputed archipelagos. Manjiro was happy to be on the *Kanrin-Maru* again. During the short voyage from Japan to the Bonins, he stood on the weather deck, felt the biting sting of the salt spray on his face, and was pleasantly reminded of his friend Captain William H. Whitfield of Fairhaven, Massachusetts.

When the small squadron reached their destination, Peel Island, they saw an American flag flying in the breeze. The island governor, Nathaniel Savory, was told that the Japanese squadron planned to claim the Bonin Islands, in the name of the Japanese government. Savory's reaction was complacent. He was tired of being harassed by brawling, fun-seeking whalers, and admitted that he could not care less what flag flew over the island. A Japanese colony was immediately established on the island, and the squadron returned to Japan.

Shortly thereafter, the new American Consul General, Robert H. Pryor, delivered to Manjiro a letter from Captain Whitfield, which he had received from the Reverend Samuel C. Damon in Honolulu. Trembling with joy and excitement,

Manjiro carefully opened the sealed envelope and slowly
read the letter, which proved to be a timely one.

San Francisco
March 9, 1862

To the Friend I Have Not Seen for A Long Time:

I have missed you for such a long time and now the newly
appointed Minister offers to take a letter to you. If you care to
send a reply after receiving this letter I hope you will take the
same means which I am sure will bring your letter to me. I too
will send more letters to you.

My wife is well and "Aunt" is married. My son Marcellus is
thirteen years old now and grown to be as big as you were at the
time of your sailing on the *Howland* years ago. I have two
daughters, eleven and nine, both healthy and lovely.

The old gentlemen next door still praises your honesty and
good nature whenever he recalls the time you were at our home.

We are now trying to overcome a trouble in our country that
may lead to serious consequences. War causes a great loss of life
and wealth in any nation, but cannot always be avoided.

You must have become an important man by now. We are
looking forward to the time we can trade with your country, and
your people may come here and do business as ourselves. Why
don't you come? Bring the Japanese products for sale.

Your sincere friend,
(Signed) William Whitfield

Soon after his successful mission to the Bonin Islands, Manjiro was appointed captain of the *Ichiban-Maru*. The plan was
that he would make a whaling expedition in the vicinity of the
Bonin Islands, but this venture was short-lived. Soon after the
ship sailed, Japanese and Russian relations became strained
over some questionable boundary lines. The Japanese government decided that, rather than risking a confrontation with
Russian ships, which were known to be active in the region,
it would cease all activities near the controversial boundaries.
The *Ichiban-Maru* was recalled.

Manjiro resumed his teaching duties and also began offering private tutoring in the English language. For a short time,
it seemed that he would be able to enjoy a peaceful and
fulfilling existence with his family. It was during this period
that Manjiro and his wife Tetsu became parents for the third
time, with the birth late in 1862 of the baby girl whom, as
previously mentioned, they named "Kyo."

Soon after Kyo's birth, however, Japan was swept by an epidemic of measles, and the disease claimed Tetsu's life. Thus Manjiro echoed an aspect of experience of his American benefactor Captain Whitfield, in that each lost a wife in the prime of life. The loss was devastating for Manjiro, and he lapsed into a deep state of depression. Even so, he recognized that, besides his official duties, he now faced the prospect of raising his children alone. His loneliness nearly broke his heart, but he continued to struggle.

After the signing of the first treaty with the Americans in 1854, the Tokugawa regime became increasingly unstable, and the Bakufu's internal political affairs were becoming more and more unmanageable. Many samurai abandoned their daimyos and clans and roamed freely between major cities of the empire. They soon banded together and openly opposed the admission of foreigners to their country. These samurai, known as the "ronin," were committed to the goal of overthrowing the shogunate and returning Emperor Meiji to power. Their rallying cry was, "Revere the Emperor and expel the barbarians." Their countless acts of violence against the Bakufu became commonplace rather than exceptional. Many members of the Bakufu were fearful for their personal safety. Manjiro, however, was not one to concern himself with the politics of the day. He merely went about his duties.

In 1863, he was called upon for help in the building of a modern naval force. The Bakufu sent him to Kagoshima to help organize a training school. He later developed a similar school in the city of Kochi in his home province.

Japanese resentment of foreigners peaked in 1868 with the overthrow of the Tokugawa. The shogun was deposed and the Emperor returned to power, ushering in a new era called "Meiji." The army of ronin declined rapidly following the overthrow of the Tokugawa. The name of the capital city was changed from Yedo to Tokyo. During this period of change, the government assigned Manjiro to the prestigious post of instructor at the Kaisei-jo School, which eventually became the University of Tokyo. Although there are no records available to confirm an exact date, it is known that he was married for the second time, to a young maiden named Koto. They became parents of two sons, Seijiro and Keizaburo. However, this marriage was to be short-lived, for Koto and Manjiro separated soon after the birth of their second son.

The political face of Japan was changing, and a new mode of nationalization was beginning to prevail. It was necessary to formulate a policy of enforcement, so as to maintain order both within and outside the empire. The samurai were in a state of disarray, and thus a national army was unquestionably needed. The new army would be under the influence and control of Emperor Meiji rather than committed to any particular daimyo or clan. As Japan lacked experience in maintaining a national military force, she looked to the West for help. In 1870 the Japanese government formed a delegation to study the logistics involved in maintaining a contemporary army. Their mission was to travel to Europe to investigate firsthand the Franco-Prussian War (1870–1871), which was near resolution at the time. They were to observe such military techniques as battlefield strategies and deployment, as well as the scientific methods of maintaining an army. Manjiro was included in the delegation because of his knowledge of Western ways and behavior.

The delegation traveled first to San Francisco, where they boarded a train to New York. They were scheduled to have several meetings with U.S. government officials prior to their departure for Europe, and a five-day stay in New York was planned.

Manjiro could not help but think of the Whitfields, knowing that Fairhaven was only a short distance from New York by train. He asked for and received from the head of the delegation a two-day leave so that he could travel to Fairhaven to see his old friends. He knew that this might be his last opportunity to visit them, and he wanted to thank them once again for having rescued him and his friends, and for their many kindnesses. He traveled by train to Boston and then on to New Bedford.

In October 1870, before noon on a bright sunny day, Manjiro stepped off the train in New Bedford, not far from where he had come ashore twenty-seven years earlier. He was carrying a bag that contained some small gifts for his friends. The town gave a rather different impression from what he remembered, though he did immediately recognize the bridge over the Acushnet River, connecting New Bedford and Fairhaven.

The draw section of the bridge, which he had remembered many times since his departure on the *Stieglitz*, a lumber ship, in 1849, especially caught his attention. The many ships' masts in the harbor were another familiar sight.

Adjacent to the railroad station was a large stone building called the "Wamsutta Mill." He later learned that it was New Bedford's first cotton mill, the construction of which had been begun late in 1848 but had not been completed by the time of his departure in 1849. In this mill, cotton was processed into bed sheets and other fine fabrics. The Wamsutta Mill was in later years to become world-famous for its bedding goods. A number of similar structures could be seen along the river on the New Bedford side.

As Manjiro walked toward the New Bedford–Fairhaven crossing, located about half a mile south of the train station, he was surprised to note how much progress had been achieved since he was here last. As he crossed the bridge, his attention shifted to a protrusion of land on the Fairhaven side, known as "Poverty Point," which was where he had stayed, in the home of Captain Whitfield's Aunt Amelia (also called "Aunt Milly"), when he first arrived in Fairhaven in May 1843.

He continued east along the main thoroughfare to the turn-off that led to the peninsula known as "Sconticut Neck," where the Whitfield farmhouse was located. Manjiro didn't know the person who answered the door, and he was surprised to learn that the captain and his family had returned to 11 Cherry Street in Oxford Village—the same house where Captain Whitfield had been raised by Aunt Milly prior to his marriage to Albertina in 1843.

The sun was casting long shadows by the time Manjiro arrived at the Whitfield home. The captain himself answered the door. He was only momentarily taken aback at the sight of his former ward.

"If it is not John Mung!" he said, and extended his hand. Manjiro replied, "I have been looking forward to this for twenty years."

William Whitfield, appeared to have aged considerably, and indeed he was now seventy-five years old. Mung himself had attained the age of forty-three. Mrs. Whitfield, upon hearing the sound of Mung's voice, rushed into the room and embraced him. The exchange of conversation was brisk, as Captain and Mrs. Whitfield enlightened Mung on many subjects, including the marriage of Aunt Milly to Samuel S. Daggett of Edgartown, Martha's Vineyard, Massachusetts, in December 1857. Since the Daggetts had made the Vineyard their home, the captain and his wife had decided to live in the Cherry Street house, where the captain had lived as a young man. Whitfield also told Mung that his son Marcellus had attempted to learn whaling but, not finding it a compatible trade, had become an apprentice carpenter. Mung also told many stories to Captain Whitfield, the man to whom he was most beholden.

John Mung spent his last night in Fairhaven at the Whitfield's 11 Cherry Street home. He was never again to return to Massachusetts. On the following morning, as the sun peaked in the sky, William and Albertina Whitfield and their world-traveled stepson Mung uttered painful words of parting.

As he retraced his steps through Fairhaven, Mung made several stops along the way. He saw his tutor Jane Allen and her sister Charity and thanked them again for their help and support. As a remembrance, he gave them several small Japanese coins. He also visited his old friend and classmate Job Tripp, who resided at 38 Walnut Street, just south of the Unitarian Church on Washington Street.

John had only a brief time for these visits with old friends, for he had to hurry along to the train station. There he boarded the Boston-bound train to begin his return to New York to rejoin the Japanese delegation. When their business in New York was concluded, the envoys boarded a ship and sailed to Europe to continue their mission.

Manjiro's leg became ulcerated while he was in London, and he was unable to participate in the activities of the official party. Because of his illness, he was left in London when the envoys traveled on to Paris.

Upon the delegation's eventual return to Japan, the government discovered that Manjiro had asked for and received permission to depart from the delegation on a private endeavor. This was not considered acceptable, and both Manjiro and the head of the delegation were chastised and reprimanded. Manjiro was relieved of some of his official duties.

The ulceration that had begun in London proved to be a serious one, and Manjiro became unable to function effectively. The decline in health weakened his spirit as well as his body. He remained in near seclusion in his Tokyo home during his retirement years. No longer was Manjiro the sought-after teacher of Western technology.

While he was in retirement, Manjiro took as his third wife a woman named "Shige," who, as his second wife had done, presented him with two sons. These children, his fourth and fifth sons, were named "Nobuyoshi" and "Hidetoshi."

In 1879, the aging Manjiro received word of the death of his mother Shio. This dreadful news further depressed him.

In 1884, he was surprised to learn that the Reverend Damon had arrived in Tokyo. The reunion with his old friend from Honolulu raised the spirits of the old whaler Manjiro.

Damon later wrote the following passage about Manjiro:

> We are happy to state that our desire to locate Manjiro was fully gratified and we found our friend the father of a most promising family numbering four sons [sic] and one daughter. He presented us with photographs of his wife and interesting family. His oldest son is now a physician of much promise, and engaged in one of the government hospitals of southeastern Japan. Another son is an educated architect. He came with his sons from Tokio to Yokohama, to bid us farewell. Long shall we cherish the memory of our visit to Japan, but among the most pleasing incidents of that visit were the repeated interviews with Nakahama Manjiro, the wrecked sailor-boy, the successful adventurer in returning to his native land and the translator of Bowditch's Navigator. He informed us that he has in his possession a single copy of this translation, and we have a copy presented by him in 1860. No other copies are known to be in existence, all having been destroyed in the conflagration in Tokio, when some government buildings were burned with the archives of Japan.
>
> He is about sixty years of age, but not possessed of a large amount of this world's goods, being dependent upon his sons for support. We most sincerely wish the Japanese government might honor itself by honoring its old and faithful servant with a liberal pension. Long may he live and prosper.

On February 14, 1886, Captain William H. Whitfield passed away at his residence in Fairhaven, at the age of eighty-one years and three months. His obituary notice appeared in the February 20, 1886, edition of *The Fairhaven Star*.

Obituary

Capt. Wm. H. Whitfield, well known in this town and vicinity, died at his residence in Oxford Village last Sunday morning in his 82nd year, and our community loses one of its most honest and upright citizens. Capt. Whitfield had made many friends by his conscientiousness in all business matters and upon the announcement of his death in circles where he was best known, his excellent qualities were the subject of converse. He was a successful master mariner. He made his first voyage whaling in the ship *Martha* in 1819, and after another voyage in the same vessel went out as boat steerer in the ship *Pacific*. Then followed a voyage in the *Missouri* as second mate, and on his next cruise it was as first officer in the *William Thompson*. The above vessels were outfitted by Seth Russell and Son. Capt. Whitfield's first voyage as Master was made in the ship *Newark*, sailing from Newburgh, New York, after which he commanded the ship *John Howland* for the firm of J. & J. Howland. He then embarked in the merchant service and at one time commanded the *Gladiator* and *Hibernia*, and afterwards purchasing a brig, took command himself, in which vessel he closed his seafaring life. Capt. Whitfield resided here all his life, having been born here and for two years represented this district in the Legislature. So conscientious was he as to being biased in any in his actions while in the Legislature that the usual compliment of a pass by the RR Company was returned by him to the railroad authorities. At one time during Capt. Whitfield's career in the merchant service, he became interested in the guano traffic, and as one of the stockholders of the company which had purchased the Swan Islands in the Caribbean Sea, he went to those islands in the interest of the company, when his friends gave him the title of Governor of Swan Islands. Capt. Whitfield had been in poor health for the past two years and about a month ago received a paralytic stroke which undoubtedly was the cause of his death. He leaves a wife, son and daughter, the latter the wife of Jos. C. Omey.

Captain Whitfield was interred in the Riverside Cemetery in Fairhaven, Massachusetts.

On September 1, 1890, just over four years later, the captain's wife Albertina died. She was seventy-nine years and four months old, and she died at her residence in Oxford Village in Fairhaven.

In 1898, Manjiro's health deteriorated still further, so much so that he had to move to his son Toichiro's home at Kiobashi Ku, Unu Cho, No. 8, in Tokyo. On November 11, 1898, Nakahama Manjiro died suddenly from an attack of apoplexy, at seventy-two years of age. Manjiro, who was a Buddhist, had made prior arrangements for Buddhist burial rites, but his son Toichiro, going against his father's wishes, had him interred in accordance with the Shinto religion. Manjiro was laid to rest in the Zoshigaya Cemetery in Tokyo.

Manjiro in the course of his life had been married three times and fathered seven children. His first wife, Tetsu, was the mother of two girls and one boy, Suzu, Toichiro (meaning "First East Boy"), and Kyo. His second wife, Koto, bore two boys, Seijiro and Keizaburo. His third spouse, Shige, also had two sons, Nobuyoshi and Hidetoshi.

Not knowing that Manjiro had died, Anne Bonney, a relative of the Whitfield family who often visited them at their home on 11 Cherry Street, wrote the following letter to him.

4 Sears Street, New Bedford, Mass.   Dec. 5, 1898

Dear John Mung.

For that is the name by which I remember you and think of you. With this, I send you a copy of a recent newspaper which told us of you, and all of us who remember you were very glad that your son had written to Marcellus Whitfield and it was very pleasant to get this message from you. This letter revived old associations and memories and I was glad to learn you were still in the land of the living. Many times have I thought of you since I last saw you. Many changes have occurred since you were here in 1870. Capt. Whitfield his wife and two daughters have died—his daughter Sybil left one daughter, who is an accomplished young lady. His only son Marcellus P. Whitfield is by occupation a carpenter and builder—a worthy son of his father. He has a wife and a family of boys. Marcellus lives in the very same house where you used to live with Aunt Milly he has done considerable in enlarging it, but still I think you would know it was the same low roofed cottage which was once your home. My father Josiah S. Bonney and my mother have both passed away. It was in my father's house you took your first meal on American soil, brought here by Capt. Whitfield. My father was Capt. Whitfield's business man and my mother was own cousin to Capt. Whitfield and there was much intimacy between the families. I remember you as a bright little fellow and we all became fond of you immediately. I was then a girl of fifteen years and am now sixty seven years old. I have always had the impression that I was older than you, but the newspaper makes you out the older and one cannot always rely on newspaper articles.

Do you recall the visits Mary Ann Post and I Anne Bonney used to make to Aunt Milly's. Those were delightful times. Once Mary Ann had embroidered on card board in brilliant colors a young rooster and brought it as a gift to Aunt Milly—it was placed on the mantel-shelf, and we all admired it—after supper the four of us sat talking and joking together till Aunt Milly said, "Time to go to bed John, and I want you to get up early." And as you left the room you pointed to the shelf and said "yes, when Mary Ann's rooster crows", and we all laughed and thought it a very good joke. Some of us still cherish as keepsakes the pieces of Japanese money you gave us, but what serves most to bring you to my mind, is a bodkin you made for me from a bit of whales tooth—all these years it has had a place in my work basket and whenever I use it I think of you.

My sister Elizabeth is a widow and lives in California with a son. My brother Josiah has been dead some years. My other brothers were young boys when you lived here—two are married and have families—my youngest brother, James has never married and his home is with my youngest sister Ada. She has a husband and two daughters. My husband and I have dwelt together in happiness lo! these many years. We have a daughter and a son. My daughter is a highly accomplished woman. She is a teacher of music and excels on the violin. I hope I have not tired you in telling so much about my people and hope it may interest you.

I am glad for the honors which have come to you, and hope you may live long to enjoy a peaceful and happy life. With loving regards, Ever your Friend,

> Anne Bonney Opheman
> 4 Sears St. New Bedford, Mass. U.S.A.

Manjiro had died twenty-four days earlier. He never had the opportunity to read this letter from his old friend.

14

The Japan-Fairhaven
Relationship Continues

When Manjiro Nakahama died in 1898, the nineteenth century was already coming to a close. The whaling industry, which had been especially lucrative in the port city of New Bedford, Massachusetts—the whaling capital of the world—was near its demise. Its decline, caused primarily by the discovery of crude oil in Pennsylvania shortly after 1850, was soon to play an intricate role in the changing course of world history. The finding of abundant petroleum beneath the surface of the earth had occurred at a very critical time in United States history—a time when America was awakening to new industrial endeavors. The whale oil that had once lighted lamps across America became a relic of the past. The new technology included the mechanization of mills, factories, and engines, which precipitated a new demand for lubricating substances. Petroleum, the newest lubricant, was hailed as the solution to the problems of mechanical friction. As the market for sperm oil dwindled, so did the number of whale ships.

The harbor of New Bedford, once teeming with deep-drafted whaleships, had become a port which primarily harbored small fishing vessels that were capable of venturing only a few hundred miles out to sea and sailing only days at a time, unlike whaleships, which could cruise for months and even years before returning to home port. The familiar riggings of the packet ships and schooners that plied the merchant trade were still visible in the harbor, but only a few whaleships remained. The days when the taking of whale had been the lifeblood of New Bedford were long gone.

Nature, working in mysterious ways, often fills a vacuum. Such was the case when whaling was brought to a close. The new era of textile industrialization had begun, and New Bedford was part of it.

Despite the passing of both Captain William H. Whitfield

Whaleships berthed at the New Bedford City Pier. Circa 1900. (Courtesy Fairhaven Selectmen)

and Manjiro Nakahama late in the nineteenth century, the relationship between their families continued to flourish. The strong bond of friendship between the two families was based in part on mutual respect. Manjiro's oldest son, Dr. Toichiro Nakahama, assumed the Nakahama family's responsibility for continuing the relationship, and Captain Whitfield's only living son, Marcellus, played a similar role in the Whitfield family. This second generation ensured the continuance of the relationship by establishing a tradition of passing along the details of the story to succeeding generations. The bond between the families became ever tighter, and the bond of intimacy persisted into the third and fourth generations. At this point, the Japan-Fairhaven cordiality was strictly confined to the two families; no government officials or other persons were involved—a situation that was to change, as time passed.

Following is an excerpt from a newspaper article in *The Fairhaven Star* dated November 26, 1898.

Bread Upon the Waters,

A Remarkable Story of A Fairhaven Shipmaster

Marcellus P. Whitfield of Fairhaven, Mass., on the 28th of October last received a handsomely engraved invitation to be present at a reception to be given on board the new Japanese cruiser *Kasagi*, at Philadelphia. The invitation was by the officers of the cruiser and included Mr. Whitfield's whole family. Not knowing anyone upon the *Kasagi*, the invitation was a mystery until the next day, when an explanation came in the form of a letter from Keizaburo Nakahama, chief paymaster of the ship. The writer stated that he was the third son of Manjiro Nakahama of Tokyo, Japan, who had been taken care of and educated by Mr. Whitfield's father, master of the ship *John Howland*, in 1841. "Under this circumstance," he says, "I have been commissioned to find your address by my father, as I have been sent in official service, and to report all about the captain's family."

The February 6, 1892, issue of *The Fairhaven Star* noted the passing of Miss Jane Allen, and the Fairhaven town clerk's records show that she died on February 2. Her demise was attributed to cancer. She was seventy-two years, four months, and eleven days old at the time of her death. Miss Allen was the first American schoolteacher whom John Mung encountered. It was she who prepared him for admission to an American classroom. When he arrived in Fairhaven, Miss Allen tutored Manjiro in the basement room of her home at 10 Oxford Street prior to his enrollment at the Point School, District 11, in Oxford Village (commonly referred to as the "Stone School House"). Miss Allen also taught at the Pease School, District 19, in Fairhaven, and when her sister Amelia, a schoolteacher herself, was married in 1849, Jane transferred to the Long Plain School, District 1.

Some years after Manjiro's death, Dr. Toichiro Nakahama decided to present the town of Fairhaven with a gift in memory of his father. After much deliberation, he remembered that his father had given the Reverend Samuel C. Damon of Honolulu one of his own personal samurai swords. Then why not a similar gift to the town of Fairhaven?

Consequently, he initiated a search for a worthy sword. He was satisfied when he discovered an ancient samurai sword in a small curio shop. A close examination revealed that the weapon was of the sort classified as a *tachi*, which was worn

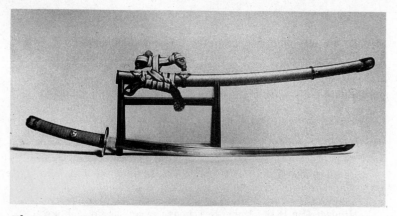

The antique samurai sword which was presented to the town of Fairhaven in 1918 by Dr. Toichiro Nakahama, Manjiro's oldest son. Circa 1918. (Courtesy Millicent Library, Fairhaven, Massachusetts)

for court ceremonies. Another type of sword, known as *katana*, was used exclusively by samurai, and was worn with the edge of the blade upward. The *tachi*, on the other hand, was worn on the left side with the edge of the blade downward. A flat string was tied around the loins to hold the sword in a horizontal position.

The characteristic features of the blade indicate that it is a pure example of the Bizen school and was thus made in the period corresponding to the early fourteenth century on the Western calendar. The blade, which was originally much longer, was shortened to adjust it to the stature of an owner, probably at about the middle of the fourteenth century. At that time, close battle formations of foot soldiers armed with drawn swords came into vogue. Presumably the part of the tang on which the maker's name was inscribed had to be cut off.

Dr. Nakahama purchased the sword in the summer of 1918 and began working through diplomatic channels to gain the interest and support of high officials in the Foreign Minister's office in Tokyo. The Japanese ambassador to the United States, Viscount Ishii, represented the Japanese government and the Nakahama family. Charles S. Hamlin, Governor of the United States Federal Reserve Board in Washington,

D.C., was the American who worked with Ishii to formalize the arrangements. Much effort and time were devoted to planning a meaningful ceremony. Finally, it was decided that the official presentation of the sword would be made on the birthday of the United States of America. July 4, 1918, was selected as the date for the ceremony. Local officials from New Bedford and Fairhaven, including the Board of Selectmen, went to the Japanese Embassy in Washington to work with the Japanese ambassador and members of his staff on a plan for the specifics of the presentation ceremony. The Fairhaven High School stadium was selected as the site where the gift would be presented. The festivities were scheduled to begin at two-thirty in the afternoon.

On June 9, 1918, *The Fairhaven Star* offered the following solicitation:

The Schoolmates of Nakahama sought by Fairhaven Committee

Anyone who attended school with Manjiro Nakahama during the latter's residence in Fairhaven is requested to communicate with Henry D. Waldron, secretary of the Fairhaven committee having in charge the arrangements for the exercises on the Fourth.

At last evening's meeting of the committee, sub-committees were appointed and the following committee chairmen named: Decorations, P. C. Headley; music, I. N. Babbitt; parade, George N. Gardiner; entertainment, Harry L. Pope.

The committee will meet again Sunday evening at 7:30 o'-Clock.

On July 2, 1918, *The New Bedford Evening Standard* featured the announcement reprinted below, which was accompanied by pictures.

Will Attend the Exercises

Two of Three Surviving Schoolmates Will Be at Fairhaven

Remember Japanese Boy Well—Was Known as John Mung.

The coming of Viscount Ishii to Fairhaven July 4th, is fraught with more than ordinary interest for Mrs. Amanda A. Southworth of 280 Kempton Street, Miss Annie W. Carsley of 166 Campbell Street, this city and Mrs. Elbridge A. Morton of 41 Middle Street, Fairhaven. For these three women, so far as

known, are the only persons living who attended school with
Nakahama at the Sconticut Neck School in 1845. Nakahama was
known as John Mung in his school days, and it is as "John" that
these classmates speak of him. All say that he was not only a
bright boy in school, but that he was always a well behaved boy.

"The thing I remember about John," said Miss Carsley yesterday, "is that he was always a good boy in school. I do not
think that he ever cut up with the other boys. He was very
studious and seemed to try as hard as he could to make the most
of his opportunities."

Like Miss Carsley, Mrs. Southworth had only words of praise
for John, and that he readily made friends with the children.

Mrs. Morton and Mrs. Southworth hope to attend the exercises in Fairhaven, July 4th, but Miss Carsley is not able to go.

The planned event brought much attention and acclaim to
the town of Fairhaven. Several days later, on July 9, 1918, *The
Fairhaven Star* gave a full account of the formalities, as follows:

Viscount Ishii, Ambassador of Japan to the United States, was
accorded a most enthusiastic welcome by the people of
Fairhaven on July 4th, and the unique and important occasion
will long be remembered as Fairhaven's most wonderful Fourth
of July.

The town was in gala attire and on no previous occasion had
it looked so attractive or had taken on more of a holiday
appearance. American flags and bunting with Japanese flags
liberally distributed were seen everywhere. The whole length of
the bridge was adorned with the flags of both nations suspended
from wires overhead and along Washington Street for three
miles from the Mattapoisett line, banners were displayed. The
Town Hall, the library and the churches as well as the stores
and the blocks in the business section were liberally adorned
with colors and at the stadium was a mass of red, white and blue
with the national flags conspicuous. At the memorial monument
at the end of the bridge Japanese and American flags were
placed at each corner of the shaft. Flags were displayed at
hundreds of homes.

Viscount Ishii, the Viscountess, a member of the ambassador's
suite and a military attache of the legation, accompanied by
secret service men, arrived in Providence Tuesday afternoon
and were met there by Mayor Ashley and Hon. Charles S.
Hamlin. The party went to Mr. Hamlin's home at Mattapoisett
where a reception in honor of the ambassador and his wife was
held Wednesday afternoon. From 4:30 to 6:00 Viscount and
Viscountess Ishii received the guests as they arrived. With them

(Top) *Viscount Ishii with a delegation of American government and local officials, July 4, 1918. Circa 1918.* (Bottom) *Sword presentation ceremony at the Fairhaven Stadium, July 4, 1918. Circa 1918.* (Courtesy Millicent Library, Fairhaven, Massachusetts)

in the receiving line was Mrs. Charles S. Hamlin, Mr. Hamlin
and Miss Anna Hamlin, assisting in the presentation of the
visitors.

Soon after nine o'clock Thursday morning Viscount Ishii and
his party were met at the Fairhaven end of the bridge by
Lieutenant Governor Coolidge, members of the Governor's staff
and a delegation of members of the New Bedford city
government. There was an imposing military and naval escort
including regulars from Fort Rodman, Naval Reserve force
under command of Lieutenant Washburn; and the first
battalion of State Guard. The parade proceeded to the New
Bedford High School where there were addresses by Mayor
Ashley, Lieutenant Governor Coolidge and Viscount Ishii.

After the exercises in New Bedford the Viscount and his party
were met on the bridge by the following committee from
Fairhaven: Phineas C. Headley, Jr., Isaac N. Babbitt, Morris R.
Brownell and William M. Allen. Ambassador Ishii proceeded to
Riverside Cemetery accompanied by members of the Whitfield
family where he placed a wreath upon the grave of Captain
William H. Whitfield. Returning from the cemetery,
Ambassador Ishii called on Mrs. Eben Akin, at whose house,
Nakahama was entertained the first night he was on shore.

The party next proceeded to Tabitha Inn where a buffet
luncheon was served to the guests and members of the
committee. After the luncheon the guests, accompanied by
Harry L. Pope, Mrs. Walter P. Winsor and John H. Stetson,
visited the Memorial Church and Millicent Library at which
latter place the visitors registered. They then went to the Town
Hall where a short reception was held and an opportunity given
the guests to inspect the log book of the ship *John Howland* and
other things bearing on the life of Nakahama while he lived in
Fairhaven.

After the reception the parade formed in front of the Town
Hall and marched through William, Union and Green Streets to
Cushman Park, through the park and Park Street to Huttleston
Avenue, to Green Street and into the stadium by the west
entrance.

The parade was made up of a battalion of regulars from Fort
Rodman, Naval Reserves from the local barracks, the Fairhaven
State Guard Company and the Naval Reserve Band from
Newport.

Lieutenant Loring Washburn was in charge of this feature
and it was carried out in a manner that frequently won the
enthusiastic applause of the thousands who witnessed the
movements. The national salute at the Town Hall and the
assembly of the men at the stadium. Nothing as impressive was
ever seen in Fairhaven in its whole history.

The sword given by Dr. Toichiro Nakahama found a permanent home in the Millicent Library, located across the street from the Fairhaven Town Hall. Many Japanese visitors to the library have signed a guest book which was set up for that purpose. Even the Imperial Crown Prince Akihito and Princess Michiko signed it when they visited on October 4, 1987, which was before they became the Imperial Emperor and Empress.

In June 1919, Marcellus P. Whitfield of Cherry Street in Fairhaven received the following letter from the Japanese Embassy in Washington.

Imperial Japanese Embassy

June 9, 1919

Mr. Marcellus P. Whitfield
Fairhaven, Mass.

Dear Mr. Whitfield:

It is with a great pleasure that I inform you H. M. the Japanese Emperor has been pleased to grant my request to decorate you with the Sixth Order of the Rising Sun, under the date of May 16. It may be added that this action of the Emperor's is in recognition of the generosity and good will which your late good Father showed toward a Japanese subject and which to this day is remembered with gratitude by the Japanese people.

The Order is now on its way and shall be sent forward to you as soon as it reaches this Embassy.

With congratulations, I am

Yours truly,

K. Ishii

Accompanying the letter and written in Japanese was the official document of decoration, which has been translated as follows:

Imperial Japanese Embassy

Washington

By the Grace of Heaven, Emperor of Japan, Seated on the Throne occupied by the same Dynasty from time immemorial,
We confer the Sixth Class of the Imperial Order of Meiji upon Mr. Marcellus P. Whitfield, a citizen of the United States of

America, and invest him with the insignia of the Imperial Order of the Rising Sun pertaining to the said class, in expression of the good will which we entertain towards him.

In witness whereof, we hereunto caused the Grand Seal of the Empire to be affixed, at our Palace in Tokyo, this sixteenth day of the fifty month of the eighth year of Teisho, corresponding to the two thousand five hundred and seventy-ninth year from the coronation of the Emperor Jimmi.

Seal of the Empire

The sixteenth day of the fifth month of the eighth year of the Teisho.

[Seal] Countersigned:
Count Hiedo Kodama
President of the Bureau of Decoration

This diploma is examined and recorded in the Register of Decoration as No. 5311

[Seal] Signed: Gozube Yokoto
[Seal] Signed: Tetsuo Akamine
    Secretaries of the Bureau of Decoration

Dr. Nakahama's gift to the town of Fairhaven in memory of his father inspired a resurrection of interest in the deeds and accomplishments of Manjiro Nakahama. This renewed interest has had far-reaching effects.

Eighteen months after the sword presentation, the Millicent Library received a mysterious package, which proved to contain a special gift from the Japanese ambassador, Shidehara. The following news article appeared in the February 13, 1920, edition of *The New Bedford Morning Mercury:*

Ishii Makes Gift to Fairhaven Library.

Four Marvelous Manuscript Volumes, Quaintly Illustrated, the Story of Nakahama Manjiro.

The story of the rescue by Capt. William H. Whitfield of Fairhaven, of Nakahama Manjiro, the Japanese boy, which hastened the opening of Japan to the United States, is still vivid because of the holiday made for Fairhaven and New Bedford on the occasion of the visit of Ambassador Ishii on the Fourth of July in 1918, when he came to present to Fairhaven a sword, the gift of Dr. Nakahama, a son of Manjiro.

The Japanese government was so pleased at the reception accorded the ambassador that it has since conferred decorations upon representatives of the town of Fairhaven and New Bedford.

Viscount Ishii was recalled to Japan several months ago, but that he still holds in appreciation the welcome accorded him, is manifested in a token he has conferred upon the Millicent Library of Fairhaven, Charles S. Hamlin of the Federal Reserve Board.

G. W. Hill, librarian of the Fairhaven library, has just received the gift which is of great value. It is a manuscript record in four volumes, the story of the voyages of Nakahama, his experiences in Fairhaven, his shipwreck and voyages on a whaler. An outline of the story accompanies Ishii's gift, prepared by Ambassador Shidehara, who is Japan's representative at Washington at the present time.

The four volumes are bound in covers of choice Japanese silk. The record is written on Japanese paper—paper so thin that each sheet is folded to comprise two layers. His chief interest to those to whom the record is a sealed book by reason of unfamiliarity with the Japanese language, is in the illustrations, beautifully executed by a Japanese artist who worked obviously from sketches and description furnished by Nakahama. Never having seen the scenes he pictures, the artist has saturated them in Japanese atmosphere and this gives the illustrations a strange character. There are many views of the whaler *John J. Howland* in which the hull is ornamented after the fancy of the artist giving the ship the appearance of a Japanese junk with rig and boats of a whaler. The eagle which formed the tailpiece on the stern of the old ship, undoubtedly worked up from a sketch by Nakahama, is typically Japanese. There is a scene in water colors of the waterfront of a town and certain characteristics of the tower of the Congregational Church as it was before the gale destroyed the spire and the gothic ornaments of the tower were ruthlessly sacrificed a year ago, are preserved in the drawing. But otherwise it is imaginative and confined [sic] with the attempt to reproduce the architecture of a New England church are dreamlike sketches of Japanese villas, which make a curious combination. There are pictures of whales of different species, scenes in the Pacific Isles all in the style familiar on Japanese fans. There are drawings of alleged American railroad trains under description by Nakahama with innumerable cars running across several pages, drawings of toy works and whaling paraphernalia and paintings of flags and private signals of New Bedford whaling merchants. Some of the spelling of the titles is weird. These are pages in Nakahama's handwriting, written in English, copies of letters to Capt. Whitfield. One page contains the English alphabet, another the name of some of the states. Nakahama, it will be remembered, visited this country at a time when the penalty of death maintained for any who left Japan and returned from the outside world. A concession was made in his case and his writings were a revelation to a benighted land of what civilization was accomplishing outside the realms.

These volumes appear to be similar to those who came into the possession of Stewart Culin, curator of the Museum of Brooklyn Institute. Mr. Culin learned that his volumes were written and illustrated from Manjiro's descriptions by artists in the service of the Lord of Tosa and it is probable the volumes now given Fairhaven were part of the same extraordinary work. The volumes are enclosed in a beautiful case of silk covered board. Librarian Hill will arrange for a public view of the volumes in a suitable glass case, later on.

Although, in the years that followed, the notability of the Manjiro-Whitfield story began to fade in the minds of most Fairhaven residents, it remained fresh in the memories of the Whitfield and Nakahama families.

The New Bedford Evening Standard printed an editorial in August 1924 on the occasion, part of which is reproduced here.

Nearly 80 years ago, the late Captain William H. Whitfield of Fairhaven, rescued five starving Japanese fisherman from an uninhabited island in the Pacific. He brought home and educated one of them, who later became a Prince of Japan and because of his American experience was influential in opening the door of the Flowery Kingdom to Commodore Perry.

Today Kiyoshi Nakahama of Tokyo, grandson of the celebrated Manjiro Nakahama whom Captain Whitfield rescued, is the guest of Captain Whitfield's son, Marcellus P. Whitfield, in the house at 11 Cherry Street, where his grandfather passed some weeks during his stay in America, and is reverently visiting landmarks associated with the history of Manjiro and his rescuer.

The most dramatic moments for the young man, came when he opened this morning the treasured yellow logbook of the *John Howland* and read the entry recording the rescue of his father on June 27, 1841. "This day light wind from S.E.," the entry reads. "The Isle in sight. Found five poor distressed people on the Isle. Took them off. Could not understand anything from them more than that they was hungry."

Visits Captain's Grave.

The gratitude that Manjiro Nakahama expressed all his life to the Fairhaven seaman who took him in as a member of his family and gave him an education that made him a great man on his return to Japan, has been handed down from father to

(Top, left to right) *"Allie" (Whitfield) Omey, granddaughter of Captain Whitfield; Marcellus Whitfield, son of Captain William H. Whitfield; and Toichiro Nakahama, son of Manjiro Nakahama, shown standing in front of the Whitfield home at 11 Cherry Street in Fairhaven. Circa 1924.* (Courtesy Dr. Hiroshi Nakahama) (Bottom) *Looking north on Cherry Street. The Whitfield home is in the right foreground. Circa 1924.* (Courtesy Dr. Hiroshi Nakahama)

son, and from son to grandson. Kiyoshi Nakahama has looked
forward all his life to the time, when having graduated from the
University of Tokyo, his father would send him to Massachusetts where he might visit Fairhaven and perfect his knowledge
of the language and customs of the country to a degree worthy
of his distinguished ancestor. Arriving in Fairhaven early yesterday afternoon, he went directly from the train with Mr. Whitfield to Riverside Cemetery, to visit the grave of the kind Captain Whitfield with whom his grandfather lived for more than
ten years." Commenting that he would go again to the grave
today to place a tribute of flowers, Mr. Nakahama explained
that it was his first duty to go straight to the cemetery yesterday,
without pausing by the way to purchase flowers.

Seems Familiar.

Later in the evening, Mr. Nakahama retracted [sic] his steps
past the old house and walked alone down to the water's edge.
"You can imagine what my thoughts were in the streets of this
very interesting old town," he said this morning. "I was thinking
of how it must have seemed to my grandfather as he walked
these same streets at the end of his eventful trip. It all seems
familiar to me. I have seen so many pictures and read and heard
so much about it."

"There are still two things I want very much to see, and Mr.
Whitfield has promised to show them to me," said Mr.
Nakahama. "I want to see your old whaling ship, the *Morgan*,
so that I may know what sort of ship my grandfather sailed on.
Mr. Whitfield has a painting of the *John Howland* in the next
room. And I want to go to the old house at Sconticut Neck where
my grandfather spent most of his time when he was here.

Loves the Sea.

Young Nakahama is the elder of his father's two sons. It was his
ambition to become a seaman, following in the footsteps of his
grandfather, but his father said that with only two sons he could
not spare one for the sea. He yielded to the young man's pleading that he be allowed to go to sea for at least a few months, and
following his graduation from Tokio University in 1921, Mr.
Nakahama entered the passenger service of the Oriental Steam-
ship Company for ten months. He has specialized in the study
of political economy and when he has perfected his English he
plans to engage in foreign trade.

"I am in this country principally to learn English well," he
said, apologizing for his speech, which is far better than his
apology indicates. "My father although he has never been here,
speaks English very well for he studied with my grandfather. He
has spoken English fluently since he was ten years old, and
always is scolding me because I do not speak better. But it is
very hard, for the most of the teachers in Japan are Japanese,
and the pronunciation is not good."

May Go to Brown.

Mr. Nakahama came to New Bedford from Harvard summer school, where he concentrated on the study of English. At the same time he was making inquiries as to Universities in Massachusetts which he may enter in the fall. He does not wish to go to Harvard, which he ranks highest of all, because there are so many Japanese students there that he fears he would speak too much Japanese with them. He will probably choose one of the smaller colleges, or perhaps go to Brown. He left Japan in June of last year, spending a year in study in England and touring Europe before coming here.

"Every year on June 27," explained Mr. Nakahama, his eyes shining with the recollection, "my father gathers our family and our relatives together and tells us the story of how our grandfather was rescued and how, if it had not been for the kind Captain Whitfield we would not be living today as we do."

His grandfather died in 1898, when Mr. Nakahama was but three years old, and he remembers the distinguished old gentleman but faintly.

Father Coming.

"Do you know." said Mr. Nakahama, "I have visited Fairhaven even before I visited the native home of my family. My grandfather was born in the little town of Nakanohama, on the Island of Shikoku. When I go back I shall go there too. My father has wanted to come here, but he has been so busy all his life that he has not had time. He is a physician, but now he has retired from the private hospital he has had for 20 years, and is traveling with my younger sister. I expect him here in November, and then I will come again to Fairhaven with him to see Mr. Whitfield."

Mr. Nakahama is very optimistic over American-Japanese relations. He believes that the Japanese exclusion policy of the United States is too strongly emphasized in some quarters of Japan, but he anticipates no serious trouble growing out of it. He feels that Japan has the name of being a military nation, but the wars which have given her that name have not been of her own making. He says his country wishes to participate sincerely in movements for world peace. Personally, his feeling is one of great friendliness for the United States, and of warm gratitude to the community in which he is now a guest.

"Grandson of Nakahama sends message
through *Star* to people of Fairhaven."

The Fairhaven Star, Fairhaven, August 22, 1924.

To the Townspeople of Fairhaven and New Bedford:

It is my very great pleasure to tell you our earnest thanks for the kindness which was shown to my grandfather by you or your parents or your grandparents.

Eighty years have elapsed since my grandfather bade goodby
to the benevolent Captain and Mrs. Whitfield as well as to the
very kind neighbors. I am now living with Mr. and Mrs. M. P.
Whitfield with the feeling that I am quite at home in the same
house in which John Mung spent some time before he went to
the old Whitfield homestead on Sconticut Neck with the captain
and his family.

You would guess my feelings upon receiving even a piece of
stone from this town.

It is also my great pleasure to meet every person who knew
my grandfather. He heartily welcomes me just as he did my
grandfather more than half a century ago.

I am glad to tell you that my father is coming here in November and at that time he can have the opportunity to express his
earnest thanks to all the kind townspeople.

K. Nakahama

More than eighty years have elapsed since the late Captain
William H. Whitfield of this town rescued Manjiro Nakahama,
a starving Japanese fisherman, from an island in the Pacific
Ocean, and now Kiyoshi Nakahama, grandson of the rescued
man, is visiting here with relatives of Captain Whitfield and is
making himself acquainted with the town which was once the
home of his grandfather.

Kiyoshi Nakahama is the elder of the two sons of Dr.
Nakahama. His home is in Tokio, but he recently finished a
course at the Harvard Summer School. In the fall he plans to
enter one of the smaller colleges, as he fears that if he enrolled
at a large institution where there are many Japanese, that he
would soon get into the habit of talking his native language too
much. Kiyoshi was graduated from Tokio University in 1921,
and then entered the passenger service of the Oriental Steam-
ship Company for a period of ten months. He was anxious to
follow the sea as his grandfather did, but his father was not
willing, so he has specialized in the study of political economy,
and after he mastered the English language completely, he will
undoubtedly engage in foreign trade.

Such is the description of the distinguished visitor who is
spending the week with Marcellus P. Whitfield, 11 Cherry
Street, and Selectman Thomas W. Whitfield of Fort Street. He
has already visited the points of interest of the town, and has
also been to the grave of Captain Whitfield in Riverside Cemetery, where he placed a tribute of flowers.

He also visited the grave of Job C. Tripp at Riverside where
he also placed a floral tribute. Mr. Tripp was a schoolmate and
intimate friend of Manjiro Nakahama and until his death was in
correspondence with the family by whom he was addressed as
"grandfather."

As Kiyoshi had promised, he and his father did visit Fairhaven together, arriving on November 29, 1924. Toichiro and Kiyoshi stayed on the second floor of the Whitfield home. They knew that it had been a single-story house when Manjiro was there and that he had stayed in the attic room. Memories of Manjiro must have dominated their thoughts and their conversation. Toichiro presented to Marcellus Whitfield a gold cigarette case and a very rare, delicate lacquerware work of art.

Dr. Nakahama says Fairhaven is his "Second Birthplace."

The New Bedford Evening Standard, December 2, 1924.

"The United States is my second country, and Fairhaven my second birthplace." In such courtly fashion did Dr. Toichiro Nakahama of Tokio, Japan, this morning express the debt of gratitude he has come to Fairhaven to voice to the family of Marcellus P. Whitfield. Dr. Nakahama is the eldest son of the Japanese prince, Manjiro Nakahama, whom Mr. Whitfield's father rescued 80 years ago from an island in the China Sea, where Manjiro, then but a poor fisher lad, had been eking out a starvation existence following a shipwreck many months before.

All his life Dr. Nakahama has wanted to come to Fairhaven, but his arrival this morning from Providence was his first realization of that ambition. His son, Kiyoshi Nakahama, visited the Whitfields this summer, while his father's round-the-world-tour had progressed as far as France. Young Nakahama is a graduate student of political economy at Brown University, and his father went directly from New York to Providence, paying a brief visit to his son there and then coming on to New Bedford, escorted by the young man. The two are guests until Thursday at the home of Mr. Whitfield, 11 Cherry Street, Fairhaven.

Studied Medicine.

Dr. Nakahama is a genial, active man of 67, gray haired, but looking younger than his years, and beaming pleasure at his experiences. His title of doctor is the result of his medical studies, pursued first in Japan and completed by four years, about 1880, in the foremost medical schools of Germany. For many years he has conducted a sanitarium in Tokio, but this spring, feeling the weight of his years entitled him to a more moderate program, he turned it over to a colleague and allowed himself a half year of travel. His entry into the medical profession was the result of advice of his father who, during the years he lived with the Whitfields and eagerly absorbed an American education, realized how valuable to Japan men trained in Western medicine could be, and what a splendid path for advancement it would offer them.

After the first welcomes, which were more like reunions, since the Whitfields and the Nakahamas know each other well through photographs and correspondence, Dr. Nakahama unpacked gifts he had brought to his host's family. Precious small carved ivories from his daughter, lacquered boxes of many sizes and designs, culminating in a wonderful big one intricately embossed in gold, representing two years' labor by the artist who made it, emerged from their dainty tissue wrappings. They gave an Oriental touch not suggested by Dr. Nakahama himself, with his European clothes and his English speech and knowledge of American forms of intercourse.

Dr. Nakahama says his principal object is to meet the family of his father's rescuer, to see Fairhaven, which he has seen so often in pictures that it has a familiar look, and to lay a wreath on the grave of Captain Whitfield. Incidentally, he expects to greet again Charles S. Ashley, who was his guest in Tokio. After his brief stay in Fairhaven he will go on to Washington, where he expects to present letters of introduction to Charles S. Hamlin, of Marion and to several physicians. Then he will go to New York for a brief visit, thence to Niagara Falls, of whose wonders he has heard so much, and on to San Francisco, for he is to sail on the 18th of this month for Japan.

Never Will Forget.

The story of the rescue of Manjiro Nakahama by Captain Whitfield will never be forgotten so long as a member of the Nakahama family lives," said Dr. Nakahama. It is a familiar one to many people of Japan, and one that Dr. Nakahama retells to his family many, many, times. For Manjiro was the first Japanese to sojourn in foreign countries and return home without incurring the death penalty. It was his good fortune that Japan, already considering the opening of its hitherto closed gates to foreign countries which culminated a year later in the admission of Commodore Perry, exercised leniency in his case. The government confiscated most of the souvenirs of America which Manjiro brought home with him, and a flood later swept away the rest, so that Dr. Nakahama has no material relics of his father's first stay here, but he has an almost photographic familiarity with all the events of that adventure that meant so much to his family.

Dr. Nakahama, although he has given up his hospital, has by no means retired into private life. His card indicates the numerous activities to which he will return for it lists these titles: Commissioner of the Tobacco Monopoly Bureau of Japan, which sees to it that the tobacco industry is conducted sanitarily; member of the Central Board of Health, Medical Adviser of the Pension Bureau of Japan, president of the Insur-

ance Medical Society of Japan, Medical Director of the Hinode
Life Insurance Company, and president of the Medical Society
of Tokio.

Dr. Toichiro Nakahama guest of the Whitfields

The Fairhaven Star, Fairhaven, December 5, 1924.

Dr. Toichiro Nakahama of Tokio, Japan, and his son, Kiyoshi
Nakahama, a graduate student of political economy at Brown
University, have been the guests of Mr. and Mrs. Marcellus P.
Whitfield, this week. Dr. Nakahama leaving on Thursday after-
noon for Providence. He will visit Niagara Falls, Chicago and
San Francisco, sailing from there for Japan, completing a trip
around the world.

On Thursday, at 12, he was given a luncheon at Tabitha Inn,
which gave him an opportunity to meet a number of town
officials and several citizens, including former mayor, Charles S.
Ashley of New Bedford, who visited Dr. Nakahama at Tokio
during his recent trip around the world. Wednesday evening
Mr. Ashley entertained Dr. Nakahama and his son at a luncheon in New Bedford. Members of the Whitfield family and Miss
Allie Omey were among the guests.

Dr. Nakahama is a son of Manjiro Nakahama who was rescued from a rock in the China Sea by Captain William H.
Whitfield, who was master of a whaler. The boy was brought to
Fairhaven and educated in the schools here afterwards returning to Japan and was the first Japanese to return to the country
without being put to death. He afterwards became one of the
leading statesmen of the country and it was mainly through his
influence that the ports of Japan were opened to the world.

Dr. Nakahama has always wanted to visit Fairhaven but he
never realized his ambition until his arrival on Tuesday. He is
a genial, active man of 67, gray haired, but looking younger than
his years. He pursued his medical studies in Japan and then in
Germany. He has conducted a sanatorium in Tokio for many
years. He became a doctor on the advice of his father who
realized, as a result of his training here, how valuable men could
be who were trained in western medicine.

Dr. Nakahama brought many gifts for members of the Whitfield family. They included small carved ivories from his daughter, lacquered boxes of many sizes and designs. There was one
intricately embossed in gold, representing two years' labor by
the artist who made it.

Dr. Nakahama's principal object was to meet the members of
the family of his father's rescuer, to see Fairhaven with which
he has become familiar through photographs and pictures he
has seen in *The Star* and other papers, and to lay a wreath on
the grave of Captain Whitfield, which duty he performed on

Wednesday. "I wish you would express to the people of Fairhaven my appreciation of your beautiful town," he said, "and my thanks for the generous hospitality shown me during my visit." He admired the beauty of the town and its residence and its clean streets. The Town Hall building particularly impressed him.

After visiting the grave of Captain Whitfield Wednesday morning Dr. Nakahama visited the Misses Dana. He then visited the Rogers School where he and his son and Superintendent Prior gave talks to the children. Willard Delano Whitfield, son of Selectman Thomas W. Whitfield, welcomed the visitors in behalf of the children. They then visited Fort Phoenix and the home of Selectman Whitfield. Thursday morning the party visited the Wamsutta Mills and William B. Geohegan also arranged for a visit to the Sassaquin sanatorium. At noon he arrived at Tabitha Inn to meet the town officials and other guests at luncheon. Those present were: Dr. Nakahama, Kiyoshi Nakahama, Marcellus P. Whitfield, Thomas W. Whitfield, Willard Delano Whitfield, John I. Bryant, Charles S. Ashley, John H. Stetson, Elton S. Wilde, Rev. William H. Parker, Clifton A. Hacker, Charles I. Drew, William D. Champlin, Henry D. Waldron, David L. Kelley, Walter H. Francis, George H. Tripp, Galen W. Hill, George B. Luther, Thomas A. Tripp, Daniel C. Potter, William F. Delano, Charles H. Striley, and Charles F. Prior.

On April 9, 1926, nearly two years after the visit to Fairhaven by Toichiro Nakahama and his son Kiyoshi, the following obituary appeared in *The Fairhaven Star*.

Marcellus P. Whitfield

His Death Recalls Rescue by His Father of Manjiro Nakahama

Marcellus P. Whitfield, one of Fairhaven's best known citizens, died at his home, 11 Cherry Street, Saturday night, aged 76 years. He had been ill with pneumonia for two weeks, and previously had enjoyed very good health. He is survived by his widow and four sons: Thomas W. Whitfield, a member of the board of selectmen; William H.; Joseph O.; and Edgar J.—all of Fairhaven.

Deceased was a son of the late Captain William H. Whitfield, a well-known whaling master, and early in life made two or three voyages whaling, one of them with his father. When he gave up the sea, he engaged in the carpentry business which he carried on all his life.

Marcellus P. Whitfield was the possessor of the insignia of the

Imperial Order of the Rising Sun, and a diploma conferred upon him, the Sixth Class Order of Meiji, which he received in 1919 from the Emperor of Japan.

These decorations followed the visit of Viscount Ishii, ambassador of Japan, to Fairhaven on July 4, 1918, when the viscount presented to the town of Fairhaven a beautiful Samurai sword of the 14th century, to commemorate the act of Captain William H. Whitfield in saving the life of Manjiro Nakahama, and giving him an education. The sword was the gift of Dr. T. Nakahama, a son of Manjiro Nakahama.

On November 10, 1928, the coronation ceremony of Emperor Hirohito took place at the ancient city of Kyoto. On that occasion, His Majesty posthumously conferred upon Manjiro Nakahama the second grade of the fifth court rank, for the distinguished service he had rendered to Japan during his lifetime. This is one of the highest honors of Japan.

On June 3, 1937, an article appeared in the local newspaper, *The Fairhaven Star*, which read as follows, in part:

NAKAHAMA, SON OF PROTEGE OF FAIRHAVEN DIES
IN JAPAN

Selectman Thomas W. Whitfield recently received an announcement of the death in Tokio, Japan, of Dr. Toichiro Nakahama on April 11. Dr. Nakahama was the son of the Japanese boy rescued by Mr. Whitfield's father, a whaling captain, from a desolate Pacific island.

The formal announcement of Toichiro's death had been sent by Kiyoshi Nakahama. It was beautifully printed in English and bore a heavy black border, and it read as follows:

Mr. Kiyoshi Nakahama
No. 120 3-chome Denen-chofu,
Omori-ku. Tokyo

Mr. Kiyoshi Nakahama begs to announce the death of his father, Dr. Toichiro Nakahama, which took place on April 11, 1937. The cause of his death was cancer from which he had been suffering for some time. The deceased was 81 years old and is survived by his wife, two sons, and three daughters.

Dr. Nakahama had led a very distinguished career. He had been director of a hospital and was president of the Medical

Society of Tokyo. In addition, he had served as a medical
adviser to insurance companies. He was a member in good
standing on the Central Board of Health. Dr. Nakahama had
received his medical training first in Japan and later in Germany.

In August 1940 Fairhaven Selectman Thomas W. Whitfield
received a letter from Kiyoshi Nakahama telling him of his
intention to send to the town of Fairhaven 1000 cherry trees.
The letter read, in part:

July 31, 1940

I have succeeded in acquiring 1000 pieces of your cherry trees
from one of the most famous nurseries in Japan. The Yokohama
Nursery Company, Ltd. This firm has experience in exporting
trees, seeds, etc. But a certificate issued by your department of
agriculture is absolutely necessary to export the trees to your
country. Please pay our immediate attention to get the permit.
I shall make a buying contract of the trees with the nursery upon
receiving from you the certificate.

According to expert advisers, the best way to transport trees
is via Seattle, thence overland route to Fairhaven, and the best
season to send is from December to February. The trees will be
sent in two boxes, each containing 500 pieces of them and
weighing about 500 pounds each. The nursery is not responsible
for any risk in transit.

It is our estimate that about half the trees will not be survived
either while they are in transit or after they are planted due to
climatic conditions, etc. But I shall be very happy if even one of
them get root and if you and your people understand my motive
in seeing beautiful cherry blossoms every Spring to come.

With all good wishes to you and to all Fairhaven citizens.

Sincerely yours,

Kiyoshi Nakahama.

Kiyoshi Nakahama's goodwill offer was rejected by the U.S.
Department of Agriculture. The department's Bureau of En-
tomology and Plant Quarantine cited its concerns in a letter
addressed to Mrs. Thomas W. Whitfield in February 1941, as
follows:

Due to the danger of introducing injurious pests, plants of the
genus Prunus, which includes the various cherries as well as
plum, peach, apricot and almond, are not allowed entry into this

country from any East Indian or Asiatic source, for which reason a permit for the importation of these flowering cherries from Japan would be out of the question.

It is with greatest reluctance that we impose these plant quarantine restrictions in a case such as this where a fine effort to promote international good will is apparent, but we feel sure you will understand very well the necessity of protecting our country against further introduction of the many serious insect pests and plant diseases which exist abroad and which we have every reason to fear could bring serious damage to our American orchards and gardens if allowed to establish themselves here.

Despite this discouraging refusal, the Whitfields and the Nakahamas continued their communication and their friendship until December 7, 1941, when it was interrupted by the bombing of Pearl Harbor in the Hawaiian Islands. The subsequent declaration of war between the United States and Japan disrupted mail service between the two countries, thus severing the long-established communication between the Whitfields and Nakahamas. As Americans reeled in the wake of the attack on her naval fleet at Pearl Harbor, every city, town, and hamlet across the United States began to mobilize young men to respond to the call of arms.

In Fairhaven, a typical small New England town, the Board of Selectmen began receiving protests from families whose sons were fighting and dying in the Pacific theater. They expressed outrage because the town continued to exhibit on public view a picture of the Japanese boy Manjiro Nakahama, as well as related Japanese memorabilia.

A letter from the Fairhaven Board of Selectmen reads as follows:

May 15, 1944

Mr. Thomas A. Tripp, Chairman
Trustees of the Millicent Library
Fairhaven, Massachusetts

Dear Mr. Tripp:

At a meeting held in this office tonight of the heads of the town departments and members of the finance committee, it was the general feeling that the picture of Nakahama Manjiro now hanging in the Selectmen's Office be removed for the duration of the war in consideration of the feelings of families having

boys in service. The Selectmen will have this picture removed
and packed away, as was suggested.

The matter of removing the Samurai Sword was also suggested and we are passing this on for the information of the
Board of Trustees.

Yours truly,

[Signed] Harold Kerwin

[Signed] Charles W. Knowlton

Though Thomas W. Whitfield, a grandson of Captain William H. Whitfield, was a member of the Fairhaven Board of
Selectmen, his signature did not appear on the official letter.
Whether this was by his choice or otherwise cannot be determined. The possibility exists that Mr. Whitfield may not have
attended the meeting, and thus may not have voiced an opinion.

A meeting of the Board of Trustees of the Millicent Library
was held on Tuesday evening, June 2, 1944. Thomas A. Tripp,
Vice President of the Board of Library Trustees, read the
letter from the Board of Selectmen. The minutes of the meeting are as follows, in part:

> Mr. Tripp read a letter from the Board of Selectmen regarding
> the removal of the Samurai sword from public display for the
> duration. He read a letter he had drafted in reply, this being
> approved heartily by the Board as being very satisfactory. The
> opinion was expressed by several that the removal of the sword
> was a foolish idea, as it had nothing to do with the present war
> lords of Japan.
>
> Meeting adjourned at 8 P.M.

Avis M. Pillsbury
Secretary

On the following day—Wednesday, June 3, 1944—the letter that Tripp had drafted was sent to the Fairhaven Board of
Selectmen. The letter is reproduced below.

June 3, 1944

Board of Selectmen
Fairhaven, Mass.

Gentlemen:

In reply to your letter of May 15th, we would say that the
Samurai sword is the property of the Town and its location is

entirely subject to direction of the Selectmen. It was placed in
the library because the location was conspicuous and the envi-
ronment excellent.

Since Pearl Harbor the public criticism of the location has
been too meager to merit notion. In the opinion of the Trustees
the removal of the sword is uncalled for.

We await further instructions from your Board.

Respectfully yours,

Vice Pres.

Trustees of the Millicent Library

The Board of Trustees of the Millicent Library remained
steadfast. No other letters of concern were received, and the
Japanese sword remained on display. The reasoning of the
Board of Trustees was that the sword was a symbolic gesture
commemorating a noble deed and that it had no political
significance.

In a 1987 interview, Willard D. Whitfield, great-grandson
of William H. Whitfield, corroborated the fact that when
Japan joined the war, siding with the Axis against the Allies,
Whitfield's correspondence with the Nakahama family
ceased. "We couldn't write any more," he explained.

Willard Whitfield joined the Coast Guard and served as a
chief radioman. After the war, during the occupation of
Japan, he often inquired, through military channels, about the
status of the Nakahamas. When he was asked about the war
and his relationship to his Japanese friends, he would only
say, "War is not personal, but strictly a family relationship"
(meaning that his relationship with the Nakahamas had nothing to do with politics but was a matter of long-standing
friendship between the families).

Slowly at first, correspondence between Fairhaven and
Japan was reestablished after the war, beginning nearly a
year after Japan's surrender in August 1945.

In the years that followed, the number of members of the
Whitfield family who resided in Fairhaven family was gradually reduced. Finally, only Captain Whitfield's granddaughter, Allie (Whitfield) Omey, resided in Fairhaven. Willard
Whitfield, at the time of the death of his mother, Marie L.
(Gunn) Whitfield, in May 1966, was residing in Bowie, Mary-
land. The town was left without an active member of the

Whitfield family to carry on the tradition of communicating
with the Nakahamas.

Fairhaven's only contacts with the Japanese then took
place through the Millicent Library. Avis Pillsbury, Library
Director, was the curator of the Whitfield-Nakahama relationship until her retirement from the library in 1952, when
she was succeeded by Rita E. Steele. Miss Steele was at once
captivated and intrigued by the tale of the Manjiro odyssey.
She carried on the tradition of entertaining the countless Japanese who continued to visit the Millicent Library in Fairhaven, as though they were on pilgrimage, retracing Manjiro's steps.

At last even Allie Omey of 13 Cherry Street, the last surviving Whitfield in Fairhaven, died. On June 1, 1959, Benson and
Mary Morris purchased the Whitfield house at 13 Cherry
Street from Allie Omey's estate. Shortly thereafter, a letter
arrived from Dr. Hiroshi Nakahama of Japan, addressed to
Mrs. Omey. Mrs. Morris was well aware of the relationship
between Japan and Fairhaven, and after consulting with Miss
Steele at the Millicent Library, she answered Dr. Nakahama's
letter, indicating her willingness to continue the tradition of
communication between the Nakahama family and Fairhaven. In the meantime, Willard Whitfield continued his correspondence with the Nakahamas.

On October 27, 1960, *The Fairhaven Star* noted the following story:

Japanese Honor Whitfield's Memory

In commemoration of the centennial of Japanese-American diplomatic and trade relationships, Mitsuo Tanaka, Japanese consul general in New York, was a visitor in Fairhaven last Thursday. He was accompanied by LeRoy Kajiwara, his economic
assistant, and Alan B. Smith, cultural assistant.

The visitors arrived at the town hall about 10 A.M. and were
escorted to the grave of Captain William H. Whitfield in Riverside Cemetery by the selectmen, Walter Silveira, James B.
Lanagan and Walter J. Borowicz, and Police Chief Norman D.
Shurtleff.

Mr. Tanaka placed a wreath on the grave of Captain Whitfield, whose rescue of an obscure Japanese fisherman, Manjiro
Nakahama, from a Pacific island in 1841, and education of him
in Fairhaven led to his taking an active part in the development
of Japan as a modern power after his return to his native country.

The party was then escorted on a tour of historical sites in
town and was then honored by a reception at the Millicent
Library, where a Samurai sword presented the town in 1918 by
the Nakahama family, and examples of Japanese art were on
display.

On Tuesday, December 19, 1961, the following article appeared in the New Bedford *Standard-Times*.

Fairhaven to Weigh Plan
For Japanese "Sister City"

A three-man committee was appointed by the Fairhaven Board
of Selectmen last night to investigate possibilities of linking the
town and Nakanohama, Japan, as "sister cities."

The idea was suggested in a letter several months ago by
Willard D. Whitfield, a former native of Fairhaven, now with
the Executive Office of the President for Emergency Planning in
Washington.

Committee appointees are John R. German, chairman; Miss
Rita E. Steele, and John A. Walkinshaw, all of Fairhaven.

A recent follow-up letter from Mr. Whitfield states, "I have
received recently a communication from Miss Emily Warinner
of Honolulu in which she suggests the possibility of establish-
ment of sister cities with the village of Nakanohama, birthplace
of Manjiro Nakahama."

Japanese Rescued

Mr. Nakahama was rescued in 1841 from an isolated Japanese
island by Captain William H. Whitfield and crewmen of the
New Bedford whaling vessel *John Howland*. He returned to the
United States with his new friends, changed his Oriental garb
for Western clothes and for 10 years resided in Fairhaven.

Educated in Fairhaven schools, Mr. Nakahama assisted in
negotiating the Treaty of 1854, in which Commodore Matthew
Perry and a personal representative of the Emperor of Japan
participated.

I understand from friends on the West Coast that this idea of
"sister cities" is quite popular there, and perhaps the idea proposed by Miss Warinner does have some merit.

I am forwarding her letter in order that you might take this
up with the board to see if they feel it is something they would
like to undertake. I am also sending a copy of this letter to Miss
Warinner because of her interest in this proposed program.

Contact Possible

I feel sure that the Japanese Embassy in Washington and the
New York Consul's office would be interested in entertaining
such a proposal, and would be willing to contact the embassy if
the board felt there was merit in the idea.

Although there were no longer any Whitfields living in Fairhaven, interest in the Manjiro story was increasing, especially on the part of the Japanese, many of whom visited Fairhaven each year.

In 1967, a simultaneous live television broadcast was produced via telecommunications media between the New Bedford Whaling Museum and Tokyo. The event was received with great excitement in both Massachusetts and Japan. Nakahama family members were among those involved in the simulcast in Japan, along with historians, writers, and other interested parties. Participating from the New Bedford Whaling Museum were local dignitaries and Whitfield family members, who traveled from Fort Lauderdale, Florida, for the occasion, as well as Millicent Library officials and other notables.

In 1968, at Cape Ashizuri in Tosashimizu City (Manjiro's birthplace), Kochi Prefecture, on Shikoku Island, a large bronze statue of Manjiro Nakahama was erected. The ceremony was well attended by Nakahama family members and local officials. The statue was purposely placed overlooking the vast Pacific and facing east, as though looking toward Manjiro's adopted American home in Fairhaven, Massachusetts.

15

The Visit to Fairhaven by the Imperial Crown Prince Akihito and the Sister City Relationship

In 1976, a renewal of interest in John Manjiro was sparked by actions of the U.S. State Department. In planning the Bicentennial celebration of the United States, the State Department decided to recognize individuals who had had a direct impact on this country's history during its 200 years of existence. Manjiro, alias John Mung, was credited with having played a major role as an interpreter or consultant when Commodore Matthew C. Perry and his Black Ships entered Japan for the purpose of opening ports to foreign trade. In recognition of Manjiro's role, the State Department invited his descendants to come to the United States for a testimonial.

Hiroshi Nakahama, a great-grandson of Manjiro, was one of those invited to the ceremony. A practicing physician from the city of Nagoya, Japan, Hiroshi had followed in the footsteps of his father Kiyoshi and his grandfather Toichiro by continuing the tradition of maintaining ties with the Whitfields. Hiroshi and his wife Grace were invited to Fairhaven as guests of the U.S. government.

In May 1976, Dr. and Mrs. Hiroshi Nakahama arrived in Fairhaven, the town where Hiroshi's great-grandfather had received his American education. It was on this occasion that I, the author of this book, first met the Nakahamas. The meeting was arranged mainly through the efforts of Rita E. Steele, who, as director of the Millicent Library, was acting as hostess. Since that time, the Nakahama family and I have developed a warm relationship.

Accompanying the Nakahamas on their American visit were two Japanese newspapermen from *The Chunichi Shimbun*, of Nagoya, Japan. They had been assigned to cover the historic significance of the Manjiro story for Japanese readers. These newsmen were Kazuo ("Jim") Narita, a writer, and

Minoru ("Mike") Tanaka, a photographer. Jim Narita's assignment was to write up the continuing story of the visit in a daily newspaper column, and Mike Tanaka was to make a photographic record of the events and places included in the story. I formed a strong bond of friendship with these two newsmen which has continued through the years and is still flourishing.

The visit of Dr. and Mrs. Nakahama to the greater New Bedford area, in company with Jim Narita and Mike Tanaka, brought new attention to the long-standing Japan-Fairhaven relationship, but the revival of interest on the part of local people in the Manjiro adventure was not long sustained. However, any lingering hostility toward the Japanese on account of World War II was weakened by the public recognition of Manjiro's descendants.

Suddenly, in the summer of 1977, the symbolic samurai sword that had been given to the town by the Nakahama family was stolen from the Millicent Library. This incident had a devastating effect on Rita E. Steele, who felt that she personally had failed to protect the sword. She never seemed to be able to recover fully from the humiliation and embarrassment she suffered as a result of the incident. Even at the time of this writing, the whereabouts of the missing sword and who stole it are still unknown.

On June 12, 1982, a replacement sword was presented to the town of Fairhaven through the efforts of Dr. Tadashi Kikuoka, a professor of Japanese studies at Seton Hall University in South Orange, New Jersey, with the help of various Japanese-American businessmen. The presentation of the replacement sword took place in front of the Fairhaven Town Hall. Even though the ceremony was not as grandiose as the original presentation in 1918, a surprising number of people did attend the noteworthy occasion.

The Japan-Fairhaven relationship was dealt a severe blow with the passing of Fairhaven's popular curator of the Manjiro legend, Rita E. Steele, in July 1985. Her death left a void in the long-term relationship.

I had already begun researching and compiling information on the amazing story of Manjiro Nakahama and his relationship with Captain Whitfield. After the death of Rita Steele, I began to play host to the many visitors who were curious to see the places in Fairhaven where Manjiro had lived and studied.

Two years later, in October 1987, because of an unprecedented visit to Fairhaven by Japanese royalty, the previously little-known story of Manjiro received news coverage throughout the United States and abroad.

This surprising development started when Takuji Yamaguchi, of Bun You Associates of Tokyo, was assigned by Funio Watanabe, head of Bun You Associates, to act as his emissary. Yamaguchi was instructed to make a side trip to Fairhaven during a business trip to Boston. His mission was to investigate the possibility of forming a Sister City relationship between Fairhaven and Tosashimizu City, Japan. Yamaguchi said nothing of his mission to anyone in Fairhaven, but when he reported back to Watanabe, he stated that conditions were favorable.

In February 1987, Minoru Tamba, the Japanese Consul General in Boston, visited Fairhaven and New Bedford to suggest forming a Sister City relationship. After some informal discussions, Tamba and officials from both Fairhaven and New Bedford agreed to begin the groundwork for a Sister City alliance in a tripartite arrangement.

Mayor John Bullard of New Bedford suggested that, because the John Manjiro story was more directly related to Fairhaven than to New Bedford, Fairhaven should take the lead in the Sister City plan. He also offered New Bedford's assistance and cooperation.

In June 1987, the Fairhaven Board of Selectmen consisted of Walter Silveira, Joseph Cataldo, and Kenneth Wood, Jr. Acting on a recommendation from the Fairhaven Historical Commission, the board appointed me to form the Sister City Committee. The committee that was eventually formed included fourteen representatives from Fairhaven and six from New Bedford. The Fairhaven members were Donald R. Bernard; Carolyn Longworth; Roland Seguin; Mary Morris; Louis Veilleux; John Medeiros, Jr.; Daniel Mello; David Gilbertson; Priscilla Wright; Marian Mitchell; Michelle Crotty; Karen Garnett; Alice Torres; and Marinus Vanderpol. The New Bedford representatives were Maria Tomasia; Ayako Rooney; Cindy Yoken; Mel Yoken; Edward Camara, Jr.; and Amelia Cabral.

In September 1987, a delegation of city officials from Tosashimizu City, Kochi Prefecture, Shikoku, Japan, led by Honorable Mayor Kiyoshi Izumi, visited Fairhaven and New Bedford. The delegation extended an invitation to their
Massachusetts counterparts to visit Tosashimizu City before
the end of the year to sign a Sister City agreement.

Their invitation was submitted as a proposal to the Fairhaven Town Meeting, a representative forum of local government officials. At a special Town Meeting on September 24,
1987, the following resolution was passed:

Article 19

Sister City Relationship

a. Moved to authorize the Board of Selectmen to establish a
Sister City with the city of Tosashimizu in Japan, for the
purpose of creating mutual understanding between the people of our two great communities, and further to adopt a
resolution for this purpose to be presented to the government
of Tosashimizu. Seconded.

Voted unanimously.

b. Moved the sum of $15,000 to pay for the expense involved
with sending a contingent of persons to the city of Tosashimizu, Japan, for the official signing of an agreement between the two communities to establish a Sister City. Seconded.

Voted the sum of $15,000.

In the meantime, Consul General Minoru Tamba conceived the idea that a visit to Fairhaven by the Imperial
Crown Prince Akihito and Princess Michiko would generate
much interest in and acclaim for the Sister City relationship
and the Manjiro legacy. Tamba worked successfully through
political channels to have Fairhaven included in the itinerary
of the Imperial couple's upcoming visit to the United States.

Their visit took place on October 4, 1987, which was a
cloudy, damp, and cold day. A light drizzle was falling. The
site chosen for the meeting was 11 Cherry Street in Fairhaven, the house where Manjiro had spent his first few weeks
in Fairhaven in 1843. The official entourage, led by U.S. and
Japanese Secret Service, as well as state and local police,
arrived at approximately 1:45 P.M. As Fairhaven's official

coordinator of the event, I was on hand to greet the sixteen-limousine motorcade of the Imperial Crown Prince and Princess.

I greeted Crown Prince Akihito and Princess Michiko on behalf of the townspeople. The delegation accompanying the Imperial couple included former U.S. Senator and U.S. Ambassador to Japan, Mike Mansfield, who had joined the Crown Prince's entourage in Boston. After the significance of the house was explained to the Imperial couple, I rode with them past the ancient schoolhouse in which Manjiro had attended classes while he was living on Cherry Street. The motorcade continued along Green Street past the Fairhaven High School stadium, where the official presentation of the samurai sword to the town had taken place in 1918. When the motorcade arrived at the Fairhaven Town Hall, we were greeted by American and Japanese schoolchildren waving Japanese and American flags, and singing the cherry blossom song, "Sakura." (The Japanese schoolchildren had been brought from Boston to Fairhaven in honor of the occasion.) As Tamba had predicted, the event inspired development of a new local interest in the Manjiro story. Nearly 2000 townspeople enthusiastically hailed Prince Akihito and Princess Michiko as they emerged from their limousine under the watchful protection of both American and Japanese Secret Service.

Roland Seguin of the Sister City Committee introduced the Imperial couple to the state and local officials who were on hand for the historic occasion. I then introduced State Senator William Q. MacLean, Jr., who served as master of ceremonies. Senator MacLean's remarks were as follows:

Imperial Crown Prince Akihito, Crown Princess Michiko, Selectman Silveira, Mayor Bullard, Distinguished Guests:

It is with a great deal of pleasure that I welcome the Imperial Highnesses Crown Prince Akihito and Crown Princess Michiko to the town of Fairhaven. We are honored by your presence.

The bond of friendship between Japan and the United States is further strengthened by your visit. We are proud of the fact that your Imperial Highnesses took time from their busy schedule to honor us by being with us. I hope that your stay in our country is a fruitful and pleasant experience for you and I am sure that your stay in the United States will be a warmly

received one. I wish you a safe journey throughout your visit
here and on your return trip to Japan.

**Fairhaven Selectman Chairman Walter Silveira, who was
introduced by Senator MacLean, offered the following:**

Your Highness Prince Akihito, Princess Michiko, Dr. and Mrs.
Nakahama, Ambassador and Mrs. Mike Mansfield, Mr.
Whitfield, Mayor Bullard, Mayor Viveiros, my fellow Selectmen
Joseph Cataldo and Ken Wood, Chief Bernard, ladies and
gentlemen.

It is with deep humility and great pride and honor that, on
behalf of all our residents, I welcome you and your wife to the
town of Fairhaven to continue the friendship and goodwill of
our two nations that began 146 years ago.

In the spirit of kindness and concern for his fellow man,
Captain Whitfield began a friendship that has endured from
generation to generation.

We are particularly grateful that you and the people of Japan
continue to visit our community to view first hand the area
where Manjiro was welcomed and received his education that
helped him play a major role in helping our two nations.

Within the past month we have taken another step to cement
our bond with the nation of Japan and will, in the near future,
sign a Sister City agreement with the city of Tosashimizu,
Manjiro's birthplace.

We appreciate the fact that you have taken the time from
your very busy schedule to honor us with your presence and
open our hearts to you and your people. The "welcome" mat
will always be spread out to all the people of Japan.

Please enjoy your stay in our country and we wish you a safe
journey for your return to Japan and pray for your father's
speedy recovery. [The Emperor Hirohito at the time of this visit
was gravely ill.]

**Following Selectman Silveira's welcoming remarks, Sena-
tor MacLean introduced His Highness, the Japanese Imperial
Crown Prince Akihito, who delivered the following oration in
English:**

Senator MacLean, Selectman Silveira, Mayor Bullard, Mayor
Viveiros, Mr. Bernard, ladies and gentlemen.

It is with a great pleasure that my wife and I have been
invited by President and Mrs. Reagan to visit the United States.
I am particularly happy that our first formal meeting with
Americans on this trip should be here in Fairhaven, at a site that

is symbolic of the everlasting friendship and goodwill that is shared by our countries.

One hundred and forty six years ago, in 1841, even before diplomatic relations were established between Japan and the U.S., a 14 year old Japanese fisherman was rescued by William Whitfield, the captain of a whaling ship.

It was to this town of Fairhaven that Capt. Whitfield brought young Manjiro Nakahama and treated him as his own son. The story of Whitfield's kindness and humanity is well known among Japanese today. Ten years later, Manjiro returned to Japan, became a teacher, and over a long career, played an important role in helping Japanese officialdom form a correct understanding of the United States.

The kindness and goodwill of this one American toward Manjiro have borne a fruit of inestimable worth in Japan, a land of a very different history and culture far across the Pacific. This fruit is the affection and respect of the Japanese people for Americans, feelings that have been passed down over the generations and are very much alive today.

I take great pleasure in knowing that the friendship that existed between Manjiro and Whitfield during their lifetimes is still alive today in the hearts of the Nakahama family, the Whitfield family, and the citizens of Fairhaven. I am particularly grateful that Hiroshi Nakahama and Willard Whitfield, the great-grandsons of the two pioneers of U.S.-Japan relations, were able to travel from afar to be present today. I would also like to express my appreciation to the people of Fairhaven for carrying out the historic mission of cherishing and passing on to future generations the spirit of this first friendship between Japanese and Americans.

The relationship of friendship and trust that exists between Japan and the U.S. is based entirely on the goodwill and warm feelings that exist between our peoples. To strengthen the ties that bind us in the future, it is opportune that we should gather here today to remember those two pioneers in the U.S.-Japan relations.

Finally, on behalf of my wife and myself, I would like to express to the city and people of Fairhaven our appreciation for the warm welcome we have received. I pray for the continued good health and prosperity of all.

Prince Akihito's speech was followed by words of greeting from the great-grandsons of Manjiro and Captain Whitfield—Dr. Hiroshi Nakahama, Chief Surgeon of the Chunichi Hospital, Nagoya, Japan, and Willard Whitfield, of Fort Lauderdale, Florida, both of whom attended the historic ceremony as guests of the Japanese government.

Crown Prince Akihito's visit to Fairhaven, October 4, 1987. (Courtesy Cathy Bernard)

Earl J. Dias, Trustee Chairman of the Millicent Library, made the following gift presentation to Prince Akihito:

> Your Imperial Highnesses:
> Your visit to Fairhaven is a welcome illustration of the close ties between this community and your great nation.
> On behalf of the town of Fairhaven, I should like to present to you a wash painting of Fairhaven harbor by a distinguished local artist, Arthur Moniz.
> The painting depicts the port at which your countryman, Manjiro Nakahama, landed with his rescuer, Captain William Whitfield, in 1843.
> Your Imperial Highnesses, please accept this gift with our affection, goodwill, and admiration. May it bring to you happy memories of your visit to wind-cooled Fairhaven (and I do mean wind-cooled!).

In response, Prince Akihito presented to the town of Fairhaven a collection of prints by the famous Japanese artist Kaii Higashiyama. A bouquet of flowers was presented to Prince Akihito by Elizabeth Hoekstra, daughter of Fairhaven school superintendent Ron Hoekstra. Chad Thomas Santos, my grandson, presented a bouquet of roses to Princess Michiko. The Imperial couple then walked among the children and waved to the shivering but enthusiastic crowd.

Earl Dias guided the Imperial Highnesses into the Millicent Library, where they signed the Japanese guest book. After a brief tour of the Millicent Library, the Imperial couple left Fairhaven, to travel by motorcade to Boston.

This unprecedented visit to Fairhaven by members of the Japanese Imperial family lent much credence to the proposed Sister City arrangement between Fairhaven, New Bedford, and Tosashimizu, Japan, the birthplace of Manjiro.

Later in October, an official delegation was selected to travel from Fairhaven and New Bedford to Tosashimizu to sign the Sister City document. Representing the town of Fairhaven were Selectman Joseph Cataldo and Selectman Kenneth Wood, Jr. (Fairhaven Selectman Chairman Walter Silveira was unable to make the trip because of poor health.) Members chosen from the Sister City Committee were Donald R. Bernard, Chairman; Maria Tomasia, representing the Honorable Mayor John Bullard of the city of New Bedford; Roland Seguin, Vice Chairman of the Sister City Committee; Carolyn Longworth, committee member and director of the Millicent Library; Daniel Mello; and John Medeiros, Jr. In addition, Ayako Rooney and David Gilbertson, also committee members, served as interpreters.

The delegation and interpreters arrived in Japan on Monday, November 30, 1987. Kiyoshi Izumi, Honorable Mayor of Tosashimizu City, along with members of the City Council and the Sister City Association of Tosashimizu City, were the hosts of the Fairhaven group during our week-long stay in Tosashimizu.

On Friday afternoon, December 2, 1987, the delegation was paraded through the streets of Tosashimizu, where we visited a traditional Japanese tea school. We were then escorted to the Civic Cultural Center, where the signing ceremony was to take place.

The atmosphere was formal. The Fairhaven–New Bedford representatives were seated behind closed curtains on the stage of the auditorium. The mayor and his official staff and delegates were also seated on the stage, across from the

American delegation. At approximately 2:00 P.M., the curtains parted. In the auditorium to witness the official ceremony were more than a thousand local citizens.

The speeches that followed were genial and formal. Finally, the documents (in triplicate) were presented. Mayor Izumi signed for Tosashimizu, while Selectman Joseph Cataldo and Selectman Kenneth Wood, Jr., signed for Fairhaven. Maria Tomasia, who, as already mentioned, was representing Mayor John Bullard of New Bedford, attached his personal seal to the official documents.

The agreement which was officially signed by the representatives of the three committees reads as follows:

Twin City
Agreement and Memorandum
Between Fair Haven New Bedford and Tosa Shimizu

1. TWIN CITY Agreement

One hundred Forty-six years ago, Tosashimizu City in Kochi prefecture, Japan, and FairHaven, New Bedford City in the State of Massachusetts, the United States of America, greatly contributed to the promotion of interchange between Japan and the U.S. through the medium of John Manjiro Nakahama, a citizen of TosaShimizu, who was washed up on an uninhabited island when he was 14 years old, and was rescued by an American whale boat. After landing on FairHaven New Bedford, he learned the English language, mathematics, navigation and surveying in the U.S.A., and when he returned to Japan he played an important role in introducing Western civilization to Japan and supporting Japanese diplomatic activities during the historic turn from feudal to modern Japan. In memory of this man, both cities and their people who hope to promote mutual understanding, respect and friendship through a broad range of interchanges, as a contribution to world peace, now solemnly declare that both cities have hereby been twinned.

This Agreement has been executed in duplicate in both Japanese and English, by signature of the undersigned, subject to ratification by the legislature of each city. This Agreement shall be effective from the day when both city legislatures have completed their ratification.

2. *Memorandum on Interchange Activities between the Twin Cities*

Upon execution of the Twin City Agreement between Tosa-Shimizu City and Fairhaven, New Bedford City, both cities discussed plans for interchange activities between them. Based on the firm belief that mutual exchange between both cities and their communities will be substantially furthered by their twinning, both parties have agreed that they will push forward their mutual interchange in several aspects.

It was agreed that interchange activities in the following specific fields are to be arranged from time to time through mutual consultations.

- Interchange between youths and ordinary citizens
- Interchange in relation to the arts, culture and sport
- Interchange in relation to urban administration
- Interchange in relation to the economy and industry

IN WITNESS THEREOF, both cities have executed these documents, the undersigned representatives of both cities affixing their signature hereto, the day of

December 2, 1987

FairHaven	Walter Silveira [Signed at a later date]
FairHaven	Joseph Cataldo, Jr.
FairHaven	Kenneth M. Wood, Jr.
New Bedford	John Bullard
TosaShimizu	Kiyoshi Izumi

Once the document was signed, an innovative audiovisual telephone conversation was held between the Tosashimizu Civic Cultural Center and the Fairhaven Town Hall. Walter Silveira of the Fairhaven Board of Selectmen had been waiting anxiously for the call, so that he could extend greetings to the people of Tosashimizu City on behalf of the townspeople of Fairhaven. Mayor Kiyoshi Izumi, witnessed by members of the Japanese City Council and over a thousand citizens of Tosashimizu, reciprocated the words of goodwill.

The technology used to make this audiovisual telephone call to the other side of the world had been developed in part by the Mitsubishi Corporation of Japan. Mitsubishi had chosen to officially introduce its new state-of-the-art audiovisual telephone on the occasion of the signing of the Sister City agreement between the coastal fishing community of Tosashimizu City, Kochi Prefecture, Japan, and the communities of Fairhaven and New Bedford, Massachusetts, in the United States.

The joining of these communities as Sister Cities is a unique event, which did not occur by chance. Although there are many Japanese-American Sister City relationships between cities throughout the United States and Japan, the relationship between Fairhaven–New Bedford and Tosashimizu City is by far the most notable. Its uniqueness stems from the fact that Manjiro was the first person of Japanese origin known to have been educated in the United States and then to have returned to Japan.

This bonding relationship, the story of which is the subject of this book, was spawned a century and a half ago and has been sustained over three generations, despite a world war that threatened its very existence. The personal family relationship between the Nakahamas and the Whitfields was conceived on a barren Pacific atoll some 375 miles (603 kilometers) southeast of Edo, Japan—the uninhabited island from which five Japanese fishermen were rescued by an American whaleship from the port city of New Bedford.

The Japanese at that time were unfamiliar to most of the world. Manjiro's mere presence in Fairhaven and New Bedford thus aroused great curiosity and interest, especially among his immediate associates. After he returned to Japan, Manjiro exchanged letters with the Whitfields and others whom he had known in Fairhaven. As the years passed, the Nakahama and Whitfield families continued their exchange of letters. This broadening of the lines of communication must be credited with the development of the long-term relationship between the two families.

It is poignant to note that the town of Fairhaven did not initially participate actively in the relationship between Manjiro and Captain Whitfield. Local records reveal little about Mung's years in Fairhaven, implying that his presence and activities probably had no great significance at that time. It is likely that most of the townspeople of Fairhaven and New Bedford neither knew nor cared that Manjiro was living among them.

Today, however, both Americans and Japanese look back to a time when circumstances were quite different. We look back upon this amazing story with great pride and satisfaction—with the feeling that we are responsible for Manjiro's notable achievements and acclaim. We Americans are so enamored with adventure and folkloric heroes that we tend to romanticize and embellish stories such as Manjiro's.

In conclusion, we ask, What will be the future course of this odyssey? Will the bond between these Japanese and American communities continue to flourish within the shadow of Manjiro's memory, or will the ravages of time fade this heroic story? We can only hope that as long as the Nakahama and Whitfield families have living descendants, the relationship will endure.

This epic adventure of Manjiro, alias John Mung, is one that has been cradled and nurtured for over 150 years. It must not be allowed to wither or die, as it is a remarkable tale indeed.

Resources

Bristol County Registry of Deeds, S.D., New Bedford, Mass.
Daily Alta, San Francisco, Calif.
The Daily Evening Bulletin, San Francisco, Calif.
The Fairhaven Star, Fairhaven, Mass.
Fairhaven Town Clerk's Records, Fairhaven, Mass.
The Friend, Honolulu, Hawaii.
Kochi Library, Kochi Prefecture, Shikoku, Japan.
Millicent Library, Fairhaven, Mass.
Nakahama, Dr. Hiroshi, personal and family documents, Nagoya, Japan.
New Bedford Free Public Library, New Bedford, Mass.
The New Bedford Morning Mercury, New Bedford, Mass.
The New Bedford Standard Times, New Bedford, Mass.
New Bedford Whaling Museum, New Bedford, Mass.
The Polynesian, Honolulu, Hawaii.
The San Francisco Herald, San Francisco, Calif.
Scipio Town Clerk's Records, Scipio, N.Y.
U.S. Customs House Records, Washington, D.C.

Bibliography

Brooke, George M., Jr. (ed.), *John M. Brooke's Pacific Cruise and Japanese Adventure, 1858–1860*, The University of Hawaii Press, Honolulu.

Fairbridge, Rhodes W., *The Encyclopedia of Oceanography*, Encyclopedia of Earth Sciences Series, Vol. 1, Van Nostrand Reinhold Company, New York. Fairbridge is a professor of geology at Columbia University, New York.

Hawks, Francis L., D.D.L.L.D. (ed.), *Japan Expedition—M. C. Perry*, Congress of the United States, Washington, A.O.P. Nicholson, Printer, 1856. Compiled from the original notes and journals of Commodore Matthew C. Perry and his officers, at Commodore Perry's request and under his supervision.

Hegarty, Reginald B., addendum to *Starbuck* and *Whaling Masters*, New Bedford Free Public Library, Reynolds-Dewalt, New Bedford, Mass., 1964. Hegarty is curator of the Whaling Room of the New Bedford Free Public Library.

Judd, Bernice, *Voyages to Hawaii before 1860*, The University of Hawaii Press, Honolulu, 1974. Enlarged and edited by Helen Yonge Lind.

Nakahama, Dr. Toichiro, narrative manuscript.

Sherman, Stuart C., *Whaling Log Books and Journals, 1613–1927*, Garland Publishing, Inc., New York, 1986. Revised and edited for publication by Judith M. Downey and Virginia M. Adams, New Bedford Whaling Museum, New Bedford, Mass., with the assistance of Howard Pasternack, Brown University, Providence, R.I.

Starbuck, Alexander, *History of the American Whale Fishery*, Castle Books, Secaucus, N.J., 1989.

Stevenson, Robert L., and Paul C. Blum, "Western Views of the Japanese," *Japan Gazette*. Edited with notes by Kiyoshi Hasegawa, Noaki Tsukada, and Kirihara Shoten.

Warinner, Emily V. *Voyager to Destiny*, The Bobbs-Merrill Company, Inc., Indianapolis–New York, 1956.